MR. RIGOLETTO

In Conversation with Louis Quilico

MR. RIGOLETTO

In Conversation with Louis Quilico

By

Christina Petrowska

Captus Press

MR. RIGOLETTO:
In Conversation with Louis Quilico

Hardcover edition, 1996

Photo credits:
Front cover photo curtesy of Barry Glass
Back cover photo curtesy of André Pierre Leduc
Back cover drawing by Christina Petrowska

Canadian Cataloguing in Publication Data
Petrowska, Christina, 1949–
Mr. Rigoletto: in conversation with Louis Quilico

ISBN 1–896691–83–8

1. Quilico, Louis, 1925– – Interviews.
2. Singers – Canada – Interviews.
I. Petrowska, Christina, 1948– . II. Title.

ML420.Q6A5 1999 782.1'092 C99–931956–6

Captus Press Inc.
Mail: York University Campus
4700 Keele Street
North York, Ontario
M3J 1P3
Telephone: (416) 736–5537
Fax: (416) 736–5793
Email: Info@captus.com
Internet: http://www.captus.com

0 9 8 7 6 5 4 3 2 1
Printed in Canada

To my wife, Christina Petrowska

What is so incredible for me is to be able to say that when I met my wife Christina I found the one true love of my life. In Christina I have finally found an equal partner in love and music. She has an unsurpassed artistic quality which makes performing with her such a great joy and so wonderful that it cannot be compared to anything else. When we perform we breathe and think musically as one. In our loving, which is so beautiful and perfect, our emotional and spiritual life together has made a tremendous impact on our lives. Heaven was on my side because Christina is mine. I used to say, "God, thank you for letting me breathe one more day," because I was thinking only of myself. But now I say, "God, I thank you for letting me breathe one more day so that I can really cherish what has been given to me — my wife Christina, and my singing voice."

Contents

Foreword by Thomas Hampson

There is a tradition behind the scenes of the opera world among singers and between colleagues of recognizing, admiring and, in some ways, protecting what we all 'know' to be the real standards of good singing. Seriousness of purpose, health of voice, longevity of career and a certain indefinable skepticism about taking yourself more seriously than the forces of nature that allowed you to be what you are — these are some of those standards.

When asking some of my colleagues about Louis Quilico, the man and singer, the word that is invariably used is *GENEROUS* — certainly generous of voice, but also, probably more importantly, generous of heart, spirit, compassion, dedication and effort! What lies behind this generous artist will be glimpsed in this book through narration, anecdote, admonishment and, of course, the facts of his generous career.

I've always admired Louis as a 'forefather" baritone for the very quality that leaps from his story in this book: No Nonsense. In his tales and tips and lessons, Louis speaks firmly, directly, almost simply, with a sense of practicality that is at first disarming. Don't be fooled! The profundity of experience is yours to be had in the reflection of his words and deeds.

We live in a world more and more dominated by disposable celebrity and must always be alert to the few examples of a life dedicated to a longer vision, stable maturation and, quite frankly, a generous and gentle embrace of the human spirit.

Read on in respect; sing on in fellowship; live on in wonder!

Acknowledgements

All my thanks go to Ann-Marie Boudreau, who so tirelessly transcribed the taped conversations and helped with my editing of them.

Also, my children, Dominique and Alexandra, and my mother for their ever loyal support and patience.

Also thanks to Aldo Maggiorotti for his careful scrutiny of operatic misspellings and Lucie Kocum who researched archival material and documents at the National Library of Canada.

Introduction

It seems appropriate that I write the introduction to *Mr. Rigoletto: In Conversation with Louis Quilico*, because we met when Louis wrote the preface to my book *Opera Illustrated.* In fact, that first encounter resulted in our marriage a few months later and a professional relationship that includes a lot of concertizing together.

This book came about as a conclusion to many months of taped conversations. By comparing notes we both realized that we have the same approach, ideas and concepts in teaching and performing.

My first questions about teaching and learning occurred when I was a 14-year-old hotshot at Juilliard. I was able to play and perform any virtuoso show-piece I wanted but I didn't know how I was able to do so. I had a natural technique and facility like every other young prodigy at Juilliard. I received a wonderful education, learning not only from the school or teachers but watching such extraordinary classmates as Itzhak Perlman, Pinchas Zukerman, Misha Dichter, Garrick Ohlsson, to name just a few. My debut at Town Hall in New York was shared with the unsurpassed artistry of Murray Perahia. My teacher at Juilliard, Rosina Lhévinne, was a legend in her own time teaching hundreds of famous pianists such as Van Cliburn, John

Browning, and James Levine, the music director and conductor of the Metropolitan Opera. She was a great spiritual influence on my musical life.

Her assistant at the time was Jeaneane Dowis and I continued coaching with Dowis for many years following my graduation from Juilliard. With her I learned more about the technique and mechanics of playing the piano than from anyone else. She had an exercise in which I would look at my fingertips for hours, trying to identify separate muscles for use in particular touches at the keyboard. It was a study in meditation and self-discipline. Eventually I was able to control muscles I never knew I had.

Louis had a parallel experience discovering his vocal cords through meditation and self-learning. You must know your body and how all the muscles function to develop technique on any instrument, but in voice it's crucial because you are the only instrument through which the sound emerges. What a revelation these concepts were for me. I was able to control the most subtle touch at the keyboard and because I knew exactly how I did it was able to reproduce the touch and sound at will. It is mind over matter.

As a child, performing was very easy, a relaxing activity and at the same time exciting. I don't remember ever forcing the sound. Somehow, as we get older we become obsessed over-achievers, unable to control our intense drive. We seek perfection and we force and push the sound instead of using the nervous tension as a source of energy and relaxing into the sound. Tension should not be used as weight or strength. It is like electricity or continuous energy.

Whether it is repetitive practice by the vocal cords or the fingers on the piano, we can abuse our bodies to the extent that the ideal sound and musicality escapes us. Both Louis and I believe that vocalization by itself or scales and Czerny alone will not create a great technique. Warming up the muscles is essential but the practice of a Czerny study, for example, leads mainly to the perfection of that Czerny study. You learn Beethoven by practising Beethoven. You don't learn a Verdi opera by vocalizing all day, you learn Verdi by doing it. Only mental lethargy accounts for the monotonous repetition of exercises or vocalizations. You must focus on the concept or inner vision of the sound you want to produce.

The technique necessary is then adapted to create the sound. We need to learn exactly how to recreate a sound or musical phrase. Technique cannot be generalized or simplified. We have to know how to utilize the equipment we have. For pianists it is the size and shape of hand, natural body grace, speed of the nervous system's response, reflexes, length and width of the fingers and general flexibility that determines performance as well as musicality. Vladimir Horowitz had a remarkable nervous response. His octaves and trills were legendary and much of his unparalleled virtuosity is owed to his lightning-speed muscular and nervous responses. Natural talents are a result of our physical facilities and what we do with them.

Muscular coordination of the human body involves an entire chain of events by which the smallest movement will induce contraction and relaxation. This action will balance or reverse with the same lightning speed at that precise moment. Pianists, for example, must practise economy of movement; less is better. Chopin abhorred all overemphasis or affectation. He insisted on naturalness and simplicity in piano playing. Piano technique should be a means to an end coming directly out of an imperative need for the musical expression. You must focus on only what is absolutely necessary for the sound required.

Jeaneane Dowis, my wonderful coach, gave me many lessons on this concept. All those hours I spent in Zen-like concentration staring at my finger tips, willing a previously unnoticed muscle to move, gave me the tools to create my own technique. I learned to separate one muscle from another, to economize on movement, to balance tension and relaxation and how to breathe. Only a small amount of energy is needed to produce any kind of tone and that only for a split second. It doesn't matter which technique a pianist uses, high articulation with bent fingers or the straight and flat fingers of the Russian school. All volumes and shades of tone, pressing keys quickly or gradually can be done with ease if the pianist masters the mental process which helps to release the tension created in preparation and at the moment of tonal production. The action itself becomes invisible and the result is the illusion of continual movement.

Sound retains all the thoughts and emotions which we as listeners perceive only as a mysterious something, an intensity or edge in a performance which is almost more apparent when it is not there. We can tell very quickly when the sounds don't move or touch us. On the purely physical plane we respond sensually to a sound. Louis always says that the voice must come from the heart, not only from the larynx. Singing is a fascinating and complex mix of the concrete and the abstract, physical and spiritual, technical and intuitive. There is a marriage between sound and vocal cord. Diderot wrote that one must consider lyric declamation like a line and singing like a second line that crisscrosses the first one, and the more this declamation is interlaced with the singing line, touching at many points, the more genuine, the more beautiful the singing itself will be. As the singer creates his or her art the mind and heart must supply the intangible material which will capture the imagination of the audience. Sound is eternal. It is born and dies at the same moment, only living in our memories.

Anyone can carry a tune. It becomes difficult when you pursue perfection but I believe that every musician, in fact everybody can benefit and derive great pleasure from studying singing. All my piano teachers used to insist that I sing at the piano. Singers usually breathe at each phrase end which results in a natural and musical phrasing. They study the structure of the aria or song and observe the phrases as they follow one another leading to climaxes and cadences. C.P.E. Bach wrote that the best way to feel the natural flow of a phrase is to sing it. Beethoven's style was influenced by the orator's style, and Greeks and Romans associated music with the art of rhetorical delivery.

For Chopin, as for most Romantic composers, music was language. Chopin in his 'Projet des méthodes' wrote that for him music was the expression of thought and feeling through sound. Sounds to make music are used as we use words to make language. No wonder that Chopin was attracted to singing and based his own style and playing on it. He transformed the piano into a leading tenor or soprano and created a rubato, cantabile style and legato that creates the impression of human breathing. He used to tell his students that you must sing if you wish to play.

I also strongly suggest that my own students sing the musical line of their piano music and listen to the great singers who have that natural ease and agility that never lets the listener anticipate or feel tension in their performances. More than with instrumentalists, a good singer's effortless flow of tone has a satisfying and mesmerizing effect on listeners, whereas strained and inhibited singers are painful to listen to and watch. This effortless flow of tone in good singing or instrumental playing can be compared to the performance of a car of quality which glides noiselessly while other cars work. We experience that excess energy as tension which is ultimately communicated to the audience as a weak performance.

Louis Quilico at 70 years of age still has the agility of a coloratura soprano. Notes produced are of a pure resonance without any extraneous noises, clear, round sounds effortlessly sustained without tension. He has a remarkable natural instinct for singing which began at 6 years old but probably even earlier. The newborn baby produces unbelievably penetrating noises because inhibitions and tensions do not exist. By three or four years old babies enjoy all forms of vocal improvisation, songs and anything that is rhythmic or patterned. They speak, shout or sing uninhibitedly from the diaphragm and demonstrate a natural musicality. Some of these children will retain a singing instinct, others will lose it as they grow.

Like Louis, who was trained in a choir at his parish, young singers with pleasant voices who join a choir are given not only solfege but vocal training. Singing is made natural and not full of obstacles for young children were surrounded and nourished by singing. To sing in a church choir one must sing with a legato line and this singing must preserve a serenity in spite of virtuosity of any kind. The singer then learns to focus on the legato line and achieves a certain humility and awe when faced with the wonder of music. The natural singing ability strengthened with academic musicianship will eventually lead to a conscious control of one's voice. However, it takes a combination of natural instinct and academic knowledge to make a great singer. Attaining awareness often means retracing one's steps back to childlike unawareness and simplicity where tensions and inhibitions don't exist.

Tension is caused by stress or fear of inadequacy and we have to learn how to use this fear and tension positively. What is tension? It happens when we become strained and vocal cords, muscles, nerves, eyes, emotions become stretched to tightness and taxed beyond endurance. For both voice and piano it is necessary to maintain a balanced state of the body. You need a straight spine, freedom of breathing and a high degree of concentration which then allows for a free flow of memory which is indispensable for performance. A professional musician uses innate musical instinct to attain a balance between generating and releasing tension, giving the illusion of continuous movement. When there is too much force or anxiety one hasn't learned to control this balance and the result is muscular tension in many parts of the body which adversely affects one's performance. Nervous tension used intelligently brings intensity and excitement to a performance, giving it that special edge and adding charisma to the performer. This anticipation or controlled tension brightens the musical and academic qualities of a sensitive and seasoned artist and makes the performance unique. Tension then acts as a conduit for communication between performer and public. This tension is like electricity. Although we cannot see it, it exists and should be used. In composition, for example, it is this tension that intensifies our thrill in the thematic development, the rhythmic and harmonic interaction and gives the edge to the climaxes.

There are many performers and musicians who have a natural ability to combine moments of great tension with those of repose, making everything seem easy. Some voices float to the high notes effortlessly and some pianists make the octaves of scales ripple across the keys as if by magic. These are musicians who have an intellectual grasp of the music and know how to convey it without a barrier between their body and their instrument. This is a result of coordination between the movements of the body, music and timing in relation to tone. Above all, however, it is the breathing which gives the natural ease to the performance. You must breathe in the musical rhythm of what you are performing, maintaining a balance between creating tension and releasing it at the right moment. Music without rhythm is like a body without bones or muscles. In singing rhythm is fundamental because it allows articulation and diction and the shape and form of the music to remain flexible.

A singer uses all the muscles of the body and breath for a single sound, but the real work of singing comes from the brain. Although some singers sing by instinct, technical ideas are a result of comparison and analysis after the fact. For those who love singing everything about the voice or sound contains some kind of lesson. Virtuosity by itself is one-dimensional and real musicianship requires the dramatic tension of words and the understanding of the emotional, intellectual and spiritual content. It is a union of sound and thought and as ideas and words are illuminated by the sound, sounds are explained by the ideas and words. Singers and instrumentalists should realize that all their experiences in the world of sound are important to their art. Performers should have a repertory of sounds and emotions and draw upon it in performance.

Singing is a marriage between the singing and speaking voice and between the sound and the word. Diction and articulation give life to the spoken word and emotions and ideas are injected into speech. The voice must collaborate with the spoken word. The idea and intellectual content behind each word is what gives the music its nuance and variety. Words give life to the vocal sound. If someone sings well but we cannot understand the words and the singer doesn't understand the content behind the words, we as listeners are not moved. The mind also controls body tension and relaxation, as well as pronunciation and articulation. Because singers are their own instrument, the voice, body and intellect must work together to become fully expressive and in control. The voice, which must be flexible, has to be capable of a variety of tonal colours and pitch and react instantly to the subtleties and emotional nuances of the text.

Problems arise when physically the body and voice do not respond to these inner impulses as immediately as they should or there are obstacles of insecurity and anxiety causing tension. Facial tension resulting in frowning while singing can be eliminated easily by not frowning, thereby releasing the strain. A good singer supports his or her voice without involving other parts of the body. A pianist, for example, whose shoulders are up while he or she plays will immediately notice a difference in tonal quality when the shoulders are down and the tension is released.

Good singers sing with economy of movement and breath. Although the foremost vocal necessity is breathing, it is not so much a question of learning to breathe as it is learning to control the way one breathes naturally. There are two movements in breathing: inhalation and exhalation. The difficulty lies in the necessity of releasing only the quantity of breath required to sustain the sound. The voice is basically breath coming out of the lungs which the larynx transforms into sound through the vibration of the vocal cords. In other words, these rather thick cartilages contract in a certain fashion, and exhaled air passing through them makes them vibrate, producing sound.

The action of the vocal cords is similar to the vibrating strings on a violin or the reeds of an oboe. Different pitches are the result of changing the contour and elasticity of the cords and varying the contour of the resonating system. For example, the reeds come together momentarily and close off the expired air, then open and allow the air to escape in puffs. Repeating this process rapidly causes vibration of the vocal cords and results in tonal production and pitch variation. The air escaping rapidly is what produces the sound. The pitch is altered by the vocal cords in the same way pitch is changed by the lips of a trumpet player. A trumpeter plays different notes by enlarging or diminishing the size of the opening made by his lips, by changing their firmness and shape and by changing the force of expired air.

All vocalized sound is the result of air being expired through the cone-shaped narrowing of the phonatory tube at the apex of the trachea. The vocal cords, which vary in length, tension and contour, can interrupt the flow of this expired air partially or completely, but because they are elastic they yield under pressure. Singing or speaking is an aerodynamic phenomenon in which the muscles adjust and hold the vocal cords in a certain position, shape and tension, i.e., the laryngeal muscles do not produce vocal sound. The changes in the expired airstream caused by the movement of the vibrating vocal cords make the sound, and the changes of pitch in singing occur in part due to the variation in length, tension and mass of the vocal cords.

For example, each string of a stringed instrument is tuned to a specific pitch which is determined by the tension, length, mass and elasticity of the string. As the tension becomes greater, the pitch produced when the string is plucked or bowed is higher. If tension is doubled the pitch will rise one octave. Shorter strings produce higher pitches than longer strings. The thickness of a string affects both pitch and timbre. If the width or mass of a string is decreased the pitch will rise and if the mass is increased the pitch lowers. Elasticity also plays a part in producing pitch. Less inertia is produced in a flexible elastic material and more mass may be used before the limit of its tension is reached. Notes of the same pitch can be made with a string of varying length, tension, mass and elasticity as long as the ratio between these elements is correct. This will account for the differences between two different makes of a violin, and this idea of vibrating strings is the same for singers with the same tessitura. The vocal cords are able to produce tones the same way violin strings do. The force of expired air provides the energy with which the sound is made at the larynx.

Breathing in singing should not attract any more attention than speaking. When we speak we do not think about breathing. It is a natural reflex. Breathing brings about expression. It is the strength and control behind our breath and the amplitude we give it with the larynx, soft palate, tongue and lips that make the nuances in the singing line. For example, one musical phrase can be flowing and another divided. Some words may be accented and some fading in the shadow of a breath. One must be natural in singing, especially so as not to place any strain on the vocal cords. There are several ways of breathing: abdominal, which is accomplished by lowering the diaphragm and allowing the air to penetrate to the very bottom of the lungs; thoracic, which is accomplished by expanding the rib cage; and breathing which takes place at the top of the lungs. Louis says that the most important things in the production of the voice are the vocal cords. It is vital not to overtax them with forced breath.

The most recent research into vocal cord action proves that the 18th- and 19th-century bel canto composers, teachers and singers knew what produces good singing. They felt that a note is correctly produced if it can be swelled or contracted. Listen to the crescendos and diminuendos of Montserrat Caballé and marvel at her easy flow of sound and tonal colour. This means that the tightly closed vocal cords are activated with a minimum of air. The ends of the vocal cords are attached to cartilages which are linked to the vocal box. This vocal box is directly connected to the root of the tongue. This box must remain in a low but flexible position, otherwise the throat and the width of the pharynx will be closed or too narrow, resulting in the production of sharp, edgy sounds and singing off pitch. The voice sounds squeezed and dull due to the displacement of the voice box. Sharp singing is caused by forced production and flat singing by undue tension.

It is sometimes difficult to control those muscles which contract and determine the pitch of a sound, especially if you can't see them. By forming in your mind a precise visual image of the pitch you might be able to control these muscles. It is also necessary to develop and train an inner ear. Instrumentalists don't need to rely on this but singers need to imagine pitches at the speed they want to sing them. This flexibility comes first from the mind, then the inner ear, and finally the voice. It is vital to perfect a technique that works for you and that can be used repeatedly, because even good voices can sound bad if used incorrectly. Singing is a complex vocal act consisting of the physical position of the body, fixation of the larynx, sensation of the degree of support in terms of breath pressure, mechanical fixing of the tongue to determine vowels and the mental actions of conceiving the pitch, pronunciation, singing the correct note values, enunciation in relation to spatial demands, as well as the degree of vowel stress determined by the musical phrase, emotional and spiritual content.

Teaching voice, therefore, is both aesthetic and scientific. Science and anatomy supply the artist with the means to develop the technique to interpret. One has to avoid those teachers for whom technique and dogma are more important than the music. The mind has to be trained and the resulting awareness and technique will control only the muscles necessary for producing the desired sounds. There are many teachers who think that their way alone will create a great singer and some talentless people who have no understanding of the complex process involved in singing. Some voice teachers are unable to sing professionally or even sing. There are also piano coaches or repertoire pianists who label themselves voice teachers or vocal coaches. This can be dangerous for the uninitiated vocal student, for although these pianists are invaluable to the world of singing they have a different expectation of voice students than professional singers do. If you haven't experienced singing an opera with orchestra it is difficult to explain the stamina required, the sensations elicited or the balance between voice and orchestra. In reality, one learns by doing. Just as a pianist cannot teach a singer how to sing, but can help with musicianship, repertoire and an awareness of mistakes, a singer cannot be a piano teacher, but can help with musical line and phrasing.

Singing is so ephemeral that to try to communicate to another human being sensations in unseen vocal cords is extremely difficult. A sound may be called 'liquid' by one person and 'dry' by another. Some teachers do comparative teaching by metaphor. If you have a poetic nature, creative imaging for a student may work. What I do is to communicate the 'feel' of a sound by comparing it to another similar sensation. Some interesting phrases that I've heard and collected throughout the years, and with apologies no longer know whom to credit, are:

- feel the breath in the knees
- shape the throat like a pear
- sink through the floor on a high note
- feel soap bubbles rising in your throat
- feel as if your throat was on top of your skull
- feel as if the tone is elliptical and is arched between your pharynx and the top of your head

and my own personal favorite

- see your tone wedged between your teeth.

I have similar, almost surrealistic jargon for pianists. To this day I remember Rosina Lhévinne telling me to use my 'ghostly fingers to caress the keys', or to 'make love to the piano; the keys are your lover's skin'. That metaphor certainly made me want to practise more. By visualizing my usually mundane work at the piano as an imaginative erotic treat, the sounds I elicited from the keyboard always sounded warmer and more exciting.

Certain qualities of sound produced by the human voice are communicable, and there are words to describe these sounds that are generally agreed upon, such as 'closed sound', 'warm, cold, edgy, sharp' and many more. Although there is no tried and true method of vocal teaching the most flexible teacher will garner the best results. When the student can develop a way of singing in which there is mental imagery of sounds and knowledge of how to reproduce these sounds as well as the sensations resulting from these sounds, the student will be free to interpret the music without tension or fear.

Opera makes high demands on the singer's body coordination, balancing strength, flexibility and relaxation guided by the music and character of the text. Singing should be the ultimate joyous intellectual and physical experience. In the beginning, the young artist has to be guided to find his or her true voice. Often by listening to much-admired singers and working with great artists one learns the most. Enjoying music and loving art is the ultimate gift we are given as musicians. We learn by doing, experiencing, teaching ourselves and forever searching for more knowledge.

Biography

Even after celebrating 25 years at the Metropolitan Opera during the 1996–97 season, Montreal native Louis Quilico is still proving himself a force of nature in the operatic world. Having appeared in every important theatre from Anchorage to Tokyo and in operas ranging from his role-defining turn in *Rigoletto* to his recent recording of *The Most Happy Fella* in London, England and in New York City, Quilico is well-established as one of the foremost operatic stars of the century. He continues to perform and the assured quality of his still-strong voice is a testament to his personally devised vocal technique.

Mr. Quilico's expressive vocal powers and humanistic characterizations have reinforced his reputation as one of the great Verdi singers of the century. Still a favourite with opera lovers nationwide, Mr. Quilico is frequently recognized from his many performances in "Live from the Met" telecasts and videos.

Since his marriage to pianist Christina Petrowska in 1993, Mr. Quilico has continued recording and performing as a soloist and in joint recitals with his wife. The couple have collaborated on a series of recordings devoted to arias, art songs and operatic transcriptions. Their latest CD recording, *Chants Francais et Russes*, has received several glowing reviews. Arthur Kaptainis, respected music critic for the Montreal Gazette wrote: "Youthful at 72, baritone Louis Quilico still has a few tunes up his sleeve and he delivers them robustly on a disc of French and Russian tunes. Verdi baritones are not supposed to sing French art songs. After 70 they are not supposed to sing anything. Yet these self-evident truths have not stopped Louis Quilico, the former stalwart of the Metropolitan Opera, from issuing a successful Franco-Russian recital with his second wife, Christina Petrowska at the piano."

Opera Canada Magazine awarded the disc five stars: "Now in his 74th year, Quilico's rich, powerful baritone seems undiminished by the passage of time. Indeed, he makes one wonder how his younger colleagues could match his vocal scope and sheer beauty of tone."

Mr. Quilico's performances with Ms. Petrowska have also been applauded. The Toronto Star wrote: "The great Canadian baritone, Louis Quilico, is still deeply in love with musicmaking. He also seems very much in love with his wife, distinguished pianist Christina Petrowska. Both these objects of his affection helped make Quilico's recital on Monday night a special occasion."

The couple have given recitals throughout Canada and the United States, most recently in Philadelphia and in New York City. The Philadelphia Inquirer wrote: "Now in his 70's, Quilico sings with the assurance of a man fully in command of his craft. His top notes are there when needed. His articulation ensures each word is clear as his voice weighs its meaning. His program reminded listeners of the breadth of his singing life. He showed that singing and dramatic emphasis are graduations of expression. He was always the singer in these, even at the height of towering passion."

From the Canadian newspaper the Winnipeg Free Press: "Quilico showed powers undiminished in a program of familiar operatic arias. He was partnered by his wife Christina Petrowska, who also took a solo turn in three operatic realizations by Liszt. You need a singer capable of instantly fixing the character in the mind's eye and Quilico did just that in splendid voice with bloom and power to spare."

Born to an Italian father and a French-Canadian mother on January 14, 1925, Louis Quilico spent his formative years in Montreal, Canada. He was a solo chorister in the choir of St.-Jacques Church in Montreal and while a student of Frank H. Rowe won a prize, which allowed him to continue his studies with Teresa Pediconi and the famous baritone Riccardo Stracciari, at the Conservatoire Santa Cecilia in Rome.

On his return to Montreal in 1948, he trained with Martial Singher at the Conservatoire de Montréal and sang supporting roles at the Variétés Lyriques in the *Barber of Seville* and *La Traviata.* With the help of a scholarship from Mannes College in New York City, he continued his studies, from 1952 to 1955, with Singher, Ralph Herbert, Désiré Defrere (staging), and Emil Cooper (repertoire).

In 1953, he won first prize in the radio competitions, "Nos Futures Etoiles" and "Singing Stars of Tomorrow" and went on a Jeunesses Musicales tour with mezzo-soprano Rolande Garnier. He also participated in the CBC-TV programs, "Music Hall," "Serenade for Strings," and "Silhouette."

In 1954, Louis Quilico made his professional stage debut with the Opera Guild of Montreal as "Rangoni" in *Boris Godunov.* The following year, he won the *Metropolitan Opera Auditions of the Air* competition, and made his New York City debut, October 10, 1955, with the New York City Opera, singing "Germont" in *La Traviata.*

In 1957, he sang the title role in a televised program of excerpts from *Wozzeck* for CBC-TV and was "Masetto" in a production of *Don Giovanni* for the Montreal Festivals. The following year, he sang in the North American premiere of Nicolas Nabokov's *Symboli Chrestiani* with the Montreal Symphony Orchestra. At the 1959 Spoleto Festival in Italy, he sang the title role in Donizetti's *Il Duca d'Alba.*

In 1960, Mr. Quilico made his Covent Garden debut as "Germont" in *La Traviata* opposite Dame Joan Sutherland and remained a member of the until 1963. In 1962, he debuted at the Bolshoi Theatre in Moscow, USSR, as "Rigoletto." In 1963, he made his Paris Opera debut as "Rodrigo" in *Don Carlos* and at the inauguration of the ORTF Auditorium, participated in the premiere of Milhaud's oratorio *Pacem in terris* under conductor Charles Munch in Paris, France. He was a member of the cast for the Geneva premiere of *La Mere Coupable*, by the same composer.

In 1967, Mr. Quilico performed in a solo recital at the Stratford Festival Theatre in Stratford, Ontario. He returned to Stratford in 1970, with soprano Lois Marshall. He gave several recitals at Expo '67 in Montréal and was "Iago" opposite Jon Vickers and Teresa Stratas in *Otello*. In May 1967, he played "Creon" opposite Ernst Haefligher, Marilyn Horne and Joseph Rouleau in a performance of Stravinsky's *Oedipus Rex* with the Toronto Symphony Orchestra. The production was led by conductor Robert Craft with Stravinsky present. The same year, he appeared as "Rigoletto" with the Vancouver Opera and sang in "The Messiah" with the Toronto Mendelssohn Choir. In January 1968, he participated in a concert performance of Verdi's *Alzir*' with the American Opera Society at Carnegie Hall.

Beginning in the 1960s, Mr. Quilico appeared regularly at many of the world's great opera houses — the Vienna Opera, the Teatro Colon of Buenos Aires, the Teatro Massimo of Palermo, and the operas of Rome, Venice, Turin, Florence and Paris. He performed frequently with the Canadian Opera Company in a variety of roles ("Iago" in *Otello*, "Germont" in *La Traviata*, "Amonasro" in *Aida*, "Scarpia" in *Tosca*, "Enrico Ashton" in *Lucia di Lammermoor*, "Michele" in *Il Tabarro*, and title roles in *Rigoletto*, *Macbeth* and *Simon Boccanegra*) and appeared regularly with the Opera du Quebec (the "High Priest" in *Samson et Dalila*, "Germont" in *La Traviata*, "Tonio" in *I Pagliacci*, and the title role in *Falstaff*).

In 1961, 1969 and in 1972, Mr. Quilico sang at the Bolshoi Theatre. In February 1972, he replaced the regular "Golaud" (Thomas Stewart) in *Pelleas et Melisande* during a run at the Metropolitan Opera in New York City. In December 1972, he stepped in again at The Met, replacing Tito Gobbi as "Otello" opposite fellow Canadian, Jon Vickers. In January 1973, he opened at the Metropolitan Opera as "Germont" in *La Traviata*. Thus began a long and prestigious career with the company which lasted for 25 consecutive seasons, until he retired in 1998.

His roles at The Met included title roles in *Rigoletto*, *Falstaff*, *Macbeth* and *Gianni Schicchi*, "Don Carlo" in *Ernani*, "Di Luna" in *Il Trovatore*, "Iago" in *Otello*, "Renato" in *Un Ballo in Maschera*, "Amonasro" in *Aida*, "Rodrigo" in *Don Carlos*, "Ronio" in *I Pagliacci*, "Barnaba" in *La Gioconda*, "Scarpia" in *Tosca*,

"Michonnet" in *Adrianna Lecouvreur*, "Golaud" in *Pelleas et Mélisande* and "Dr. Bartolo" in *The Barber of Seville.*

During the 1950s, 1960s and 1970s, Louis Quilico sang regularly with the New York City Opera and with most of the major opera companies in the United States and Europe. During the 1974–75 season, he performed in various cities, including London, England (Covent Garden) San Francisco, Hartford, New Orleans and Baltimore.

He reprised the role of "Germont" in *La Traviata* and played "Pandolphe" in Massenet's *Cendrillon* for Festival Ottawa in 1978 and 1979 respectively. In 1979, he starred in the CBC-TV special "Portrait de Louis Quilico." In the late '70s, he and his son Gino became the first father/son team to perform at the Metropolitan Opera and with the Canadian Opera Company.

Mr. Quilico has been acclaimed for his performances in many televised broadcasts of "Live from the Met." Following the telecast of *Rigoletto*, the New York Times wrote: "Louis Quilico, as "Rigoletto," was at the centre of the drama ... his passions and fears could be heard in his voice as well as seen in his face and body." The New York Post wrote of another performance as "Renato" in *Un Ballo in Maschera:* "Louis Quilico was the vocal star. His aria, *Eri Tu*, proved the high point of the evening."

In November 1991, Louis Quilico again sang the title role in *Rigoletto* at the Opéra de Montreal. Two months earlier, he had triumphed in the role of "Tony" in a new production of the lyric drama, *The Most Happy Fella*, presented by the New York City Opera at Lincoln Center. Among his recent performances at the Metropolitan Opera, in the 1990s, were *Adriana Lecouvreur*, *Tosca* and *I Pagliacci*. During the same period, he appeared as "Falstaff" in New Orleans and as "Dr. Bartolo" in *The Barber of Seville* in Palm Beach and Fort Lauderdale. For his 70th birthday he performed at the New Israeli Opera House in Tel Aviv, Israel in *The Barber of Seville.*

His final performance of "Rigoletto"' — his 510th — was at the National Arts Center in Ottawa on September 17, 1994. Opera Canada Magazine wrote of the event: "Louis Quilico, in his 69th year remains a vocal and dramatic marvel. His "Rigoletto" will be remembered for decades and it was no surprise when the entire sold-out house instantly rose to its feet as the curtain descended on Act II."

Louis Quilico has taught at the Faculty of Music, University of Toronto (1969 to 1987), at McGill University (1987 to 1990) and most recently at the Academy of Vocal Arts in Philadelphia (1994 to 1999). He is currently a teacher at the Glenn Gould Professional School, Royal Conservatory of Music in Toronto.

Mr. Quilico received an honorary doctorate from the Université du Quebec in 1987 and in May 1999 was awarded the first "Distinguished Visitor Award" by the University of Toronto, Toronto. He has been honoured by the Sarasota Opera Guild and was given the keys to the city of Sarasota, Florida in 1996. He won the Prix de musique Calixa-Lavallée in 1965 and received the Canadian Music Council medal in 1985.

In 1974 he was named a Companion of the Order of Canada and in November 1999 will received one of Canada's highest awards, The Governor General's Performing Arts Award. The municipality of St.-Leonard in Montreal has named a street in his honour.

The Conversation

ℬ ⌑ ℭ

This section contains the conversation between Christina Petrowska ($\mathscr{C}$) and Louis Quilico ($\mathscr{L}$).

Some Personal Thoughts

𝒞: *When did you discover singing and what does it mean to you?*

ℒ: The most incredible moment of my artistic life was when as a very young child I discovered my musical instrument — my singing voice. It was, for me, a unification of body, mind and spirit. It grew to become second nature to me for I had found a love, a true and pure love for singing that drives me and inspires me to this day. That is why I have been able to achieve what I have during my career. It is not only the singing that is so wonderful, but the music that drives one to discover and comprehend the emotions and passions that exist within oneself and in one's life.

𝒞: *Can you explain this in more detail?*

ℒ: In art, as in life, you must give yourself up completely, meeting challenges with integrity, despite risks. Love of singing creates its own future and embodies everything a singer can hope for in an artistic life. When you are performing you are drawn into the mystery of creation. You experience that special moment of magic that is not given to many people but which can transport you into another dimension, just as love does in one's life.

𝒞: *Who was your inspiration for singing?*

ℒ: Deanna Durbin and Leonard Warren. When I was about 17 years old I saw Deanna Durbin in one of her many films. I had a mile and a half to walk home and I don't remember ever touching the ground. I was very impressed by Leonard Warren the first time I heard him on the radio on Ruby Mercer's program from the middle 1940s. I went right away to buy a recording.

𝒞: *What was it about these two singers that inspired you?*

ℒ: The voice, the charisma, the beauty. They moved and excited me.

𝒞: *If they were your inspiration who were your vocal teachers?*

ℒ: Riccardo Stracciari and Walter Brunelli in Rome and Martial Singher at the Conservatoire in Montreal and at Mannes School in New York.

𝒞: *Explain the difference between vocal coaching, voice teachers and repertoire pianists.*

ℒ: One must define and refine the title 'voice teacher'. Vocal students should realize that there is an enormous difference between a voice teacher, vocal coach and repertoire pianist. Although pianists are of enormous value to the singer, an accompanist is not a voice teacher. Making suggestions and playing through repertoire does not make you a 'master teacher of voice'. I feel that to be a 'voice' teacher you must psychologically and physically know your voice as you sing, especially on a big stage, if you're teaching opera. The experience you achieve from singing with orchestra, costumes and chorus is crucial, especially in learning how to achieve proper balance and stamina. It's not the same in a studio. There were many wonderful coaches and pianists at the Metropolitan Opera, Covent Garden, Paris Opera and at other companies whom I should credit for helping me.

Their experience with the operas, their advice, was incredible for me. Also, the artists I have worked with: Luciano Pavarotti, Placido Domingo, Mirelli Freni, Beverly Sills (to name just a few) have contributed enormously to my artistic life. One must not forget that opera is an ensemble art. However, the vocal technique that I have which allows me to sing in my seventies is my own unique creation and was a personal development which I am still working on. A true artist never stops searching.

𝒞: *Pianists are extremely valuable to singers. How did your first wife help you?*

ℒ: In the beginning of my career she taught me solfege (not voice) and encouraged me to pursue a career, which is why I was always grateful. In her student days, Lina had hoped to become a concert pianist but said, "I did not have the strength." Instead she chose to work on operatic scores and do some accompanying. She always said, "He (Louis) was the master of the voice — he is the singer, I am not." I say that to clarify the always confusing problem of vocal coaches, voice teachers, and accompanists.†

𝒞: *Why did you choose Thomas Hampson to write a foreword?*

ℒ: I have sung with Thomas at the Metropolitan Opera and admire and respect his integrity, vocal technique and artistry. He is also very literate and a singer whose musicianship and use of language is impeccable. Not only is he a consummate performer but he respects the art of singing and teaching as a personal and spiritual journey. Of all the younger baritones, it is Hampson's attitude towards vocal art which reminds me of my own. I wanted a kindred spirit, a baritone, who will carry on the tradition of great vocal art in performing and teaching to write the preface for this book which is so personal to me.

---

† Ruby Mercer (MUS 278, Boxes 7–9, Folders 59–82), "Interviews with Lina and Gino Quilico," Archival material, National Library of Canada.

𝒞: *You retired from the Metropolitan Opera after 25 consecutive years. What are your favorite memories?*

ℒ: 'Don Carlos' and 'I Pagliacci' with Placido Domingo; 'Rigoletto' and 'Ballo in Maschera' with Luciano Pavarotti; 'Otello' with Jon Vickers. (There were so many that I hate to pick and choose.) Singing with the greatest sopranos of the time, 'Adriana Lecouvreur' with Montserrat Caballé; Renata Scotto and Mirella Freni and 'Falstaff' with James Levine, conducting. The audience, fans, backstage crew, dressers, ushers — everyone was always wonderful and made the Met my happiest home. I should mention the New York City Opera where I also sang with Beverly Sills and José Carreras, and Covent Garden with Joan Sutherland. Too many great memories to list.

𝒞: *After such an incredibly successful operatic career, what makes you happy now?*

ℒ: I have to say that it is magical doing concerts with you and listening to your concert tours. We think as one soul. We have also received such wonderful reviews for our recitals and CDs together that I take back any thing negative I ever said about critics. I also love being home. As a father to our two daughters, Dominique and Alexandra Delphine Brégent, I have had the opportunity to see them develop and grow into lovely young women. I treasure the relationship I have with both of them. I regret not being there enough for my son, Gino, and daughter, Donna. But being an opera star made it difficult to parent and survive the pressures of a career. However, Gino and I did have some wonderful moments on and off stage.

𝒞: *Any final thoughts or advice?*

ℒ: Enjoy every minute of everyday, as I do with you. Love and music make me a *Most Happy Fella.*

On the Voice

𝒞: *How did you develop your technique and your laws of singing?*

ℒ: I had six months to prepare for a performance with the San Francisco Opera. I was not happy with my singing and decided to go back to the basics and study by myself. You have to use your mind because you must develop a feeling for the voice, intellectually as well as physically. I lived in an empty room and stood about eight inches from the bare wall and meditated for at least 5 or 6 hours a day on the process of how one sings. The less singing you do while studying, the better it becomes. You have to discover yourself and your own identity. The voice will not do anything by itself. It has to be commanded. As a teacher, I never talk about sound, because for me the sound is the least important of all. You have muscles that might be obstructing you and you have to eliminate any problems these muscles might be causing by knowing where they are. We should be master of our body; therefore I developed my own way of teaching which I call the 'Nine Laws'.

1. *The way to stand on your feet:* If you don't stand in the right position you create tension. Never stand on two feet. Either you create complete tension, or you transfer the tension to one place. As you shift weight from one foot to the other, your shoulders settle and relax.

2. *Support:* If you place your hand on your abdomen and you press the lower abdomen in, the stomach area comes out. You have two sets of muscles there. The lowest muscles of your abdomen give the support. It's a small, supple action. It's like the shock absorbers of a car that absorb the bouncing. You don't take a breath by using the chest. There's only one way of breathing. Whenever you breathe, you go down there to the lower abdomen. Instead of pushing against the muscle you use it as a protective floor.

3. *Breathing:* The most important thing for a singer is his mental approach. A student working with me might not make a sound for several months. The concepts must come first. As for breathing, you don't take the air in, you shoot the air out. Don't inhale the air. Believe that the air goes towards the brains, not that you are taking the oxygen into the lungs. Singers tend to overdo, to overemphasize. If you do the opposite, and don't emphasize, the right amount of air will come in. Otherwise, overdoing it will make you take too much air in. Sometimes I tell my students to imagine that they have a little pipe between their teeth, the two upper front teeth. The air goes just behind the teeth. You don't take the air in and you don't swallow the air. You should de-emphasize the process of taking the breath in. Thinking about shooting air through the little pipe makes the process gentler. Never think that you are going to inflate your lungs. Just say yes, without thinking of any hint of expansion in the lungs. They will inflate themselves. Also, never breathe only by the mouth or by the nose. Use both. As you say 'yes' feel the breathing you are using.

4. *Opening the throat:* Everything has to be done with a certain amount of flexibility. To bring down the larynx is not a natural thing. You can move your Adam's apple, for example, independently of the jaw, which shouldn't move

in this exercise. When you ask a child to wink, at first the child squeezes both eyes. You have to learn to use only one eye. Similarly, you must learn independent motions within your larynx. You have to come to the point where like Mr. Universe or body builders you can move different muscles, one at a time. At some point, everything becomes one action, but you realize that each one is an individual action. In one's career, if you're faced with vocal trouble, like everyone is from time to time, you must find and understand the trouble spots and learn how to fix them. As for the opening of the throat, you must try to feel the expansion, it's not only a movement up and down but you must try to feel the expansion. Think of an expanding pipe that will go up and down. It should feel as though it's expanding in the area of the larynx, the Adam's apple, not in the back of the throat, the pharynx. You must also watch the position of the head. The throat has to feel as if it is in its proper 'socket', otherwise it will not function correctly. It cannot be up or down. If you bring your head down, the throat cannot function anymore, because you collapse the larynx. It collapses not only down, but also up. If you want a pipe to give you a tremendous jet stream, make it straight. Bend it and it is not the same. Your larynx has to be in its own sockets and you have to eliminate obstructions. Your larynx cannot be extended or bent backwards or forwards. It's vertical. You want to be able to sing out to the balcony.

5. *The tension of the cords:* People should realize that when you are using the vocal cords there is a very simple thing that can be done with the slightest sound. If you make a tiny, raspy, scratchy sound the tickling it creates in your throat irritates you. That irritation will show you where the cords are. Using the muscles alone will not enable you to find them but you come to the point where you develop a certain feeling for finding them. I like to sing sensing the cords going through the air. Actually, you're compressing the air. You have to have the sensation that the cords are going down, like elastic or the feeling of suspension. It's the cords that make the pressure, not the wind or breath. The voice is the most flexible part of ourselves and the

pressure we use should never be great but extremely flexible. They have to go down into the air. The cords have to be tense, like a violin string with air for a bow.

6. *Broadness of sound in the cheekbones:* We're taught that we sing with resonance. What makes the resonance? Collapse the cords and there is none. Tense the cords a little bit and there is more resonance. The upper palate lifts. It gives more space. At the same time, in your imagination, you have to think that you are giving more facial space. This is elasticity, more than getting space. A singer must have a lot of imagination. You have to feel that you become very, very broad in the face. The actual sound is a little point about eighteen inches in front of your nose and you sing into that little hole, except that everything has to be very spacey. It is the bone cavities that you have to reach, as much as possible. To that, add the sensation of feeling the cheekbones.

7. *Lifting of the eyes:* To feel space, if I bring my eyes down, I don't have any sensation of the ceiling. But when I take a breath, and by lifting my eyes and eyebrows I am aware that I take the air from this whole roomful of air. Just lifting the eyes makes me more aware of the space around me.

8. *Combination of the intake of air and sensation:* While I take the air, instead of swallowing the air, I absorb the air, which goes towards the brains. Oxygen goes into rotation and at the end of the rotation, goes out. There is a suspension. A cycle and a suspension. The air that goes in is being suspended in your whole body, bloodstream, everything. It becomes a tremendous circulation. It creates an incredible force in the human being. It's like yoga. There is a suspension between the intake or inhaling and exhaling. It transfers itself into a tremendous power. If I push it out, I lose what I want. If I'm not pushing it out, I'm using the actual strength of it. That gives me the power of my voice. To achieve this suspension and equilibrium think of a tightrope walker. When he starts to walk on the wire, he touches the wire with his toe to find the feeling then he slides into the wire. He wants to know exactly where it's

supposed to be touching with feeling. He's like a blind man using only his feet. It's supreme concentration.

9. *Making a sound:* When you make the right sound it becomes like ecstasy. Then you can sing. Your sensation goes in rotation. The rotation has to be done by your hands and has to come from the inside to the outside. With your hand you also make a rotation. The rotation is not coming to your face but the opposite.

𝒞: *You often talk about the violin and compare the vocal cords with the bow moving across the strings.*

ℒ: Yes, if you really think carefully it's a very simple thing. The violins have a chord or string. Singers have two vocal cords. The bow of the violin is like the breath for us. The breath is not as important as the cord. This is the point that's so difficult to explain. When you take a breath to bring the air up to the cord, the cord tenses exactly the way it has to tense. And that is very difficult for young singers to control. That's why singers become great, because they understand the communication between the breath and the vocal cords. If you give too much breath then the cords get too much pressure and the first thing you know, the cord becomes very tense. It's like a runner. When you look at a runner you see that he runs and is very flexible. He doesn't try to find strength in his body, he tries to find flexibility in his body. This is what happens with the voice. You have to find the flexibility of your voice through the cord. The cord indicates to the breath, give me so much air not more, then give me less air, more air, less air, and that's all it does. And that's what makes the cords vibrate.

Look at the violin. When the bow goes across the string you will see that the string is vibrating by the friction of the bow. For instance, the bow always has to have a certain rosin on it. It creates more touch for the string. The string vibrates so well because the pressure or weight of the bow on the string is never a big. If you want a bigger sound then you will see the violinist play even more with his bow. But, in general, when he wants to make a very delicate sound on his violin, he will practically not touch the strings on the violin.

𝒞: *That concept works for many instruments and other techniques. You also mentioned that when you were sick you could still sing. Is it not true that sometimes you give your best performances when you're sick because you only focus on what you need to do and you don't overanalyze?*

ℒ: Well, the point is, you're very right about that. I'm not sure if you call that focus on technique. At that point, it's like I said before, the pressure is the thing that is very treacherous. Very often when people are sick they press too much. For instance, when you're singing and you have phlegm on the cords. What do you think is the best way to get rid of that phlegm? It's to press a little bit more with the air, which dislodges phlegm from the cord. The cords are the most sensitive nerves of our body.

𝒞: *I heard an interview with Luciano Pavarotti on PBS saying that he had laryngitis and couldn't speak but he could still sing. Could you explain it?*

ℒ: When you speak your concentration is not really on your vocal cords. But when you sing your concentration is completely on your cords and you don't really put tension on the cords. When you sing, your subconscious activates your reflexes to focus tension on the vocal cords enabling you to sing but maybe not speak.

𝒞: *This is a very abstract concept which is difficult to explain to a lot of people. With orchestral or keyboard instruments and in dance you can see the body movement, but with singers you can't see the vocal cords.*

ℒ: That's exactly what it is.

𝒞: *Does that not make teaching difficult?*

ℒ: It would be easier if a singer could have the sensitivity to imagine himself or herself as a blind person. By touching your face with their hands, they feel something that is tickling at the end of the fingers and make an image inside their mind. Singers should be able to feel mentally. For me personally, I practically see what I'm doing. But my mind has been so accustomed to it that I practically see my cords.

The only thing that I cannot do is to see to give commands to my vocal cords. I give commands to them only by feeling. And this is why I say, act like a blind person. With the violin, you see the violin, you can touch it, you know where you're going to press, you see where the bow goes and you know how to press on the bow, and because it's all in front of you it's like the piano. But there's still something inside of these instruments, not physical but mental, that's exactly like my instrument. Your mind has to produce what it wants. And that is very difficult, to be able to convince a person, especially if they always had in their mind that making a sound is more important. It's to make them understand that the less you do the better it is.

𝒞: *This is a very spiritual approach. Mind over matter — less is better — meditation not over-practice. What is the story you told me about not vocalizing?*

ℒ: This was said to me by Jussi Björling. I was doing a performance with him in San Francisco in 1956.

𝒞: *What opera?*

ℒ: I was doing *Manon Lescaut* and all of a sudden I said that I had to vocalize. And the first thing he asked me was, "Do you vocalize a lot, young man?" "Oh yes!" I said, "I have to vocalize a lot." He says, "Do me a favour. Remember this one thing I'm going to tell you. God has given you two little vocal cords. He gave you those to sing, let's say 3,000 performances. Well, each time you vocalize you use up several of those 3,000 performances. Do you prefer to do a performance or vocalize?" Another thing he said to me I did not understand at first, but only much later. He said, "Young man, vocalizing is made for you to understand what you are doing." And I said, "But what am I supposed to understand?" At first because I did not understand much about the vocal approach, I used to sing and I had a nice voice. But I did not know the real technique or how to produce a voice. And this was the reason he was trying to anchor in my mind how to think to be able to sing. I thought about it so many times that the first thing I know, it was coming out of my ears. But I never got tired because it was very important to discover my technique. When I say this to people I know it makes them laugh, but I put myself against a wall for 3 to 4 hours a day. And in that time I would make maybe one, maybe two sounds. The rest of the time I didn't make a sound. I wanted to discover, to feel the sound. Nobody ever told me what you have to try to feel to discover the sound. This came from my own deduction. I watched the great artists sing and I heard what they were doing but it seemed too easy. What was it they were doing? Finally, my wall served its purpose. All of a sudden, I felt the sound and I heard the sound that I made.

C: *And that spiritual experience has allowed you to sing for so many years.*

L: Absolutely. I have to say that the most important thing in singing is that if you want to make a beautiful sound, you have to feel beautiful inside. If you don't feel beautiful, don't try to make a beautiful sound. If mentally you are frustrated, what do you think is going to come out? A frustrated sound! Why do you think a man like Pavarotti, for instance, sounds so wonderful? I'm talking about him because I'm so used to him, and I know him better than anybody else and I sang with him for so many years, but there are a lot of others as well. When it was the time for Luciano to sing, nothing else counted in life; that was it. When you make this kind of sound there's only one way to make it. You *have* to be very beautiful inside. Because it gives you freedom. When you are frustrated there's no more freedom; your mind is preoccupied. For myself, when it is the time to sing, during the afternoon, I would have to forget everything else.

C: *You sometimes sound like a Buddhist monk when you talk about singing.*

L: If that's the way I've got to be, I'll stay like that. It's very important.

C: *For every artist it's necessary to find an inner peace to be able to communicate to the audience, because you're the physical instrument and although you can have great anger or rage emotionally in the music, technically, and therefore physically, you have to be at peace with yourself.*

L: Absolutely. It's like I said and I'll repeat it: The only way to make a beautiful sound is to be beautiful inside. And you see it all the time, people who are kind of frustrated and cannot get out of their frustration. Listen to them. You will notice one thing: it doesn't work. Unless you're working too much. Then it's not a frustration, you're just too tired. But what happens at that point, when you're tired, you become frustrated very easily. However, if you are intelligent enough, the moment you feel the frustration taking over, it's time for you to stop and think, be like a computer machine. When I have problems vocally, what do I do? I stop and start to think from my toes to my hair. I remember one season at the Met. There was a wobble in my voice, and I did not like it. It took me about three or four performances before I realized that I had it. When I started to listen to myself I began to think, not to listen but to think, what is wrong with me? And I discovered right away that the support wasn't there. I realized that I was too heavily anchored and that I was not beautiful enough in spirit. That means I had started to do what many singers do, pull in the stomach not to show that you're a little bit fat, eh? But the first thing I knew, I had no more control of the air and there was a little wobble. I corrected that quickly, I tell you.

C: *When we hear young singers singing out of tune is it the technique or the ears?*

L: I think it's a combination of the two. Most of the time they don't have a good technique and they don't know how to use it. They don't know how to feel vocally. Ears maybe, but I'm not sure about that. I'm always reticent to accuse the ears. Some people have a problem. I remember in London there was a woman who would always sing a third up or down. She couldn't sing the right note. And you know something funny, she was in the chorus. I don't know how she was managing, but she was managing very beautifully. She was in the chorus for something like 15 years if not more.

𝒞: *What about this gift of certain tenors to hit the high C's?*

ℒ: Well, I'm going to tell you one thing: if your technique is good you should be able to hit it. But you see, when young artists prepare themselves they are satisfied to say, well I've got a high C, that's what I need in my life, and they stop there. Me, what I always did was to sing about five or six notes above the notes that I needed. If I needed an A natural, what do you think I did? I went to an F above high C. Some singers don't complete the potential of their voice.

𝒞: *Can tenors have a career without a high C?*

ℒ: I would say that today they all have a career without a high C because the pitch went up so high.

𝒞: *In Vienna for example?*

ℒ: No, in Russia. And, ah, it's terrible, because when you start to sing you're practically a tone higher.

𝒞: *So this is not a myth, about an orchestra or a piano being tuned too high.*

ℒ: Oh no, no, no. People like von Karajan, for instance, always wanted to have brilliance in the orchestra. But, you know, the thing is that we are human. There is only so much you can do with the vocal cords. Do you want to tax that more? You are already taxing something that should not be overtaxed. What I mean by this is: To give that kind of a high pitch you have to tense the cords more than usual. Now what is happening is that usually you can sing at 440 which is about the right pitch. Then all of a sudden you go up to 450! Now what is happening is that you are singing one performance here — let's put it at 1 inch for the cord. Now you go and sing in Vienna, where the cords are not 1 inch anymore, but must be an inch and one-eighth or an inch and one-sixteenth more and then the following performance you go back to 1 inch. You see what you're doing with the cords? And that is the danger, because you're taxing something of your body that cannot be taxed at any moment like this.

𝒞: *What would be the ideal tuning for singers?*

ℒ: Well, I'm going to tell you one thing: it depends on the singers. Lately I've heard that 420 would be the best thing. Some other place it's 440. I'm not sure, I never asked, but I think the Met is lower. They don't want to have so much brilliance.

𝒞: *And yet the Met orchestra sounds wonderful under James Levine.*

ℒ: It sounds good. You know, I don't think the higher tuning of the instruments made a difference in the orchestra. Play music the way it's supposed to be played. I'm not talking about anybody in particular, but some of the conductors hold a baton in their hands and that baton is more human than they are.

𝒞: *If you had a young artist to train, to develop into the next Rigoletto, what would be the program you would suggest?*

ℒ: First of all, he would have to be a young artist who has the voice for it. But the big problem with some of the young artists is that they are interested in fame or money. The young artists are creating a little bit of a problem. They sing the wrong things or too much heavy repertoire too soon.

𝒞: *Would you train an artist for a year?*

ℒ: Well, it might be even more than that but not only train them vocally, groom them, make sure that they're ready for the public. You have some people that can't go in front of the public. You see it all the time. But that is the most beautiful thing there is if you can understand.

𝒞: *The communication with the audience?*

ℒ: Yes. Artists sometimes cannot absorb the pressure. You think there's no pressure up there! To be a man like Pavarotti or Placido Domingo, it takes will, stamina and determination like nobody else has in this world. And that's why they succeeded because they're strong people inside. And that is the thing that you have to discover.

𝒞: *And both of them are very much aware of the quality of their performance rather than just the fame and publicity.*

ℒ: Well, I have to say that they are so strong in their beliefs that it is not difficult for them to survive. The pressure of performing is a tremendous thing. But at the same time the willpower of the man or woman, call it the way you want, is just as strong. Men like Placido Domingo and Pavarotti! They have a will and it's their mind and soul that are committed to what they are doing.

𝒞: *Yes, we don't hear many stories about opera stars getting involved in violent situations or drug abuse.*

ℒ: No! No! In general I don't think so. You have to come to the point where you are independent of any crutches.

𝒞: *What was your great inspiration?*

ℒ: My great inspiration? Well, I think Leonard Warren was really my inspiration more than anyone else because he had something in his voice that was so incredible. And, he was like my patron saint, you know. I always remember him. And I have to say, there's something similar in his voice to my voice. I did not try to make my voice like his, but it was very close to mine. And it was a very good model for me. It was wonderful!

𝒞: *Do you think that maybe students aren't listening enough to great singers? Are they relying on coaches, vocal teachers, and vocal techniques or schools rather than developing their own artistry as you did?*

ℒ: I have to say that today there is a big problem with pupils. Pupils expect to have a teacher who is going to hold their hand till doomsday. You have some people with voice teachers, and the first thing you know, 20 years later they're still going to see their teacher. You should have somebody to help you vocally but you have to come to a point where you have to understand your own instrument. Because let's face it, this is an instrument like another. Very often people have no conception whatsoever of their own instrument. And that is a real tragedy, because what happens when they land in big trouble? They don't have the foggiest idea how to fix their problems. They were very dramatic singers, incredible on the stage, but when it came to vocal problems, they didn't know what to do. A person who walks on the stage has to be able to explain what goes on with their voice. Ninety-five percent of the singers don't really know what the technique is! And you know, it's not written in books, it's not given to you through examples or anything like that. No, *it's you yourself* who has to discover it. If you cannot discover it by yourself you're in big trouble.

C: *You yourself only had a few formal lessons.*

L: Well, I had, from a real voice teacher, maybe 40 voice lessons. I had a good ear and I listened. But I was a master. When I say this it's not because I want to brag about myself, but you have to become the master of your own instrument. You, why do you walk? You know how to walk, you know how to run, that's exactly the same thing. You have to know how to walk, how to run, because it's a thing that's all inside, it's not outside. And it's not written in books. When you read a book your imagination works, your mind is travelling in a stratosphere that helps you to understand what is happening and you see it in your mind. That is the point. You see things. But when you sing, you don't see anything. You have to feel, you have to see, not with the eyes but with your soul, with your mind. And that is the thing that is very difficult to achieve.

C: *So, in fact, it's not enough to have a vision, or to say this phrase has to be legato, or sing this more musically. You have to know how to approach it technically and vocally.*

L: Actually, a legato, a diminuendo, a crescendo has nothing to do with the vocal technique. We always think that these crescendos are done with the support of the breath. But how is the breath working, how are the vocal cords working? What is in your mind? These are the things that are not always there!

C: *What about these so called famous master classes? Is it valuable to the young singer to have an opinion from several masters? And will these masters actually divulge some of their secrets or not?*

L: Well, I will tell you one thing: it's very difficult to divulge vocal secrets because it's too personal. How do you explain to a person your love towards another person? Only you feel it. And that is the point. For instance, it's very interesting to watch these master classes, but in the master class the man or the woman who does the master class does not really have the time to work on the voice. They will tell you how to do certain phrasing, but in general they don't often touch the voice. Now if they can teach the voice, that's one thing.

C: *Are there any good vocal teachers who don't sing on the operatic stage but know the technique well enough to teach professionally?*

L: If you are a psychologist maybe you will be better as a teacher, because you have to translate for someone. Voice teachers generally make you vocalize, and vocalizing doesn't give you what you want. You see, for the piano or the violin the construction of the instrument is already there. If we go back to the piano, you have to get the tree, cut it and make the form of the piano. After that they come with a piece of metal, the strings, all the material things of the piano. But singers don't want to go to back to that, and I'm sorry to say that's exactly what we should do. Naturally we don't think of wood, but you have to think of certain things, mental things, feeling things, e.g., how to use the breath, how to use the vocal cords. Even more simple than that, ask any young artist, any young voice student, how they stand. Since I have been teaching, there's not one of them that can tell me the reason you have to know how to stand when you sing. I will repeat it to doomsday: if you don't know how to stand, forget about singing.

C: *So the answer to the question is yes, you should be a singer to actually give the technique. For example, you can learn repertoire from a vocal/piano coach or from a conductor, but to relate properly to the students you should have had some of those experiences yourself by performing on the stage.*

ℒ: Yes, but I would like to meet a psychologist or psychiatrist who could tell me how you train the brain to be able to have the feeling before the word. And that is the thing that is very difficult. Because what we do in singing is say the word, but we don't care what is happening before we say it. You have to go into a sphere that is not the usual. Like I said before, you must go by feeling, but how do you train yourself to try to find the feeling? That is the thing that is very difficult. If you don't train yourself for that, how can you really hope to train others? In the old days there were some singers who would wake up in the morning and all of a sudden they were singers because they had a feeling for it. But how many times does it happen?

𝒞: *I feel that with piano teachers if they haven't had the experience of playing with orchestra on stage they can't teach a piano concerto as well. They can only teach from imagined sensations and not experienced ones, acoustical and physical.*

ℒ: I agree. The only thing is that maybe some people from outside the profession could help you to discover your inner physical being.

𝒞: *I understand what you mean. There are several techniques, for example, the Alexander technique, which teaches how to breathe. There are also general how-to books that can build confidence. Would this help the voice too?*

ℒ: Well, I'm going to tell you one thing: voice is different but not that different. In general, 95 percent of the people taking voice lessons think that to sing is to make a big noise and to push until the hair comes out. But who uses speech as a voice lesson? They don't. And for me that is the most important thing. People have to know what the sensation of voice is. There are also so many little things that are involved. And when I hear a voice teacher tell me, 'Oh, please never talk about the vocal cords!' I want to kill them. Between the cords and the breath, don't choose the breath, choose the cords. It's the cords that make everything. It's like the violin. You don't press too much on the string that you're playing on. If you look at the piano for instance, you press the note but it's not the hammer that you hit that keeps on repeating. No! It has been done. And our cords are exactly the same. If they are too tense they're not good, they don't function!

𝒞: *Are there any opera schools that you like or dislike or meet with your approval?*

ℒ: I will tell you frankly, schools are not my favorite subject. It's when they finish school that students become singers. They have to learn their trade. And I find that very treacherous that people go to a school to learn how to use a voice. And the first thing you know, they go to that school and they don't learn how to use their voice.

𝒞: *And then their voices are overused and ruined by the time they get out of the school. Does that happen?*

ℒ: Well I would not say that they are overused. The point is, very often, the voice is not used enough. You see, they don't have time to learn about the voice and that is a tragedy. They should know everything from A to Z. It's a very special thing and I feel very sorry. Because even the students themselves don't like to do detailed and arduous work on their voice. They make a face and then they'd rather go to somebody else who will say, "Oh, vocalize," and the first thing you know, "Oh it's so beautiful." You shouldn't expect compliments about your voice.

𝒞: *Is there hope for young singers? Is there hope for opera? Do you think it's going to survive in today's times?*

ℒ: Well it's an art form that will definitely survive because there seem to be more people who have a special instinct for it. And I think that's the reason why opera will survive. But it's not because the school will be there to really make these people into singers.

𝒞: *Can you explain tessitura?*

ℒ: You want me to talk about tessitura?

𝒞: *Yes, and a very simple and clear explanation of why, if a singer says, "I've got a high C," you might say to him, "But you're not really a tenor although you can hit a high C, because your tessitura is lower." Explain.*

ℒ: The voice is not a thing that you can play with. It's not a thing that you can do what you want with. It's not something that you have in a juke box, put a nickel in and anything can play, no! You see, we have our tessitura. We have the range of our voice, and tessitura means approximately the same thing. The range doesn't mean that you are a tenor. Because when I was a young man and I was not lazy, I could very easily hit an F above high C, but that doesn't mean that I was a tenor. You see, there are a lot of people who think because you have a high note you can sing *Otello*, you can sing *Trovatore*, you can sing this, you can sing that. No! That's not the way it works! The tessitura in your voice, yes, but at the same time your voice must guarantee the fact that you can sustain the range. If you try to make a tenor out of a baritone the voice cannot sustain that.

𝒞: *All right, you were talking about tessitura. Does that work for all the voices?*

ℒ: Tessitura is the same for all the voices. The director of the theatre sometimes thinks that the range of a person makes the repertoire he sings. It doesn't work that way. Because you might have a wonderful range, but it doesn't mean you can sing everything. They never understood, for instance, that if I do Scarpia, you wouldn't get me to sing Rigoletto the next day. No way! It's humanly impossible! Both of them are in my range, yes! They are both in my tessitura, yes, but it doesn't mean that I can sing both of them one after the other, because one lies in such a way that it brings your voice down, because the cords don't need the tension. You go towards *Rigoletto* and all of a sudden the tension of the cords is tremendous because it is higher. Young singers don't have any idea how to be able to control themselves. And that is a tragedy because directors, or very often conductors, take advantage unwittingly. They're not aware; they've never studied the voice. If I were a conductor or a director I would really want to know which voice can do certain roles.

𝒞: *Is this why so many singers aren't lasting as long as they should? They begin to have vocal problems.*

ℒ: Absolutely! For instance, I remember very well, José Carreras told me that he was asked by von Karajan to sing *Carmen*, *Tosca*, *Don Carlos* and *Aida*. I have a funny feeling that von Karajan did not know much about voice. And I'm sorry to say it, you see, you cannot do *Aida* and the next day try to record a *Tosca*. It is not the same tessitura! And that is the tragedy! You know, young artists don't know how to cope with these things, and all of a sudden, because men like von Karajan ask them to record, they say yes! I remember when Carreras said to me, "Louis, I have to record *Aida*, *Tosca* and *Carmen*." I said, "What are you doing?" He said, "What do you mean?" I said, "Don't accept that!" He said, "You cannot refuse von Karajan." I said, "Yes! Because with your kind of voice, you've got such a beautiful voice, what do you want to do with these operas that are made for people who have voices that are already matured." And what happened? He says, "Well, I cannot refuse." Well, I said to myself, this is your funeral! Because the voice was not any more the same as it was before.

𝒞: *He had a glorious voice.*

ℒ: Ah! It was beautiful!

𝒞: *Did that not happen to Pavarotti? I remember he did an* Aida, *a* Radames, *in San Francisco and that was maybe the only time he had done it, although he did sing* 'Celeste Aida' *in concert from the Lincoln Center.*

ℒ: *Otello*, too, in Chicago . . .

𝒞: *. . . and he stopped. I don't see him doing* Aida *since then.*

ℒ: No, he does it very, very, very little. I don't see it in his repertoire. You see, it shows the intelligence of the singer. You cannot play with your voice. The voice you have is the one that has been given to you, and it will serve you for the rest of your life. It means that it is your duty to say to yourself, wait a minute. There's the most beautiful word written in the dictionary that's ever been invented in this world, NO! And this is the point with young singers. They're afraid to say no! They think by saying no it will not be advantageous to their career. The first thing you know is that they sing these operas and by the time they finish they go to sing another kind of opera and they can't. This is where they start to go down the hill. And the first thing you know they are criticized. The public doesn't accept it.

𝒞: *Another thing I've noticed, is that a lot of the young singers don't know how to sing quietly.*

ℒ: Well the point is, young singers believe that to make yourself heard you have to sing with the full power of your voice, and very often if they sing that way it's because they don't know their instrument. A singer should learn how to use his or her voice like an instrumentalist would use it. The piano is not complicated, it's there, but how to approach the piano is the difficulty that I'm talking about. And to make a great violinist, you need a good violin. But singers are the instrument. We have two cords, and we have the bow. The bow is the air. That is exactly like the violin. Singers always play with two cords, but it's still the same thing. For the violinist, what is more important is not his bow, it is the chord, the string. How the violinist will touch the string with his bow. If he presses too much with the bow he doesn't have the right sound he wants. If you want a fat sound, or something like that, that he's going to go flat with the bow. But in general, it's always on the side of the bow. Why? Because it's not touching the string very much and it gives it more pizzicato. It's more metallic and that is the thing that is very important. And us, our instrument is exactly the same. You don't see the violinist pressing. No! You see him doing practically nothing on the string with this bow.

And for singers, the breath has got to be exactly the same thing. It's not the breath that commands the voice, it is the cords that command the breath. You expand the cord, the air goes in, then the cords come back to unify, together, with a certain tension. Then the air starts to come up. The secret of the voice is a very simple thing: the air is never compressed. And what I mean by this is that you don't force the air inside of your body. No! The air has to be very flexible, and the moment that you're going to start to sing and there's no pressure you say to yourself, well I'm going to push the air now. No, No! The opposite. When you speak in a gruff voice you don't speak this way, you don't press the air, no! It's the opposite. It's very light, the air. If you think very carefully you don't do this (deep growl) you do this (light growl) and this is singing. We don't use our speaking voice to our advantage and that is the tragedy of it. We have to use our speaking voice in the singing voice. I always say, you want to learn to sing, learn how to speak.

C: *I wanted to ask a question about acting. Do you find that the acting has improved from the time of the golden oldies?*

L: Well, like anything else, the singers have become more aware that drama is very important in music. That's what I call opera today. For me opera is drama put into music. And if you are going to do a drama you have to act it, you have to express it. And the way to express it is with your hand, with your face, maybe your body. This has to have had a certain effect on the singers today.

C: *What about your favorite, Leonard Warren's acting?*

L: I never really had an opportunity to watch him. I heard him more than I saw him. And I think he was trying to do the best he could. I'm not sure. You know, I don't want to criticize because it's too long ago. I remember I saw him in *Rigoletto* and, naturally, from my own experience at that moment, I was very satisfied with it. Maybe seeing him today, I would say no.

C: *What about teachers, stage directors and coaches? They seem to travel around the world as well. Is there a special school now for singing anywhere that you would recommend?*

𝓛: Right now, I think it's a problem. Because what is happening starts with the person who has the voice. Singers often search to find somebody that can help them more in their career rather than their voice.

𝓒: *What about competitions? How helpful are they for the singers? Do people from the various opera houses prefer to hire somebody who has won a competition?*

𝓛: Well, it does happen that they will help somebody more if they have won a contest. But at the same time I notice that it's not only the matter of competition but how much money you have. Some people try to buy their career. I could not buy my career because I had no money for it. In reality it creates a big problem, because you will have somebody who might be much better than another person but because of publicity, because of a helping hand, the less gifted one might end up with a career. I don't like to talk about it because when you talk like this people think you're jealous. It's not a matter of jealousy, it's a matter of integrity, and I feel that there's a lot of it that's missed all over the world. For instance, at the Paris Opera I refused to sing *Rigoletto* in French because I did not like the translation, but they gave the role to a Frenchman even though he was less successful.

𝓒: *So discrimination knows no bounds in the world. Getting back to operatic houses, you've sung in Canada for the COC, Montreal, Vancouver, Edmonton, Calgary, Ottawa, Quebec City.*

𝓛: When I first started in Canada, there were very few opera companies. There was an opera company in Montreal. In those years they called it an opera guild. They used to do one performance a year. Now it's marvellous to see the amount of opera. However, I have to complain about one thing: it's about time that we search in our own ranks for people who could direct our opera companies. Go to France, you will have the Paris Opera directed by a Frenchman. Well, maybe Paris is an exception, but go anywhere else in France and you have to be French. And I think in Canada we have enough people who are fully qualified to direct a company. It's about time that we helped Canadians. And when I say this it's not because I have anything against a foreigner, unless you have somebody that is really, really incredible, for instance, Placido Domingo, who just took over Washington. You have to respect that, because Domingo has a great concept of what the theatre is and he's got great ideas of what opera should sound like.

𝒞: *Getting back to vocal technique, you gave me an example about pronouncing the word 'trouble' or 'dumb-bell', stressing the importance of consonants. You also mentioned that the first syllable is important in shaping phrases. Can you explain why this is important?*

ℒ: The voice is very capricious. If you are not the master of the voice, the voice becomes the master. And problems arise when the voice becomes the master. You have to give the voice certain things that will help it. For instance, we were talking about the first syllable. When a singer sings, the very beginning of the sound is very often a consonant. Sometimes you have a vowel, but in general it's a consonant. Let's say you have a T but you don't say TRAAA, you say Tr-ble. The thing is to make the 'T' sound well pronounced, not the 'trouble'. More or less, you go from the 'T' to 'Trou-' and now 'Trou-' then '-ble'. Now why 'ble'? The point is, we have to put in our minds that if a vowel doesn't work or a consonant doesn't work, the thing is for us to try to change the real pronunciation of that vowel or consonant. For instance, if you say '*Trou* — ble', this is completely anti-vocal. What will make the vocal effect strong is to be able to pronounce the T-R-O-U- and not be afraid to say trouble. You have to really accentuate 'T — Trou . . . ble'. The -BLE finally gives you a tremendous explosion. The secret of singing is to be able to help the voice find a kind of explosion, because it creates that tremendous vocal effect. The voice is a funny thing. I go 'Aah, aah,' it doesn't have any starting point. But if you go 'Haa, haa', it's easier. I will often start a vowel with a little 'h'. It's always dangerous to put just 'aaa', it's too dry, but 'Haa', gives much more to the sound.

𝒞: *What about shaping phrases?*

ℒ: Shaping phrases is a little bit like the words, if you're not careful. I always say to my pupils, when you start a word in a phrase, the very first thing that will come out of your mouth is the thing that's important and it is going to make the rest of the phrase. Let's say that you have a beautiful way to begin a phrase and you keep on feeding the rest of that phrase with the intelligence you feel. That even if the beginning is A you must feel AAAA to bring it exactly to where the A exists. And this is the problem. Singers, when they articulate, think that they have to sing like you speak. No. There's no such thing. The speech in singing is a vocal speech and not like you would speak a language. Often, speaking a language is very weak. Singing it makes it much more truthful and intense. That's the way it is.

𝒞: *You are very concerned about the position of the head. You say it cuts the vocal cords. Are there some ways in which the head can go back if the body moves with it?*

ℒ: Talking about it is difficult if you don't see it. But the thing is, your larynx, which is where your vocal cords are attached, has to be in its own socket. That means the position of the head will create either a right or wrong vocal approach. What I mean is you just have to think about the vocal cords. Let's say they're an inch long now and tense. Now from that you have up to a sixteenth of an inch to make the voice two and a half octaves. What happens if you are not careful is that when the head moves you're more or less changing the position of your throat or the larynx and the cords, and the first thing you know, your vocal approach is completely wrong.

𝒞: *Tell me how to get a real focus and intensity in the voice without spreading the sound and how one gets the special resonance and 'ping' that you hear in the great singers like Domingo and Pavarotti.*

ℒ: This is at the same time a very difficult and very simple thing. There's always one thing that's never discussed by 95 percent of the teachers and that is the vocal cords. This is the most important thing there is. Try to understand by watching Itzhak Perlman playing the violin. He holds the violin in such a way that you practically feel that there are two strings that hold the violin up in the air. There's no effort, it's so relaxed. His right hand goes on the string and that's it. But watch the way he uses the bow. He will use it with harder pressure once in a while, for the bigger, fuller sound, but in general he always uses maybe a quarter, or it might be even less than that, of the pressure of the air.

Now I always ask my pupil, what is the most important thing in the voice, is it the air or is it the cord? And the answer always comes up the same way: It's the air. And this is false. The most important thing is the cord because the cord dictates how much pressure of air that you need. And that creates a tremendous problem because people do not understand. But the great, great singers know exactly the right amount of tension that is necessary to put on the cords and the right amount of pressure from the air. What is happening is that our nervous system is very ticklish. Try to touch your eyes. You cannot. But if you go slowly you are going to come to the point where you can touch them. The voice is exactly the same. The moment you overtax the intake of air a tremendous tension is created on the air and the cords. By creating the right amount of tension, you have to try to liberate your cords and give them a certain flexibility that is required when you sing. And this is very difficult, to be able to feel in your mind the tension of the cord and at the same time feel the pressure of the air. And this is where the great singers have succeeded so beautifully. They found exactly how it feels. And this is the problem with young singers. It's very difficult because it's not tangible and it's a thing that you have to understand individually. You see, the point is, the teacher often makes you vocalize, hoping that automatically you're going to find the feeling of liberating your cord and liberating your air.

Singers often don't have the foggiest idea about what I'm talking about. I try to talk to them about the vocal cord and the air, for instance, how to take the air, and I give a simple example. Say 'yes'. Repeat that very, very slowly. Analyze what is happening with the air when you say ‘yes’. You don’t do ‘He-yes’. No! It’s like you’re throwing out the air. It’s exactly like singing. I challenge anybody in this world to tell me the contrary. Singing is like talking. Singing is a combination with the talking voice. Very often I will take some people that speak very badly and I tell them, learn how to speak and you’re going to know how to sing. Because it’s a coordination. When you speak you don’t think of the air going in. No! The air is always there to serve itself automatically. If you listen to what I’m saying right now you will notice one thing: breathing the air is very simple. We don’t make enough correspondence between air and speech and air and singing. It’s exactly the same thing.

The thing that is very important in singing is rotation. The greatest thing that was invented in this world was the wheel but I’m going to tell you one thing: the wheel is the best example there is for a singer. The wheel comes towards you and the wheel goes away from you. Just imagine a car. Look at the front wheel when it starts to roll and watch it. When it rolls forward, this is breathing. When the wheel goes under the car and up, up, it goes forward. When the tire goes forward and touches the asphalt that’s where you take the air and you sing. But it’s difficult to try to envision this because you have to have a vision of a wheel, but you can to do it with your hand.

The ping in the singing sound is done by tension on the vocal cord and nothing else. If I loosen the vocal cord the first thing you will feel is a shallow sound and no more ping. I disagree with the teacher who says to the pupil, please sing with resonance. What is the resonance? The resonance is a cage, is a space. But they won’t say that to the pupil, they’re going to say, sing in the resonance. What do you think the pupil does? Goes and sings in the nose and the first thing you know you are doing something that is against natural singing. Because what is happening at that moment is that you’re not only trying to put it in the nose but at the same time you are giving pressure to the cord and the cord loosens. What makes the resonance is a hard cord. You loosen your cord, you lose the resonance. It’s a very simple thing, but you have to know where your cords are. Otherwise you don't how to work them or work the breath and you're in trouble.

It's not something that comes with vocalizing, believe me. Some people have succeeded doing it without thinking about the cords or the real technique. But to save your voice it's necessary to have the knowledge of vocal technique. Very often even if you know exactly what to do with the voice you get lost. The thing is to be like a computer from your toes to your hair. You must discover what you're doing, what the problems are and how to solve them technically so you can keep singing way past your seventies, like me.

𝒞: *What advice would you give to young singers about handling bad reviews. How important are they?*

ℒ: Well, there is one thing I have to say. A review is one of these things that is the opinion of one person. If the review tells you exactly what you have done wrong, take it with a smile. If there is anything that is wrong forget about it because it is not worth it. Use it constructively. If a suggestion works, use it. But at the same time don't let a review get to you. I know some artists who gave up singing because of a bad review. I don't think it is fair, because you have something that very often a reviewer doesn't have. Why do you think they became a reviewer? Sometimes they are frustrated. And another thing that I notice, in some cities where there are three reviewers, two of them will write the truth about the performance and the third one will write the opposite. Sometimes these people are so frustrated that they try to destroy people with a pen. I always say: Freedom of the press, yes! But at the same time if a critic does a bad review against an artist, the artist should be able to answer back. But today, with the union, it's like anything else. We are at the mercy of their criticism and nobody can say anything.

Only once in my life I thanked a critic. I had done a concert at the very beginning of my career. The reviewer came out and said some negative things but it was very concrete criticism. It was not criticism because he had something against me but constructive criticism which I used.

He was himself a composer and at the same time everything he said was right. At first I got very insulted, but later I realized that everything he was saying was helpful. I remember meeting him and he expected me to give him a punch in the nose. Instead I said that I was very happy with what he had written because it was very right and that the next time I would sing he would be very happy with me. He was surprised to hear this because usually what the artist wants to do is to kill the critic.

𝒞: *When I teach piano, for me the sound always comes first. I tell the student to imagine the sound they want or need for the piece. Try to picture and hear the sound in your inner ear before you think about the hand position or what you have to do physically to get the sound on the keyboard. What about voice?*

ℒ: Maybe that is the thing that is a must in the instrument, but I think vocally it is the opposite. It's to have everything function before you do anything. What I mean is that the sound is practically the least important thing, because the sound is the finishing touch of what you've been doing. You have to create through expansion, fighting a muscle and fighting tension. You listen to the sound but you don't really care about what the sound is, because the sound is the natural result of what you are trying to do.

𝒞: *But do you have to have the sound in your inner ear?*

ℒ: The problem for singers is that we don't see the sound, we don't touch it. On the violin you can see it, you can touch it. On the piano you can see it, you can touch it. And that's why in certain ways the sound indicates exactly what you are doing with the voice but at the same time the sound is there already. You are the instrument. Naturally you have to create a beautiful sound. A beautiful sound is created by the way you would touch the note, the way you would touch the cord. Our ears will definitely help you to understand and distinguish the sound that you're going to make. But, like I said, everything is done before the actual sound is done.

𝒞: *I'm not talking about the physical sound. I'm talking about imagining the kind of sound that you would like to hear and the pitches.*

ℒ: On the piano, you don't have to imagine the sound that's going to come out because the moment you touch the note it's automatic that the note plays exactly what you expect. If it's a C, you play a C and you know you have touched the C. Like the violin, you know if you touch the string and the position of the C it will sound, hopefully in tune. Singers go through the complete process of fabricating. But the fabrication is by creating the opposite of what the instrument does. Because on the instrument it's automatic.

𝒞: *I'm talking about the quality of the sound, the ability to imagine the sound.*

ℒ: The ability to imagine the sound . . . yes.

𝒞: *I mean the emotion behind the sound, the colour, the quality. Don't you hear that before you actually make it?*

ℒ: I have to say I don't think so. I think it comes by feeling more than by actual touching. It's like when you're going to start to walk. You know that one foot will start to go forward but just imagine for one minute that you're going to walk. You don't have to think. There's a command in your mind that gives you the opportunity to start to walk. It's not that there's a note that would say to you . . . ping! Walk. No. It is there. And this is the point with the voice. It's very difficult to be able to translate these things. To be able, before you do anything, to get rid of this, get rid of that, do this, do that, expand here, expand there. To have the vision, the immensity and the perfect instrument ready to make the sound.

𝒞: *The piano, for example, is almost a mechanical percussion instrument. We have to work very hard to imagine a tonal colour and get it. Because if you just press the key, yes, the sound comes but there is more to it than that.*

ℒ: But if you go back to the basics of it, without touching the key you will not create the sound.

𝒞: *I know. So in a way it's hard for us to create a sound too, because we're not using our body. W're using our imagination.*

ℒ: Oh, I didn't say that it's more difficult. No. It's the opposite. I would say sometimes it comes to the point that your second nature, your third nature, your fourth nature will create it, giving you the opportunity to be able to do everything right. And this is very difficult and why the great singers are rare. Because they found exactly what has to be done even before the sound comes out. And that is the secret. Some singers never discovered the ability to find how to create the beautiful sound. Some vocalize. It's going to give you flexibility in the voice, but your mind is more important. You must know what to do with your voice. But you have these people who vocalize let's say for 5 or 10 years and all of a sudden they lose the voice. Why do you think they lose it? Because they never possessed it. Their technique helped them discover their freedom. But they never really discovered what their freedom was.

𝒞: *This is where I find that singers have an advantage over pianists. We could have that ability, but we are at the mercy of the instrument. Whatever piano we get at a concert, that's the sound we're going to be able to make. Whereas if you've got a wonderful voice and you know what to do with it you're assured, more or less, of getting a beautiful sound or the same quality of sound at every concert. Unless you've got a bad cold or something. If you've developed the proper technique you can rely on it.*

ℒ: This is exactly what I'm talking about. You've just touched the right button. If a singer has understood his technique, his vocal technique (I'm not talking about how to learn a score or anything like that, but his vocal technique), the moment that this artist knows what to do with it he's on easy street. That is very difficult for the instrumentalist because it's not very often second nature.

𝒞: *No. Because we have to adapt to a different instrument each time we play a concert.*

𝓛: That's right.

𝓒: *And a Steinway will often have a very different feeling from a Bösendorfer. We have to readapt our physical approach to the instrument each time we play a concert. It's subtle. But it is the same thing. Whereas with you, once you have that technique you can try to recreate the sound each time.*

𝓛: You see, the point is, with the instrumentalist there is a tension when you want to play that instrument. It's not a big tension but it's still the tension that will make the instrument vibrate. And for the singer it is the opposite. The less tension you're going to give the better. I would not say we don't have any tension. We have tension, but our tension is not like the instrumentalist's. It's a flexible tension. And it is not a physical tension. But for the instrument, no matter what anybody would say, you need a certain physical tension to be able to create the sound of that instrument.

𝓒: *The vocal student has to be strong enough to say no before irreparable damage is done to the vocal cords if the teacher is not giving them the proper technique. Is that not right?*

𝓛: Well, it is right. Singers sometimes never really understand their instrument. Very often they think there has to be a tremendous pressure to create the sound. But there is a way to do it. It's given to you. It's like when you watch people who are runners. You see that some of these runners are so flexible, they don't seem to be running. And others collapse. It's to be able to discover that your technique is based on only one thing, *flexibility*. And the big problem, for instance, which creates the ending of a singer, is when he comes to a certain age. All of a sudden you don't have any more flexibility. Physically it is not there anymore.

𝓒: *How did you maintain that flexibility?*

𝓛: Well, the thing is, you have to keep on singing all the time. For instance, a lot of singers think of only one thing, to make a big sound. No! Fight that big sound. Because if you make too much big sound you lose the flexibility. It is more important to be able to make a sound that's very light. You must also keep that sound on a certain level, on a certain height. Singers don't exactly favour that. What they prefer to do is make big sounds. That is the beginning of the end.

𝒞: *To push, instead of thinking about the role, and the inflection. I've noticed that when you sing a role the language makes it a different sound. I mean it's still the beautiful voice but you inflect it with the flavour of the language and the role. I would like to hear more pianissimos and emotional content in singers today.*

ℒ: Absolutely. The mind controls everything no matter what anybody will say! It controls. You touched the right button. That is part of our instrument. To be able to touch but at the same time it is not a touch. It is a 'mind touch'. It's mind over matter. If singers don't use their minds they won't last.

𝒞: *I feel there's a lot of psychological damage by virtue of too much advice. You have piano coaches who are not vocal teachers giving advice to young singers even if they never sang a note. You have diction coaches, stage directors, you've got conductors giving lessons, everybody but a real vocal teacher. It's just an observation, but in watching the great singers and knowing their backgrounds I find that most of them are really self-taught, polishing their technique and learning their roles through experience.*

ℒ: The tragedy, if I would call it a tragedy, is that the great singers should be great teachers, but in general what happens with great singers is that they achieve perfection in their instrument and very often don't exactly know how they are doing it. Sometimes they don't want to ask themselves because their voice is there whenever they need it.

𝒞: *I agree. I was talking with John Roberts about Glenn Gould and he, of course, had a phenomenal technique and John asked Glenn, "Do you ever analyze it? Why don't you teach?" and Glenn said, "Oh My God! I don't even want to know how I do it. I look upon the keyboard as a battlefield and if I start to think I won't be able to do it anymore."*

ℒ: You'd be surprised how many people don't analyze. The only problem is that you have some singers who don't analyze and yet they are able to sing a long time because of their faith and lack of analysis. They don't bother to try to analyze. They have a feeling for it. And how do you explain this to someone? For some people it's a difficult thing to explain your feeling. It's there, but it's not really there. You have to discover it for yourself and by yourself.

𝒞: *Because the action of the vocal cords is unseen it's difficult to show anyone.*

ℒ: That's what I have said since the beginning. Because on the piano, the note is there and you can touch it; on the violin you see the string. Naturally, these people who became great pianists or great violinists came to the point where they don't even see the chord or key. They feel it. But the thing is, it's a feeling of distance. It's at the very beginning of something that we can see in our mind and feel with our emotion.

𝒞: *With pianists you may have one or two bad teachers and you learn pretty quickly to leave them, but you don't have so many differing opinions. It seems that in vocal schools you have many people that don't sing teaching young singers and this tends to confuse them. In my conversations with a lot of the young students this has been their major complaint. What do young singers do when they are performing an opera and one conductor tells them to do this aria one way, the assistant conductor tells them to do it another way, and then the piano coach who doesn't sing tells them to do the aria still a third way, and then you have a diction person. What do you do?*

ℒ: It's a difficult field for that reason. You have to come to a point when you can surpass these things. For instance, just lately I was in the *Barber* (*of Seville*) and there's one coach that told me you have to do it this way and that way. I don't go according to what I'm told but what I see and feel. Certain things have to be done in a certain way. Conductors wait till the end. Very often they don't want to impose their way of doing it. And that is a dangerous thing for young singers. They will try to comply with what is asked and sometimes they are asked do something that might impair them.

𝒞: *So the idea is to think very strongly about taking a role or taking advice. You must be sure it doesn't damage the voice or doesn't contradict what you feel is right for your technique at the time.*

ℒ: Nintey-five to 98 percent of singers don't have the foggiest idea of what they are supposed to do. A conductor will come in and they'll ask a singer to do it one way. They'll go to another performance, the conductor will ask them to do it still another way. You have to come to the point where you have to say to yourself, wait! I'm learning how to do it. Learn how to do it! Most of the time they don't. It should not be done by just somebody asking you to do something. No! It's the opposite.

𝒞: *Psychologically there can be a lot of damage to young singers. In one book I read that a student can go from an old teacher to a new teacher and it seems that everything he or she learned before was bad. And the new teacher gives them a new technique even though they sound worse. And the good singer will go back to the parents and the parents will say, "My God! We're spending this money and our child sounds much worse." But the young singer believes that the instruction is the word of God. How do you battle that?*

ℒ: I will say that there is no such a thing as going to see such a teacher and saying he or she is God. The teacher is there only to guide you. You're the one who has to make the decisions. As a painter, you're the one who has to choose the colour, you're the one who has to paint the picture. You're the one who does it. The teacher can only help you in finding a technique and tell you what's missing from your performance. Students want the teacher to do everything for them and to show exactly how it is done. You have to pay your dues. You walk on the stage alone.

𝒞: *One of the singers I was talking with suggested that the difference between conductors and the coaches was like using a palette. For example, they use the singer's talent like using colours to paint a picture. One conductor or coach will say, "I don't like your colour, do this" and the other is saying do something different. I believe you should use what you have and try to work with that.*

ℒ: Something similar happened to me at the very beginning of my career when I won the Met 'Auditions of the Air' in 1955. I won some money and glory and I was very happy about it. At the same time I was given a new contract with the Met but I had to be part of the young artists program at the Met. Anyway, the first year I was listening and I was looking, I did a little bit of coaching and I was not really inspired.

By the second year it became very intense and I remember that one day I walked in and one of our teachers who was an assistant conductor at the Met said to me, "Well, what would you like to sing?" I said, "The aria of *Trovatore*." "Fine," he said. We started and I did the recitativo. I started with my clear light sound and the way I thought best how to sing it. After I sang maybe four or five phrases he stopped me. I said, "What's wrong?" He said, "Well I have to say one thing: if you're going to sing like this you're never going to sing at the Met." I said, "What do you mean by this?" He said, "You're too young and your voice is much too light to be singing at the Met." I said, "Well, let me try to see if I can change this." And I understood what he wanted. He wanted me to sing with a very, very dark voice like an old man. And then I started to sing very dark. He said, "Oh, yes! This is the way you have to sound." "Well," I said, "in these conditions, I'm deeply sorry, I don't think I'm ever going to sing at the Met because I cannot sing this way." And I took my music and started to walk out. He said, "You're never going to sing at the Met." I said, "Thank you very much, Sir. You have advised me to do the wrong thing and I am not here to do the wrong thing. I'm here to learn what is the right thing." And I said, "People like you are assassins for singers." And I walked out and it took me about 15 years to come back to the Met.

𝒞: *And here you are going to be 70 and still singing at the Met.*

ℒ: Exactly.

𝒞: *You are still singing because you have faith and confidence in yourself and the knowledge that how you sing is right.*

ℒ: I discovered what I needed for myself. And this is the thing I feel is very tragic. Young singers don't know exactly what they're searching for. You have to use a lot of imagination. You have to be able to transport yourself into the third dimension, even the fourth dimension. And very often singers don't have the imagination to conjure up the third or fourth dimension.

𝒞: *And the most important thing is that you're out there by yourself. Nobody is going to help you make that sound. Only you can do it.*

ℒ: There is nobody who can do it for you, and this is what I feel is sometimes very treacherous. When you have an interpretation and your mind is not strong enough to believe in yourself or to discover yourself, how can you keep on surviving? That is absolutely impossible. Anybody can come and destroy you very, very easily. This is why the great singers will never self-destruct. They found out for themselves what their unique quality was.

𝒞: *And your great inspiration is the music.*

ℒ: Naturally, the composer. Just be true to the composer.

𝒞: *Well, in my own experience as a pianist, no matter what happens in one's life, when you go out on the stage the great inspiration that keeps you going is the music and communicating it to the people.*

ℒ: Absolutely. You are receiving a beautiful message from the composer. You have to be true to the composer because the composer has written something so beautiful and given you the opportunity to feel sentimental. And it's not that complicated.

𝒞: *Well I think it's one of the simplest things. I agree with you. I find that a lot of people who are in music professionally sometimes don't like music.*

ℒ: Yes it's true.

𝒞: *They're there because of duty or money but they don't love it. Love of music and the joy of singing has kept you singing for so long.*

ℒ: It's a beautiful thing to be able to open your mouth and hear the wonderful sound. You become enthralled with what comes out of you. You wonder, why does it come out of me? And sometimes you don't have to ask why because you are so true to the composer and what the composer wanted that you don't do anything wrong. It's the opposite. You go towards something almost sacred. And this is the big problem with the conductors. All of a sudden the conductors will say, one-two-three-four, and believe that it's what counts. No! This is the point. You see, it is immaterial if the conductor insists that you have to do one-two-three-four. It's one thing to get together with the orchestra and the other people, but the moment you come to the interpretation the one-two-three-four doesn't exist. The music keeps on growing and creating its own feeling. We have to create. Sometimes the conductors don't understand the composer and we are at the mercy of them or the coaches and stage directors. They all want to butt in, but if you've got a great man in front of you he will not bother you, he will help you. Very seldom will a conductor say something to Luciano or Placido. If you listen to Luciano or Placido singing it's practically always right. The point is, great conductors understand.

𝒞: *And mentioning superstars, very few put on any airs. The job at hand is only the music.*

ℒ: Very often the great problem is to find the simplicity in the music. We don't very often search for that simplicity, and it's too bad because in the simplicity you find truths.

But when you start to create your own kingdom it becomes a dilemma.

𝒞: *Singers are now using pianists who are not known as accompanists of voice but have extensive solo careers. For example Cecilia Bartoli has been using Andras Schiff for wonderful joint recitals and Ferruccio Furlanetto is using Alexis Weissenberg. What are your feelings about this type of collaboration?*

ℒ: To become a great singer one has to sing and perform. I think for the pianist it's the same. You come under the spell of great interpreters. If you get somebody that has never really been an accompanist but has been performing piano, the pianist comes to the point that they're an interpreter, not just a pianist. They discovered the facility of being able to feel, let's say, a crescendo and know exactly how to create that crescendo or accelerando. A great interpreter is a great artist, period.

𝒞: *You and I hit it off right away as a team. We've had a lot of fun at rehearsals, that's for sure. And we recorded our CD, all 10 of the arias, mostly on one take. Usually, the first take.*

ℒ: That's right. There's one thing that you will agree with: the most important thing is to be able to do music for music and not to say, I'm going to put it on a CD and that's going to bring in so much money. No! You have to enjoy it first. And that's one thing I noticed with you. You really enjoy it. On top of that, your enjoyment is not only a matter of enjoyment but you have great feeling for it. That is very important. It's so easy to work with you because you know how to make music wonderfully. Because there's an automatic understanding that comes from your part and my part. And that is very important. To be able to do music with somebody else and to be able to give and take. Very often when you do opera and you come in front of these conductors or coaches you don't have flexibility. And then you have to fight.

𝒞: *The same goes for concert pianists. If you call yourself a concert pianist you should really be on stage playing with orchestra, performing chamber music and solo recitals. I feel that perhaps this is what singers are looking for now, by collaborating with artists that have separate careers aside from accompanying. It becomes a collaboration of equal artists.*

𝓛: For instance, our collaboration is a great one, you know. And not only ours but there are many other partnerships like those you just mentioned who are doing wonderful concerts together and separately. Because you have to feel what I do and I have to feel what you do.

𝓒: *You also want to perform new repertoire.*

𝓛: Oh, definitely, we have to. You know something very funny? I hate to say this, but when I met you I had to revive myself, ask myself, 'Who am I?' But it's wonderful to be able to translate yourself in so many new ways. Sometimes you lose contact with yourself and then come back and get in contact with yourself. Like the CD we want to come out with next. A different repertoire from what I usually do.

𝓒: *Why did you lose contact with yourself?*

𝓛: Well, for instance, the semi-classical music I used to like was not in fashion anymore. This kind of music is never heard by people. But if you bring it back to them you might be very surprised by how much they will enjoy it.

𝓒: *What about historical music?*

𝓛: That is a wonderful thing to do. Like the music we discovered lately. I think it would be very interesting. Why was it lost? Maybe during the time it was written it wasn't played enough. For instance, we're at the point where new music and new things that have been written are not exactly appreciated now. Maybe the kind of music that was written at the turn of the century will create tremendous interest.

𝓒: *Since marrying me you've also been initiated into 20th-century music. I drag you, unwillingly sometimes, to my new music recitals. Is that going to have an effect?*

L: I think new music, for me, is an understanding that I don't have. You understand that kind of music. This is the interesting thing about life. People understand certain things. They're able to produce, but for some people it's not easy. It's not because I didn't do new music. I did new music but at the same time I never felt very comfortable in it.

C: *Well the thing with new music now is that it's beginning to sound more romantic than anything written from the forties, fifties or sixties.*

L: Maybe that is the reason I lost interest in it. I'm a very romantic person, you know that. The thing that is very important for me is to feel the music I have to sing. Otherwise I don't have an interest in it. Some of the new music has become quite romantic. And that's very important.

C: *You said you needed to revive yourself. Why do you say that? Was it the age factor that made you feel that you might not be singing anymore?*

L: I don't think so. I think in music it's a matter of finding new things, more repertoire that can create a tremendous interest for me. Because it's very important to be able to do something you love and not talk about something you hate. Not everybody believes exactly the same way. We all believe in a different way and we, as artists, can bring to people things that are wonderful in life. Your life has been blessed with these things. I am not a man that likes to talk about evil things, to talk about ugly things. No! Life is too short and too beautiful and that is my character. It's very important that everything that I do in life has to create something beautiful for people. This is the reason why new music, if it's something romantic, I might accept it, I might absorb it. But for a while new music was very difficult.

C: *Are you happy in your career?*

L: I think what's very important in life is to come at a point where the most beautiful moment of your artistic life is to be able to still make a beautiful sound. For example, it is happening right now. It's heaven. You know, you feel like God stayed with you and this is very important, to be able to say to yourself how wonderful life is. That you are creating sounds and music that you have done all your life, and the more you do, the less it will leave you. It's always very treacherous to think that it will leave you, but I don't know. God must have been in my corner because HE still helped me. And I think it's a wonderful thing for that reason. It's very wonderful to be able to say to yourself at the age of 25, I made a beautiful sound. But just imagine that you arrive at the age of 70, you still sing at the Met, you are still respected by people and you are able to sing this great music. I think it's a blessing. It's the greatest thing that can be given to any human being in this earth. And I wish that if I could give a blessing to anybody I love or anybody I think would be worth it, I would give the ability to create till the day they die, like dying with your boots on. I think it would be a really incredible thing to happen.

On Opera

𝒞: *You've heard some amusing stories about opera performances. Tell me one about* Rigoletto *at Covent Garden.*

ℒ: I was not part of the performance, but I heard and I know the gentleman who had to carry a certain hefty soprano. And I don't know what she could have eaten that night but when this bass grabbed her and put her on his back, all of a sudden one of the loudest biggest farts you ever heard cut through the orchestra. But that was not as bad as the soprano whispering "Sorry" in a voice that penetrated through to the balcony. She was a funny person you know.

I remember doing a performance with her of *Lucrezia Borgia* and all of a sudden in the second act, it was one of these crazy evenings, I would forget things, she would forget things and the conductor was going out of his mind, when at once we had a tremendous operatic confrontation. I looked at her and suddenly I went blank. All my words were gone. All I could sing was blah, blah, blah and she looked at me, abruptly she stopped. When the maestro saw that, he stopped the orchestra too. She turned towards the prompter and said, "What's my word?"

𝒞: *And speaking of words, what's the role of the prompter?*

ℒ: The role of the prompter is to keep you in line, and that's very important. Except if you are used to singing without a prompter, it makes it a better performance, because you don't become intimidated or dependent on words. That's the thing I find very difficult with the Met. I'm so used to a prompter now that I become really, really dependent on him or her and it makes a big difference. Sometimes some people, like my son, will not understand why singers have a blank. It's because of the dependence on the prompter. I've been doing that now with the Met for 25 years. You know when you sing every single performance the prompter is there whether you need it or not.

One time for sure at the Met I needed the prompter. When I made my debut at the Met it was *Pelleas et Mélisande*. I had done *Pelleas et Mélisand*e without a prompter before but that night there was a prompter and I was happy, because I had been called at the last minute and it's a very difficult opera to do at the last minute. That night, all of a sudden, I came to a certain phrase and I had a blank. The prompter didn't give me the words and the conductor didn't give me the cue. Then the three of us were out, boom. It didn't last very long, maybe a phrase and a half, something like that. I picked it up right away. But after that, I tell you, everyone was on edge.

𝒞: *Only computers never have memory slips but they can have mechanical blips. Nothing is perfect.*

𝒞: *Your son, Gino Quilico, is also a baritone. In fact you made operatic history together by appearing in* Manon *at the Metropolitan Opera in 1987 as the first father and son duo. Any plans to sing together in the future?*

ℒ: It's difficult to be objective about one's son, especially if you are in the same career. I am very proud of his accomplishments, however, we are very different and it's important for him to pursue his own career at this time in his life.

𝒞: *What about some more funny stories at the opera.*

ℒ: Once upon a time quite a famous French tenor joined the Paris Opera and he was supposed to sing the usher in the third act. The only thing he had to sing was one line and the poor man was not very artistic. When the moment came all the people backstage said, "Don't worry about it. We will help you." I said, "Now when we say go, you go and you count one, two, three, four, turn and sing. Okay? Good. But we will tell you four measures before you have to go." The stage assistant started to count, "Be careful now! Four, three, two, one, go." He walked on and also counted one, two, three, four but twice as slow and missed his line. He said, "I turned and the man behind me was singing already. I could never sing my lines." It was funny.

I remember in one performance of mine they brought in a policeman who had been accepted at the Paris Opera. This man had never been on a stage in his entire life with an audience. He was coming in at the last minute because somebody else had done the performance already. When the moment came for the poor gentleman to walk in I turned around to watch him. He walked to the middle of the stage but when he turned around and saw the audience his mouth opened, his eyes went big and blank and he could not sing one word. He got so panicky. I have to say that the first time you walk on the stage, it's not easy! Because when you see all these people, even if you don't have a big role or you sing only one line, it's still very scary.

𝒞: *Tell me about extraneous noises that happen during out-of-doors performances?*

ℒ: I was doing *Rigoletto* in Cincinnati, and in those years there was an open-air zoo. I remember it very vividly, because it was so funny. I was, as we say, laughing in my beard because the soprano was singing a very dramatic moment, "Up there in heaven I will be with my mother" and then she speaks about a peacock. And a peacock from the zoo made his own duet with her. And there was another moment in the opera when a lion from the zoo began to roar. But the most scary thing I've been part of was in Madrid in the park.

𝒞: *The zoo.*

ℒ: Yes. I was doing four performances.

𝒞: *Of what?*

ℒ: *The Tales of Hoffman.* And during the fourth act, there was one place — it was very strange because my make-up was very white. I looked like death, I represented death, and all of a sudden the only thing you could see was a very powerful spotlight on less than half of my body and you could see only the head. I remember very well that for four nights in exactly the same place I would sing the words, "Saint Paul" and a wolf howled. There is a reason for that because I used to take one note, and you have to make it very monotonous. I think it must have irritated the wolf who had to listen to that note and that is why he would start howling. But it was quite strange, I have to say.

𝒞: *Sometimes animals are brought in to the opera performances,* Aida *for example. Any funny stories about that?*

ℒ: Well, not *Aida*, but we were once doing *Manon Lescaut* in San Francisco and there was a horse. I was very surprised to see how they cleaned this horse. They give it an enema. But apparently they do that for one reason. One time they didn't clean the horse and all of a sudden the horse walked in with the buggy and the horse went plop, plop, plop. The soprano never saw any of these plop, plops and she put her feet into it as she walked on and then she slipped and fell into the other plops. They had to stop the performance.

Well, there's a famous story of Sir Thomas Beecham doing a performance with live animals in *Aida*. The soprano was not too good during the rehearsal and the horses or the elephant, I don't know which, went plop, plop, plop, plop. They had to stop the rehearsal because the army. which had to pass there could not go through the plop of the horses. Sir Thomas Beecham asked, "What is the big problem?" (I don't remember if it was Rome or Verona, it was one of the two.) "What is wrong, why do we have to stop?" They explained about the plops. "Oh," he says, "We have the critics before the performance!" Apparently he did not like the soprano.

𝒞: *What about strange, funny things happening during rehearsals?*

ℒ: Well, one funny thing happened to me, while I was doing *Aida* in one of the cities when I went to Russia. They give me a costume and a skirt with a very high waistband. And naturally, you make up a little bit lower than the skirt but you don't make up all the way. I had my white underwear, and my legs without make-up were white. But the rest of me was painted black. Anyway, I wanted to impress the people, and when I walked on the stage I took a very large breath. When you say, "Suo Padre . . ." you hold that note. And I did not realize that my stomach was going down. All of a sudden the skirt fell, boom! My daughter was there and said, "Daddy, you should have seen your face! It was incredible to watch your face!" The thing is, I was lucky enough to grab the skirt in the front but the big problem was not the front anymore, it was in the back, because, excuse the expression, the skirt got stuck just under my bum. I couldn't raise the skirt. Finally one of the ballet dancers saw me and it was such an awkward moment that he finally got a safety pin and pinned me down. But that, I have to say, was a very awkward moment in my career.

𝒞: *You hear stories about people falling through the scenery or something on the set not being prepared properly. Did anything like that happen to you?*

ℒ: I was always very meticulous about these things. If there was something to be put on the stage, I would make sure that everything I wanted was right. One thing that happened (Thank God it was not live!) was during *Tosca* for television in Montreal. The props people asked me what I would like to drink in the second act, because Scarpia has to drink some wine. "If you want some water, well we'll give you water. If you want wine, we'll give you wine." I said, "Give me some Welch's grape juice." It has a nice colour and it would be wonderful to have the colouring, especially for television. They put the grape juice there but I did not realize that grape juice, especially Welch's, is very strong and there's a strong smell. It's very powerful and feels like a kind of a fume, in fact. During the rehearsal I poured myself a glass, sang my lines and started to drink again. The fumes were so strong that I choked and they had to stop. Five minutes later we started again. I sang my phrase again, took the glass, the fumes choked me again. God, did I feel bad because there was nothing I could do! Finally, I baptized the juice in the garbage but I was so anchored with that smell that I don't know if it was mental or what, but when I took the glass and I looked at it, I practically choked. But thank God it was television and not live.

𝒞: *What about the stabbing of Scarpia? Any mishaps?*

ℒ: I never really had a problem except for one performance. I was in Hawaii doing *Tosca* with Dorothy Kirsten and they said to me, "Mr. Quilico, please, if you go in the ocean be very careful because the sun is very, very strong. Don't go until after 3:30 p.m. and don't stay too long. Stay about 10–15 minutes and then get out of there." I took one of these catamarans and there I was on the ocean from 3:30 till 6:30. I came back red like a tomato. Anyway, the next day I had to do Scarpia. Well, I tell you one thing, it was the slowest death you ever saw in the history of Scarpia. I couldn't go down very fast because my back and everything else was so tender that I was in terrible pain. Some people who were there said, "You should have seen yourself going down! You didn't want to die!"

𝒞: *What about Montserrat Caballé blowing you down like a feather?*

ℒ: The strange thing is that the public is very funny. After Tosca stabs Scarpia, he's still not dead. His last breath comes at the end of the soprano's lines, where she says "Mori, mori, mori!" While Tosca sings this I held myself with one hand to try and lift myself up from the floor to grab her. Then she says "Mori!" for the first time. Then I do a little bit more for the second "Mori!" And the last one she cries out "Mori!" and I really go to the utmost. And I've got one measure after that and I let go, Voom! And that's it, I'm dead. But during that performance she came in and she said, "Mori!" I got up, "Mori!" I raised up, "Mori!" I raised up. The moment I was going to die she came right on top of me and she said very, very, very softly, practically with no sound, "Mori!" And people thought she said, "Mori, Mori, Mori!" and then blew at me. They thought she blew me down with a whisper! It was so funny that I heard the public laughing like mad. I was on the floor and my stomach was going boom, boom, boom! She put the crucifix on me and my stomach was still going up and down.

𝒞: *You had an interesting story about a performance of* Aida *at the Paris opera.*

ℒ: Well, that's going to be a long one. They had just done *Turandot* with Birgit Nilsson. And I have to say that the production was super, incredible, beautiful. Naturally, when they were doing a new production they would raise the price of tickets. We had to do *Aida* about three weeks later and they raised the price again. However, it didn't mean a new production. It was only another director. Our soprano was Leontyne Price. The public was so excited to see Leontyne Price in a new production and to also have seen *Turandot* in a new production! But when they opened the curtain for *Aida* and it was the old production the whole theatre responded very negatively. I was in my dressing room and I could hear the loud speaker.

Anyway, they started the performance and everything seemed to go well. They did the first scene, the second scene and the artists walked out, "bravo, bravo, bravo!" But when the tenor walked out, they booed him. We started asking ourselves, why? Why is the public doing this? Just before the conductor went down into the orchestra pit a big collective "BOO" started. And they started to yell at him. "Go home you stupid old man!" Finally he took courage and about four minutes later he began.

Then there was the ballet sequence. I don't know if it was badly rehearsed or what, but one of these girls fell down and the public started to laugh, and at the same time some other people were still booing. We had to finish the famous triumphal scene. When the curtain opened one of the biggest boo's I ever heard in my life came out of that theatre. The entire audience went, "Boo." We kept on going. I asked the stage manager, "Why don't you close, why don't you stop the performance?" He said, "And ask the people to go and get their money back?"

In the famous march scene where the soldiers parade one of the soldiers had forgotten to take off one of his shoes, and he walked out with a crooked hat. The public started to laugh and to boo like mad. I said to the stage director, "Close it." But he still refused. Anyway, it kept on going in a crescendo. I looked at the big guys who play the long, long trumpets and I could see that all the trumpets were shaking. "Oh my God! These guys, they're going to pass out because they're all white as sheets!" They tried to get some saliva on their lips. I said, "Now we just need that. If the trumpets make a cacophony or a false note we're in big trouble!" When the moment came you could hear bad trumpet sounds. I tell you one thing, it was a cacophony! I looked at the TV monitor and in the monitor you could see people behind the conductor standing up with their handkerchiefs and they're laughing, "Ha, Ha, Ha, Ha!" And I'm sure, excuse the expression, but there must have been a lot of people 'peeing in their pants' with laughter that night.

Now I was caught in it too, I was laughing. But all of a sudden I said to myself, "Wait a minute, Louis, you have to go and face these people. Now what are you going to do?" I didn't really know. But the moment I walked in these two poor guys never expected what I was going to do. I went bang, bang, voom, and these poor guys, maybe three or four guys, landed on their backs. The people were laughing, booing, clapping their hands, screaming. I was listening but I couldn't hear the orchestra because the public was louder. I said to myself, "Who am I? Listen, there's nothing I can do here." But the moment came and the only one I could hear was the King faintly from a distance. The chorus was singing and I couldn't hear them. But I noticed that the conductor was giving me the first beat with the orchestra and I shut up. And he went like this, "Come on, come on, come on!" And I shut up.

Now I had 18 steps to go down. I started to go down my 18 steps and I went to the footlights. I crossed my arms and looked on one side of the theatre and then the other. I must have had a hell of a face because I was so mad. They told me I stopped the show for 7 ½ minutes. I didn't give a hoot, because I wanted to hear a pin drop in that theatre and if I did not hear that pin drop, I was not going to sing. And all of a sudden, one side of the theatre calmed down and then the other side. Soon there was not one single sound and I started to sing, "Suo padre. . ." The next day the newspapers said, "Thanks to Mr. Quilico the doors of the Paris Opera did not close last night!"

𝒞: *You know, it sounds like Marx Brothers at the opera! I would have paid a lot to see that one.*

ℒ: Oh yes, I wish I could have been in the audience too because I think it was too funny for words. But it turned out okay after that. The soprano sang her famous aria and there was a 10-minute ovation like I never saw in my life.

𝒞: *Was that Leontyne Price?*

ℒ: Yes, she was sitting on her right leg and they were screaming, "We want more, encore, encore!" She didn't move. Not even her face would move. And she sat there about 10 and a half, at least 10 minutes.

𝒞: *Tell me about* L'Elisir d'Amore *and* La Boheme *in San Francisco.*

ℒ: I was singing in *L'Elisir d'Amore*, and in the second act I have to have a piece of paper on me so the tenor can sign his name on it, because he's going to join the army. When the moment came that I hand him the paper I realized I didn't have any. I went to the side of the stage and tried to mime that I needed a piece of paper. Nobody could understand anything I was talking about. I looked around and there was a big table right there in the middle of the stage with a huge tablecloth of paper. Instead of going to the back of the table and cutting the paper I went to the front and while I was sitting in front of the public I ripped the paper, and when I moved there was a huge big hole. The public started to laugh.

𝒞: *What about* La Boheme*?*

ℒ: That was even more funny. Because people know *La Boheme* backwards and forwards. In the second act when Rodolfo arrives and meets his friend with Mimi there's a phrase that goes, "Questa é Mimi," and a little bit before that there's a guy who sells all the little toys for the children. Then the tenor says, "Due posti, finalmente, eccoci chi qui." The bass had just arrived and although he had not sung the opera for at least 10 years the moment came and this man sang with the biggest voice he had, "Salame!" then the tenor came in "Due posti . . ." (laughter) meaning he was a Salami! And then he repeated himself and he had to do it again. When he tried to escape the public started to laugh and I never heard such a big laugh in my life. It was funny, you know, because they could see he was very upset about it. But I'm not sure if he was upset or if he didn't do it on purpose, to make the people laugh.

𝒞: *Are there any prop mishap stories?*

ℒ: Failure of props? I wasn't there, but apparently it was very dramatic. They were doing *Tosca*, and the soprano sat too close to the table where there was a candle. All of a sudden her wig caught fire. The baritone in the back drinking his wine tried to stop the fire with his wine. That must have been very funny to watch.

I was doing *Tosca* once and there's a place where I say, "Open the door so that you will hear his suffering." And naturally, I'm the one in that production who has to bang the door. When the moment came to open the door, I banged the door and the whole set fell, flop! The two stagehands had to come in and raise the wall. The audience was laughing in the hall like mad.

𝒞: *Rehearsals are quite funny. I often wish there were videos of the actual rehearsals where things are sometimes not too serious.*

𝓛: I remember one of the last *La Boheme's* I did. I was coming out with all kinds of words. You over-rehearse and all of a sudden you cannot be serious. You come up with phrases that are not right. And I remember very well, one of the sopranos walked in at the end of the opera after the big fight with the four guys. The soprano invented a phrase which sounded like, "It's Mimi, it's Mimi that makes peepee and she feels bad." I tell you one thing, it was so funny!

I had a funny thing happen doing *Macbeth* in Toronto. At the end after I'm killed, they had the brilliant idea to take me out on a stretcher. But the only thing was that they forgot to measure how tall I am. When the two guys came and put me on the stretcher my head passed over the top of the stretcher and my feet extended over the bottom of the stretcher. When they grabbed me and started to lift my head my whole face went into the crotch of one guy and my feet went into the crotch of the other guy. Everybody saw that and started to laugh. It was so incredibly funny. When I got up I made the sign that means it smells.

𝓒: *I bet they fixed that pretty quick.*

𝓛: I told them to just grab my two arms and pull me off of the stage.

𝓒: *What about some funny experiences with the* Barber of Seville.

𝓛: The *Barber of Seville* was really my great debut in opera because that's the first big opera I ever sang. And I remember we did it in Montreal. They used to do everything in French. Thank God, because that was my first language. But at the same time the words were practically Italian. I did Fiorello and my first words were "piano, pianissimo." And that's what I sang.

Something very funny happened during the performance. One night we were doing the performance and the big ensemble, soldiers and everybody, were supposed to walk onstage and Figaro was supposed to come in and stop the big argument that is happening. We sang our notes and we were holding them and holding them. No Figaro. The poor guy was so tired that he was sleeping backstage and he came in about a minute and a half after. There was a lot of laughter.

Another thing that happened that night was where Bartolo starts to make an argument with the officer and I was the officer. All of a sudden Bartolo jumped on my back and Figaro jumped on my back and they were trying to throw me down on the floor. And I held myself upright. They got so cross about it because they would have liked me to fall down. No way. That was for the *Barber*. And then another time, the first time I did the *Barber* with Gino we were getting ready for the performance and I said, "Gino, what is it you look forward to in the *Barber*?" He said, "Dad I'll be able to kick you in the pants and you won't be able to say anything." He never kicked me in the pants but it was very funny.

I was doing *La Traviata* at Covent Garden once. I got very mad with quite a few of the singers. I came to the stage director and I started to yell at him, actually for nothing, because he was not responsible. But I screamed, he screamed back at me and I stopped the rehearsal, and all of a sudden I saw the scenery and I took my foot and I hit the piece of scenery. Just behind it there was a brick wall. The top of my shoe went up, the bottom of my shoe went down and there was my toe coming out. I fell on the floor and was crying in pain. The stage director I was screaming at came right next to me with the biggest smile you ever saw and he said, "Well, Louis, who is the stupid jackass now?" And I started to laugh through my tears. After that I had to do the *La Traviata*, but when you have a broken toe and you have to step on the foot, anytime you make a movement it really hurts. I remember walking on the stage. I sang in a shaky voice and it went on for the whole performance because the moment I put a little bit of pressure on my toe it hurt me. The reviews came out a couple of days later and said, "Tonight we heard a very sentimental *La Traviata*. Mr. Quilico was completely in character."

C: *Going back to critics, there was one story about the critic's wife. Can you give some more of the details.*

ℒ: The Paris Opera was doing *Don Carlos*. The management called me, two days after they had already started rehearsals, and they said, "Mr. Quilico, we need your services." At first I was reluctant because I knew the baritone who was supposed to do it. However, I did the performance. A singer from the chorus got me all of the newspapers. And all the newspapers were unanimous in saying that I was the star of the show. Finally *L'Opera* gave me a very, very bad review. When I saw the critic, who was Italian, I was somewhat nasty to him.

About three months later I had to do *Don Carlos* in Rouen. During the rehearsal the mezzo-soprano turned around and said, "Mr. Quilico, aren't you the one who created *Don Carlos* at the Paris Opera?" I said, "Yes, it's me." And she went, "Ha!" And that was very funny because I was wondering what the "Ha!" was for. Later we were getting ready to do the performance and I was putting on my make-up. Maybe half an hour before the performance I heard her screaming at somebody in the hall. She was swearing. She hit somebody because I heard someone fall on the floor. I said, "My God, this woman has got to do a performance. I should try and see if I can stop her fighting with someone."

I got up to open my door. The moment I went to touch the door, the door opened and there was a man on the floor. The lady passed me and went towards him. She grabbed him by the hair and dragged him back towards me. I was standing there, baffled by the whole thing. She said to the man, "Kiss his feet, kiss his feet!" I grabbed her and said, "Lady, come on this is a stupid man. We have a performance to do." And she says, "No! I'm going to kill him, I'm going to kill him!" I said, "Why you going to kill him? Please leave him." "No, please!" she said, "This is my stupid husband. He is the one who reviewed you so badly and I have no pity for him." And she kept on hitting the poor guy. Finally I grabbed her and I just went out and that was it. But it was very funny to see that once in my life I had a reviewer put in his place. I tell you one thing: he never again wrote that kind of bad review.

𝒞: *Let's discuss conductors. I hear nothing but wonderful stories about Giuseppe Patané as a conductor.*

ℒ: Well, he's one of the greats. He had an understanding for music. It was not only a matter of understanding the music and conducting an orchestra, but he knew the operas so well. He knew every single word I was singing so that for him to give an impulse or a dramatic effect was easy and natural. He was one of the very special ones.

𝒞: *Did he sing himself?*

ℒ: No, he did not sing. But he came from a musical family because his father was a conductor before him. And I remember he said, "Louis, when I started to study conducting my father taught me a lot, but one thing he said to me was, 'My dear, if you want to conduct there's only one thing to do. Do exactly like the singers who are on the stage. Know the whole score by memory'." And that's what he was doing.

𝒞: *So he was one of the conductors who conducted everything from memory.*

ℒ: Oh yes, never a score. In fact somebody was telling me that at the Met he did *Lohengrin* by memory. I think that he could not be a slave to the score. If you can do it, it's marvelous because you don't have to rely on a book. You know, he was so incredible. He knew the score backwards and forwards.

𝒞: *And he had a knack for following singers.*

ℒ: Oh yes! And I have to say that if he felt that you were a little off, he did not like that. What he wanted was to give a dramatic sense to your performance. And that's the thing that was very interesting. Because many artists said that about him.

𝒞: *What do you like to see in the conductor?*

ℒ: Well, what I like to see in a conductor is very simple. He should do exactly what I do: try to do a musical performance that is not only a musical performance but a message transferred to the public. In the orchestra you do exactly the same thing. Very often the conductors don't do these things.

𝒞: *Who has the final word during performances on tempo? Is it the singer or is it the conductor?*

ℒ: In general, if you have an intelligent conductor, we're both communicating together and that's the beauty of it. Why do you think that some performers come out of the performance and say, "My God, did you hear this?" It's very, very important to have a supportive conductor. But at the same time, if you have some soloist, a pianist, a violinist or a singer, the conveying of the music, the message of what the composer received himself, is the most important thing. Don't try to fight the composer. And very often you're going to have some conductor say, "He wrote 60!" (metronome marking) "But maestro are you sure it's him?" Very often even the composer himself did not exactly understand the tempi that the certain piece should be performed at.

𝒞: *Certainly. It's a collaborative experience. Did you ever have the experience when you are doing* Rigoletto, *and you and the other singers feel a tempo but the conductor feels something else?*

ℒ: Oh God, yes!

𝒞: *What happens?*

ℒ: You have different singers. You have a singer that sings *Rigoletto* who has much shorter breath than me. Maybe I sing a performance of *Rigoletto* and I've got a long breath and one day I don't feel too, too well. All of a sudden I have to go faster or slower. It depends on the artist, the temperament of the artist. I would say for me, the artist is so well aware of his ability that you don't have to say to yourself, why am I fighting? But anyway, to come back to the conductor. In my entire life, I protested only two conductors who played me dirty tricks.

𝒞: *Do you feel that the singers today are more concerned with musical interpretation than they were before? I mean, the day of the prima donna when the singers were able to demand anything that they wanted seems to be finished.*

L: Well, I find the big tragedy today is that conductors as well as directors are not giving. They don't believe enough in the artists. Singers today are much more aware than they were 25, 30 years ago in the time of Enrico Caruso. Once upon a time we used to call these singers 'caffoni'. That means not too intelligent. They would hit a high note and they would keep it with their hand up and the hand would come down before the note. But today the artists go according to the musical score and a sense of the dramatic interpretation. There is less importance on the high notes. Singers today ask why do you think the composer put it there? He put it there to give an effect. And why not use it.

Toscanini was conducting *Il Trovatore*, if I remember well, and a great tenor of that era was singing. Toscanini never liked to hear long, high notes. Apparently the tenor had a fantastic high note and he kept it and kept it, and somebody came to Toscanini after and said, "Maestro, why did you let that singer keep the note so long?" The answer of Toscanini was a very simple one: "When you hear gold coming from a throat like that, enjoy it as much as possible." You know, that was another way to look at it, but today the artists are not in that sphere anymore. We are very well advised about everything, by coaches, stage directors, and conductors.

C: *I would like you to tell me the story about the old man at the Met.*

L: It was a wonderful evening for me vocally. After the performance of *Rigoletto* it took me a while to take off my costume and my make-up. When I walked out, there was an old man waiting for me. In the back of the Met, at that time, the corridor was wide-open, and it was January and it was cold. I said to him, "Excuse me sir, why didn't you go in?" He said, "Oh, I'm too shy, Mr. Quilico. I wanted to talk to you, Mr. Quilico, because for me it's very important. I want you to know something. Today I enjoyed your performance so much that I was in a trance about it. It's so incredible that I always ask God if ever he likes me he should make sure that the day I have to die I'm listening to one of your performances and sitting here at the Met. That would be the greatest way for me to die." I was speechless. I mean, it's a compliment. It's incredible that this is how my performance can touch people sometimes.

𝒞: *Do you study the score, completely? I know that when we work together on an opera you sing every part.*

ℒ: Oh yes, from every angle you can look at. I will say something very funny. I know the score when I know the first word and I know the last word. Like *Tosca* is "Untal," that's the first word, and the last word is "Aagh" (Death rattle). Sometimes I feel that what is in the middle is up to God. Before a performance I always say a prayer: "God, I thank you to have given me a voice. I did not ask for it. So please help me now."

𝒞: *Have you ever wanted to be a tenor?*

ℒ: I was rehearsing *Rigoletto* with a tenor at the City Opera of New York. He was not very well-known but he was a very good tenor. We were doing the last act and when the moment came to sing "La Donna e' mobile" our famous tenor was not there. I said to myself, come on maestro, play it, I'm going to sing it. And all of a sudden I started to sing "La Donna e' mobile" in the right tonality and everything. The tenor walked in and told me to keep on going and I kept on going. I held the high note with no problem. Anyway he thanked me very much. The next day we did the performance and it comes to "La Donna e' mobile" and when he sang it he was cracking all over the place. I felt very sorry for him but it was one of those things.

𝒞: *What is your vocal range?*

ℒ: When I was younger, and not lazy, I used to sing to F above high C. I was not a tenor, I know that, but I used to go up there. Control and good breathing helped me tremendously. But now my range is an F lower than middle

C and to about A flat, A natural. I have what is needed for the baritone repertoire.

𝒞: *Who are your favorite singers of the past, those that you heard live and not on recordings? Also, those on recordings.*

ℒ: The old, old singers, I don't know much about them. I know Rosa Ponselle, because I met her. In fact I knew her very well. Caruso, I heard the recordings. I liked him very, very much. But today we have some singers who are as great if not maybe greater than they were. When I talk like this I don't want people to accuse me but I'm talking as a technician. If you're going to talk about the quality of a voice, the interpretation of a voice, you might say well, I prefer this artist or that artist. But as a technician it's very different and, for instance, I would say that one of the greatest tenors that I know is Luciano Pavarotti. I know that there are a lot of people who don't like Luciano but prefer Placido. I'm talking as a technician: Luciano had the kind of a voice nobody ever had and that's including Mr. Caruso. Luciano has a vocal extension so superior that he has practically an octave higher than anybody else I know. There are some others who could do as well but their voices are not as pretty as his voice. I would say that I like the quality of certain other artists better. It's very subjective and of the 'moment'.

𝒞: *It's nice to hear that you have a fresh perspective rather than saying that the golden age of opera is unequalled.*

ℒ: Well, you always hear about this golden age and that golden age, but I think that I was born in the golden age of the voice. Because no matter what anybody would tell you, when you stand on the stage as I have with Leonard Warren, Mario Del Monaco, Jussi Björling, Giuseppe di Stefano, Renata Tebaldi, just to name a few, it was so incredible. Even today there are some of these voices, Pavarotti, Domingo, Freni. When they talk about the golden age in the time of Caruso, well Caruso was a great artist, yes, but there were a lot of other great artists. But they used to sing maybe once a week. Today they sing like mad and they have to be greater masters of their voice than in those years. When you think about Alfredo Kraus you talk about a man who is 69 and his technique is still fabulous. It's not to be compared to Caruso, but it's another kind, another type of voice.

𝒞: *You are talking about the superstars like Domingo and Pavarotti who travel every second day and still sing beautifully.*

ℒ: Yes, but sometimes I feel that's a little bit, excuse the expression, ridiculous because it's really very dangerous. It's not the voice that will not resist wear and tear, it's your body that will not resist. I know I had some similar experiences that way, singing five *Rigoletto*'s in five days in five different cities. I used to take the morning plane at 8 o'clock every morning because I used to have to do *Rigoletto* in the other city. And I tell you, I will not start that again, and I would not recommend that to anybody because it creates problems mentally and physically.

𝒞: *Tell me the story of mistaken identity by a fan following your* Rigoletto *performance on the Metropolitan TV broadcast.*

ℒ: That was a very, very funny story. I replaced a famous baritone at the Met at the last minute and it was a telecast. I had a funny feeling that they forgot to take off the name of the other baritone. I sang the performance, and approximately three months later I received a letter in my box at the Met. The other baritone said "Louis, you deserve this letter and this is why I'm sending it to you, and I want you to enjoy it because it is true." I read the letter written by a fan of this baritone, and she said "Mr. So and So, last night I saw the broadcast of *Rigoletto* and I have to say I was so, so transported because I never, never saw you acting so beautifully and you never sang so beautifully in your life." It was a great compliment. But the thing is, in life it's very beautiful to receive a cheque from the Metropolitan after a performance, but if you can receive one thing like that from the public it is worth your weight in gold. I think it's very important, because the applause is more important than the money you get.

𝒞: *Don't let your managers read that comment! It also says something about the other baritone and the healthy atmosphere at the Met among baritones for him to have given you the letter.*

ℒ: Well, I think, people are very human. I'm sure that maybe 80 or 85 years ago in the time of Caruso, a letter like that would have never gotten to me.

𝒞: *Yes, there might have been a vendetta against you instead.*

ℒ: Yes, you might be surprised. I was doing *Un Ballo in Maschera* once and I did four performances, and on the fourth performance there was a knock at the door. In came the tenor of the evening. He was older than I was and he did not know my age. He said, "Young man I will never sing in *Un Ballo* with you." We sang it after that because he was obliged to do it, but at that time he meant I stole the show. And I have to say one thing: if you are a good baritone and you do that opera I feel sorry for the tenor and the soprano, because the aria "Eri Tu" Mr. Verdi wrote gives baritones a crown just with this opera.

𝒞: *Yes, Verdi himself was a baritone.*

𝒞: *Are there claques all over the opera houses now or is that something that's no longer accepted? (Claques are fans who are paid to applaud.)*

ℒ: It's difficult to know; I don't bother to find out. In Europe, I know that it's still in existence. For instance I remember *Aida* in Caracalla, Italy. The conductor said to me before we started the rehearsal, "I hope you're not going to sing this opera here like certain people that sang it here before." I understood who he meant; I knew the previous baritone. I started the rehearsal and everything was fine and at the dress rehearsal I did exactly what the conductor wanted, but later I heard a knock at the door. "Mr. Quilico?" "Yes." "I'm Capo Claque." I said, "Thank you, how much do I owe you?" He says "No, no, it's not how much you owe me, but you've got to do something. In 'Non sei mia Figlia dei Faraoni tu sei la schiava' you have to hold that note and hold it, hold it. Forget the Maestro because if you don't hold that note you won't get the applause from us."

And what do I do? I said to myself, well, for one night let's forget about the conductor. But you should have seen the chaos that happened with the conductor. All of a sudden, I get ready to sing the high note and the conductor realized what I was going to do, because he understood that I would do exactly what the other baritone did. You go to one side of the stage and you hit the high note and then you walk to the other side of the stage, and that's where I was when the moment for the high note came. I could see him. If he had a gun at that moment he would have shot me. Anyway, I hit the high note and I walked and arrived at the other side and there's Aida. I grabbed her. I didn't look at the conductor, but all of a sudden I lifted my head and I saw the conductor with his head between his legs. Now, I said to myself, I'm a dead duck!

We finished the act and I saw him running out before the orchestra had time to get out. I said to myself, well, I'm going to go at the end of the line, because it's a long, long line and maybe he might not reach me. He passed everybody, he arrived on the stage and passed in front of everybody and all of a sudden he grabbed my hand. At the moment he grabbed my hand the curtain opens and with the biggest smile you ever saw he said to me, "You sang like a dog. You're never going to sing with me again!" And I turned around with a big smile, "Maestro it would be the greatest thing that ever happened to my life. I don't want to sing with you because you're a dog too!"

𝒞: *Why did he get so angry over one note?*

ℒ: You know, this is the point, I wouldn't have done that especially in a smaller theatre. I've done long notes at the Met; I was never criticized by the conductor. But this one had to show that he was a great Maestro. I also have to say, Caracalla is a very commercial place.

𝒞: *Are there any other fiascos that happened to you that were amusing?*

ℒ: In *Rigoletto*? You don't play around too much with that opera. Some other operas might be easier to get a little bit loose, but with *Rigoletto* you start and you say to yourself, I hope I finish. It's not an opera that's easy, because the sentiment of it is so intense. Your involvement in it is so deep because *Rigoletto* is on the stage practically all the time.

𝒞: *Are there any superstitions with* Rigoletto, *as for example with "The Scottish Play"?*

ℒ: No, No. There's one opera where something happened. It's *La Forza del Destino*. One of the greatest tragedies happened in *La Forza del Destino*, when Leonard Warren died. He was singing his famous aria. The beginning of the aria is "Urna fatale del mio destino." It means, "Urn of my destiny, please go away." Can you imagine what that means? It means, death, please don't come to me, don't come to me. At the end of this part of the aria, there's one place where somebody walks in and says, "He's going to live," because the tenor has been shot and lies dying, but all of a sudden you find out he's going to live. Warren had to sing, "E salvo e salvo, o joia!" which means, "He's saved, he's saved, oh joy!" And can you imagine, he fell right there and died after singing "Urna fatale," "Urn of my destiny." It's incredible. And another thing that happened with that opera was the first time it was going to be produced, here in the United States in New Orleans. They did the dress rehearsal and during the night the theatre burned down. They didn't know who did it.

𝒞: *And have you sung this opera?*

ℒ: I've done *La Forza del Destino* about nine times. But I was always very reluctant to do it.

𝒞: *Are other baritones reluctant to do it?*

ℒ: Oh, I don't know, I never asked. But me, I was very reticent because that opera killed my favorite baritone, maybe the most favorite voice I ever heard in my life. I said to myself, I don't want to do it because I . . . you know, its very funny, because I thought I was going to die too! I didn't die, but now I always refuse to do it. For about 15 years after Warren died, 15 years if not 20 or 25 years, I never did it. I refused to do it.

𝒞: *How did Caruso die? Did he not die on the stage as well?*

ℒ: No, he had his attack on the stage, but I don't know if he died at home or in the hospital or something. But Warren died on the stage. And it's the only time in the history of the Met, that an artist stopped a performance, because nobody could keep on going after that, no way. I spoke to the conductor. He said, "Louis you had to hear him that night. He sang like a God. Nobody could sing after he died."

𝒞: *That's an amazing story. Since then, Richard Versaille died of a heart attack onstage during the 1995–96 season.*

ℒ: Gino (Quilico) had a similar encounter with José Carreras, who was sick (he had leukemia) when he was doing the film of *La Bohème*. Gino said that the day before he collapsed, I think it was during the third act, at one moment Carreras disappeared in the fog, and the last word he said was, "Farewell, Adieu." The next day he was at the hospital with leukemia. Nobody could sing anything and it was three days before work resumed.

𝒞: *What about your first time singing in Moscow?*

ℒ: It was very, very cold. And I don't know how, but I arrived there and the day I had to sing the performance I woke up and couldn't talk. There was not a sound coming out of my throat. The first baritone of the house said, "Mr. Quilico, you have to sing, please." and I said, "No, I don't want to, because . . ." He said, "Please, you start and after that if you can't we'll get somebody else to finish the performance." And the thing I'm still amazed with myself is that I could not speak but I could sing. And I have to say, it was a good performance. But the thing is, it was very difficult for me to understand that.

𝒞: *Don Carlo or Don Carlos? Isn't that opera done in French and Italian?*

ℒ: Yes, but you know Verdi, there was one thing with Verdi, he was a little bit more attentive about his operas than other composers. For instance, what happened with *Don Carlos*, it came first in French, not in Italian. If the opera had been written the opposite way it would have made a big problem. But the funniest thing about it, in the whole opera, if I remember well, there might have been maybe one or two notes different in French and in Italian. But it could have been difficult to have a translation that would correspond to the French one. I've done both versions, and the French is wonderful, and the Italian is wonderful too.

𝒞: *Which is your first language, French?*

ℒ: French, yes.

𝒞: *And then Italian?*

ℒ: Ah, English.

𝒞: *English and then Italian?*

ℒ: And then Italian, yes.

𝒞: *When you memorize, do you memorize the words away from the music, or do you memorize the words with the music?*

ℒ: Usually I memorize without the music, because it means something. I will read the words, but what is happening? Reading the words doesn't give me enough, doesn't provide an anchor for me. The music helps me to keep having a flow. Plus, if I go only by words I miss the other phrase coming from the tenor and what is happening in this phrase musically. That's why, very often, the music takes over in helping me memorize a work. I read the words to give me an idea of the play. Also I read the libretto.

𝒞: *Having worked with you on your operas I know that you sing all the parts.*

ℒ: You have to. Because, all of a sudden you say to somebody, "I hate you" and the person might say, "No, I love you," the opposite. How are you going to have a reaction to that, you understand? It's the opposite of what you sang. That's why it's very difficult, you know. You must know all the parts.

𝒞: *You have a wonderful memory. You remember these operas for so long and you can sing them on a few days notice. What do you attribute your memory to?*

ℒ: I have to say one thing: I don't have the foggiest idea why the memory is good. Better than that, I'll tell you about my debut in opera. I mean my great debut in opera at the New York City Opera in *Traviata*. I remember studying the opera and stating to myself, I'm going to pass out for sure. I'm not going to get through it because I will not remember it to the end. I did my first act, (it was the second act in reality, because my character comes in the second act) it went beautifully, no problem, well thank God, that's one done. I did the third act, no problem. Came the fourth act and when I finished the fourth act, I said, "Oh my God! Well I think I'm going to sing opera now!" Because for a moment before that debut I was very undecided about it.

𝒞: *But you find it pretty easy to memorize.*

ℒ: Oh yes.

𝒞: *That's a gift.*

ℒ: But I have only one problem now, at the Met. With the prompter, it's very difficult.

𝒞: *It's almost getting in the way.*

ℒ: Well, it gets in the way, because you are so accustomed to it that you expect that it's going to come and you're not scared that something will happen. But if the prompter is not there, then sometimes wow! You can forget.

𝒞: *And what about perfect pitch, you always have an unerring pitch. I have never really heard you sing out of tune.*

ℒ: I think for me it's my ears. I cannot sing false. Once in a while, once in a blue moon, because I don't put enough attention to it. But in general, no. Another problem is that sometimes when one is doing an opera with, let's say, a soprano that goes out of pitch, it happens. I remember,

Rigoletto for instance, there's one part where I would always ask the prompter to listen to me very carefully, because the orchestra is loud and I don't know if I'm off pitch, and generally (I would say 75 percent of the time) the sopranos are off pitch. And that is very dangerous, because at that point you are taking your note from the soprano. I was doing *Traviata* once with a soprano at the Met, and it was a broadcast. And I asked Joan, "Joan, listen to me at every entrance and show me if I'm right on pitch."

𝒞: *That's Joan Dorneman?*

ℒ: Yes, Joan Dorneman, the prompter. And the thing is, it was terrible, because the soprano was always a quarter of a tone or half a tone lower, and you know what it is, to all of a sudden start to sing and you're the one that's out of pitch. I tell you, it's terrible.

𝒞: *Allergies can affect your voice too. Tell me about some of your experiences.*

ℒ: Well, I don't know exactly how I can say this. It's like having a pair of glasses. You have to be comfortable physically when you do the role. It will help you mentally if you are physically comfortable, because you can't concentrate if something disturbs you. Just to give you an idea, I was doing *Roberto Devereux* at the City Opera. We did the whole rehearsal and everything was fine. I had no problem. But at the dress rehearsal I had my costume on, and I had trouble with my first aria. I thought I was sick, or not in good shape. When it came to the first performance I went through hell! The voice came out beautifully but it was very difficult.

Between the first and the second performance I was vocalizing in my dressing room, and before I put the costume on everything sounded terrific. Then they put the costume, which had a tremendous fur collar, on me and I couldn't sing. I took off the coat and I sang well, put on the coat, and I sang badly. Everything was absorbed by the fur. I called the dresser and said, "You know what we're going to do with this?" He said, "What?" I said, "You're going to put it on the side!" "Oh!" he says. "The stage director will not accept it!" I said, "You do me a favour. You tell him to come here, put on the costume and go and sing the first act!" I never put it on after that. That was it!

𝒞: *Most younger stage directors should listen and learn from opera singers who have had a lot of experience doing the productions. Today, it seems that too much emphasis is given to the stage director or to the production.*

ℒ: Well, I don't want to be nasty, I don't want to say anything that will be taken the wrong way, but it comes to the point right now that when you read a review of opera, very often the performance is incredible because of the director and the conductor. For me, it's the opposite. If the performance is extraordinary, it's because you've got good people on the stage and that's what makes the opera, makes the production or, more or less, the producer himself. And if the producer or stage director has the intelligence to really want to work with people, that's when the production can become a masterpiece.

𝒞: *What about Luchino Visconti?*

ℒ: Well, Visconti! I was invited to do an opera. It was not *Rigoletto*, but it was an opera I was doing in Spoleto. For me it was the first time, and naturally we had to do what was asked of us, especially with a man like Visconti. Well, you know, he's incredible and famous. I was and still am allergic to paint, fumes and perfumes or anything like that. I did not realize it until the dress rehearsal. During that production they decided that a table onstage did not look exactly right. It needed more glamorous dressing so they put a big tablecloth on it for the premiere. They also painted a frill of gold all around the tablecloth. And what happened? Of course I was allergic to the paint.

So when I walked on the stage and I had to sing my famous aria I started to feel that there was something disturbing me, until I realized that I was losing my voice. And it's so funny, because at the end of the act the first man I met coming off the stage was Visconti, and I looked at him right in his face. I mean, I was so mad I didn't care who it was, and I said, "Who is the lousy dog that put that tablecloth on the table?" And I knew he was the one responsible for it. But I got over it you know. What can you do? But it was a real bad moment I have to say.

𝒞: *Tell me about allergies and singers.*

ℒ: The big problem with singers is that we don't realize how sensitive the throat really is. You know you cannot touch your eyes because they are very sensitive. The throat is exactly the same. Naturally, being a thing we don't see, you can only feel if you have a problem or not. Very often it's not only allergies of singers. I think in general people are allergic to dust, penicillin and perfume. People who are prone to allergies should be very careful because just the fumes of the perfume can get you sick. I know for a fact that when there's somebody around me with perfume or cologne I must tell them, if I have to sing. Naturally, I am very delicate about it because I know that all people are so touchy about their smell. But I ask very, very delicately.

For instance, I was doing *William Tell* at Carnegie Hall. And in came a lady with strong perfume. The smell of that perfume was so incredible that it overpowered me. I told her that I am allergic to perfume, and would it be possible for her not to wear this kind of perfume? She was very nasty about it and said, "Listen, this is a free country and I'll wear it!" I answered her back, "Now I'm going to tell you one thing, do you want to get fired? Anyway, tomorrow morning we have the dress rehearsal, and tomorrow night we have the performance. You do me a favour. When you want to walk in this place you come to me and let yourself be smelled." Naturally, that was a cold approach, but at that point I didn't care. I had asked her very delicately, and usually people are very nice about it. We do have a job to do. But this one really took it the wrong way.

The next morning I was sitting on the stage and she walked in. I looked at her, she looked at me, she turned around to go out. But I called her, in front of the whole orchestra and chorus, I was very nasty I have to say, but I didn't care because she was so nasty to me, not wanting to understand that I was allergic. I said, "Would you come here!" And she turned around. I said, "Come here! I want to smell you!" She came up on the stage. I wouldn't have done it, but she walked towards me and I started to smell her from her head to her feet and she did not wear the perfume. I said, "Thank you very much, we can keep on doing the performance!" That was one of the allergies.

Another one that I had was with Thomas Schippers, the conductor who usually took baths in cologne water. I was doing the *Duke of Alba* in Spoleto, and Schippers wanted me to use his studio since I had some work to do. His studio smelled tremendously of the cologne water and although it was a nice smell, after the rehearsal I started to lose my voice.

Another thing happened before this in Spoleto. In the theater at the door of my dressing room there were about 15–20 buckets of paint, some of them open, and it smelled. I got so mad that I called the stage manager and I said, "Please, clear this up!" He said, "Don't worry, Louis, we'll have this clear for tonight." I came that night, and all the paint was there. I started to scream and make a stink. Finally the manager of the theatre walked in and said, "What's the matter?" I said, "I want these buckets out of the theatre! I don't want them around my room! I said it this afternoon and they're still there!" And she said, "Oh, you singers! You're so difficult!" I grabbed her and I said, "Listen! You take out these buckets, these cans of paint because I'm allergic to paint!" and I threw her out. And exactly five minutes later the buckets of paint were all out. Apparently, my big blow-up went around Spoleto, and the next day, I was the Duke of Alba, in the opera, and everywhere I was walking people would mention me not as Mr. Quilico, but as Duke Quilico.

Another experience happened with the famous *Duke of Alba*. We had to sing it in New York in Carnegie Hall and in Philadelphia. In Philadelphia, about five minutes before the performance I went into the dressing room of the conductor, Thomas Schippers. I was in his dressing room maybe two minutes, I wished him best of luck, then from this dressing room to the stage it was a walk I would say of about 25 feet. The moment I arrived on the stage it was as if somebody had taken a pin or a dagger and stabbed my neck. The pain went straight to my brains. It didn't bother me at first because I didn't know what it was all about, but when I started to sing the performance I began to lose my voice. We finished the performance, and on my way back from Philadelphia I said to somebody, "I think I'm allergic to the conductor."

When I arrived in New York, nothing came out of my throat. "My God what is this?" I was hoping that it would go away. I didn't do much during Saturday and I waited, but on Sunday morning I woke up and my friends tried to cancel the performance for me because I was too sick. However the management said, "You've to do the performance because there's nobody else that knows the opera." I said, "I know, but I have no voice; the voice is gone!" They got me to the doctor about 5 o'clock in the afternoon. He said, "When do you have to sing?" Somebody else said, "Tonight." He said, "No way. You'll have to cancel." It was explained to him that the show had to go on. "Well, I'm going to do something for you. I don't know how successful we're going to be, but do me a favour. You go home, get yourself ready, go in Carnegie Hall but don't even try the voice. When it's time to go on the stage and when the time comes for you to sing, open your mouth and try to sing. If something comes out you can thank God. If nothing comes out there's nothing you can do about it." I went with that.

But when I decided that I was going to cut an aria, the conductor, Thomas Schippers, who was kind of inhuman I have to say, although he was a fabulous conductor, said, "You've got to sing the aria!" But I said, "Tommy, I cannot sing the aria, I am too sick!" He said, "If you don't sing it I'm going to make sure you're never going to sing again in your life." He really threatened me well. When I saw that, I didn't say anything to him and we started the performance. You could feel that the voice was not reacting. But a terrible thing happened that night. There was one place where I used to say, "Do you know who I am?" and all of a sudden right there from the corner of my eyes, who do I see but Mr. Rudolf Bing.

Anyway, the next day I went back to see the doctor. And the doctor said, "Well, I'll talk to you after the third performance." I did the third performance. It was not too, too bad. The voice was coming back slowly, slowly. Anyway, I went to see him the day after the third performance and he said, "Well, I will tell you now you should have given up singing at that moment. You shouldn't have sung the performance because you broke a blood vessel on the vocal cord." And this is why I always say if a singer is not 100 percent fit vocally the night of a performance, quit. Because it could be very dangerous for your voice or it could be even dangerous for your reputation. I was lucky enough that the *New York Times* did not recognize me. They said there was a debut of a young baritone last night, Louis Quilico, and that was it. But they did not recognize that I had already sung in New York.

𝒞: *What about other things getting stuck in your throat? You have some stories on that.*

ℒ: Well, this one happened in Santiago, Chile. It was quite close to the beginning of my career and during my song I heard a lady in the hall. She made a lot of gasping sounds, and then I started to choke, turning completely blue. We finished the concert and the lady came backstage and said, "Mr. Quilico, I'm so deeply sorry for my outbursts but at the moment you were singing I saw that from the ceiling there was a dust particle that was floating right in front of your face and I was praying, God, please don't let him swallow it. And you swallowed it!" I said, "You can say that again!" It was very awkward, I have to say. Another place was in the mountains in Montreal. I was doing a summer concert. And all of a sudden, during an aria I swallowed a mosquito or a small fly. Anyway, I choked on it too, you know. We are susceptible to these things.

𝒞: *Now what about a feather?*

ℒ: Well, the feather is coming. I'll come back to that one. Oh, another place I went to I was doing *Cavalleria Rusticana* and *Pagliacci*. And during the first opera I started to cough to try to clear my throat but there was nothing I could do.

It was terrible, because I was not choking but there was something tickling in my throat and it drove me nuts! After this I had to sing the *Pagliacci*. Finally, after I finished *Cavalleria* I went out and I started to cough. I shouldn't have done that but you get so bloody nervous that you do it just the same. And all of a sudden something came out of my mouth. I took it out and I looked at it. It was a piece of plastic! I don't exactly remember how long it took me but I realized that it was a bristle from my toothbrush that was in my throat. I must have brushed my teeth and that thing caught in my tooth and I did not feel it.

But to come back to the feather . . . I was in Santiago, Chile, and we started the rehearsal of *Rigoletto*. Everything was going very, very, very well. I walked on the stage without realizing there was going to be any problem and I opened my mouth and something went wrong. I was having trouble vocally. There was not exactly a tickling but something right there in my throat that was disturbing me. I went on and finished the opera.

Back in the hotel something started to tickle me in the throat and I practically choked, and all of a sudden I coughed and out came a piece of thread, I would say about three-quarters to maybe an inch long. I put it on my dresser. In fact, if I remember well, I kept it and I put it in my scrapbook. The next day I noticed what it really was, because during the night it dried up and I noticed it was a feather. My feeling is that these old theatres have birds that get inside the theatre and maybe even have a nest.

My third performance was a . . . I would call it a tragic one too. I went to have dinner right before my performance, and I had soup. And I remember that the soup was very heavy, a lot of oil and spices. I went on and everything was perfect, the voice was responding. Then came the moment to sing the Cortigiani. I walked and opened a door to go down three steps. All of a sudden I looked at the stage, and it was moving around me. It was terrible! I shook myself and it stopped. I walked down and kept going and the stage again started to go, but this time even faster and I didn't know where to put my feet. Right next to me there was a seat and I could have sat down but no, I was supposed to go across the stage and that's where I went. All of a sudden I put my hand out and Voom, I fell on the stage and that was it. I didn't lose consciousness but I was completely dizzy and I couldn't stand on my two feet. Finally, they had to close the curtain because I couldn't go on with the performance for the moment. They took me to my dressing room and I said, "Give me two minutes and it might pass." Finally a doctor came in and gave me some injection, and after awhile I was alright and we finished the performance. I found out through the grapevine after that somebody said I was a dope addict because he had given me a needle. I never had dope or drugs in my entire life, not even the smallest pill.

𝒞: *What about stage fright and nerves?*

ℒ: Talking about stage fright, I remember very well doing the *Trojans* at the Met. It's not an opera I've done often but I had done maybe five or six performances. I started my aria and right in the middle of the aria, whoops! I drew a complete blank! Now the soprano was right next to me and she turned towards me giving me the words. Nothing, nothing, nothing got through to me! Apparently my face was completely blank. The prompter was giving me the words and the soprano and nothing, nothing! The conductor also got in the picture, still nothing, nothing! Finally, after about 10, 15, maybe 20 measures, practically at the end of the aria, all of a sudden it came back. And I have to say it was not scary because you don't do it on purpose, but the tragedy is that at that moment nothing wants to register. You want to close up shop and say, "No, I don't want to sing anymore!" Very often that's the reason these things happen with somebody who forgets the words.

𝒞: *Does that happen often to many singers or do the prompters help so that the audience doesn't really know what's going on?*

ℒ: The prompter is a very vital thing for some singers who cannot sing without the prompter. They get lost completely; in fact, they would not go on the stage if there was not a prompter. For about 20 years I preferred never to have a prompter because I couldn't make a mistake. But now I'm so used to the prompter that it seems that I need a prompter all the time too! And that can be scary, because often you do some performances where there is no prompter and you have to discipline your memory to work again.

𝒞: *Well, the big stars have so many roles, so much pressure and travel, how do they deal with it? How do you deal with it?*

ℒ: Well, I have to say one thing: the pressure on them is tremendous, because they've learned so many operas and during a year there are so many operas they have to do. If it's a new opera and they are used to having a prompter and you take out the prompter, you can have a problem. When Jan Peerce was young for instance, he used to do his concert with his little black book in his hand because he was afraid to make a mistake.

𝒞: *Let's talk about some operas. Who are some of your favorite Tosca's and Cavaradossi's.*

ℒ: Tenors! You don't have that much to do with them in this opera, that is the big problem. First of all, you practically don't sing in the first act with them. Second act, there's a little bit with you. Ah! well, the third act, you're not there. So you relate more with Tosca. And there were quite a few of them. Montserrat Caballé was a very good Tosca. Dorothy Kirsten was also a fabulous Tosca. And Raina Kabavianska was a great Tosca. The only thing is that Raina did me in once. During a performance, after the first act I passed in front of her dressing room and there she was with a chocolate bar about a foot long. And I asked her, "What are you doing? You have to sing!"

𝒞: *Normally, chocolate is not too good for singers. It can give you 'frogs' in your throat.*

ℒ: Yes, but she said "No, I need strength, I need strength! I always eat chocolate!" Anyway, the moment came for me to start to sing and my first phrase is "Tosca e un buon falco," and what you heard in the theatre was, "Gobble, gobble." My mouth was getting all the frogs! It was so auto-suggestive. It took me several seconds before I could forget the chocolate bar!

𝒞: *What about allergies? Are some of them auto-suggestive because singers are so sensitive about their throats?*

ℒ: Well, for instance, there was a tenor wearing a very bad perfume. There's a perfume that is the very worst for me: Aramis cologne for men. What Aramis does is catch my stomach and make me sick. I told him, but he said, "No, you are crazy. It's all in your mind."

There was a soprano, with exactly the same thing. She was having a lot of problems, vocally. And I even told her, "When you sing with me don't wear this perfume!" And I could feel that the vocal problem was due to allergy, because I know what it does to me and I know what it does to somebody else. Anyway, she didn't want to listen to me. Five years later I saw her and we started to talk. Her career had already taken the plunge down. She was not singing anymore. All of a sudden, she said, "You know, Mr. Quilico, I just discovered that I was allergic to perfume." I felt very sorry for that, you know.

𝒞: *Getting back to Tosca. What did you think of Maria Callas' Tosca?*

ℒ: Well, I will not comment too much on her Tosca because I had the opportunity to see her doing it only once at Covent Garden with Tito Gobbi. It was a great performance but I cannot comment much more about Callas because she had, more or less, already made a career, and by the time I started my career we were not singing in the same part of the world.

𝒞: *You never worked with her?*

ℒ: No.

𝒞: *Can you comment on the fact that a lot is written today about the lack of great Tosca's or Madame Butterfly's in today's opera world? We keep going back to the past, we keep talking about Tebaldi's performances, Callas' performances. What is going on in the world of opera and why are reviewers commenting that young singers are not developing into great Tosca's and great Rigoletto's?*

ℒ: My only criticism of our world today is that the people who could help the young singers are not there to help them. For instance, you take Maria Callas. She had people like Serafin, Visconti, who were working day in, day out with her. I met Serafin once and he told me, "I made Maria work on *Traviata* eight years before I let her do it." And she used to say, "Maestro, why don't you . . ." "No! You don't know it enough, you don't know it enough!" Today it takes a lot of money and Maria Callas had a lot of money behind her. And this is why, in a certain way, it's very difficult. There are a lot of them who are becoming superstars. But in the old days it seems that they had more intelligence to understand the needs of an artist than today.

𝒞: *Do you think our jet-set superstars are overexposed and oversung?*

ℒ: No. You need the right exposure. For instance, if you have an artist who's going to perform and if they are well prepared, publicity is what they need! Let's say 50 percent is publicity, then 50% is the artistic sense of the singers.

𝒞: *Is it not true that it is the record companies who are creating superstars today?*

ℒ: Definitely! Why do you think it is? It's publicity! I'm not afraid to say it. The recording companies are the most treacherous people there are in the business. The problem is that they get the same singers to do all the records. In the last 25 years you have maybe five, six or seven Rigoletto's. Same people over and over again. That's not right.

𝒞: *The same artist or artists record the opera five times.*

ℒ: That's exactly right. In my opinion, I'm sorry to say, that's no good. Because you know, you eat a steak today, you might not want to eat a steak tomorrow. And I think music is exactly the same thing. Give variety to the public! They will say these are the artists who can sell, but there are a lot of other artists who could sell. Give them the opportunity and create the publicity for them too. That's exactly like the agents. They're not there to make an artist. If the artist doesn't have a hundred thousand dollars behind him today, the agent is not interested. He's going to make him work, yes, but that's it. But the real ones who could help the others very often don't. And I have to say one thing: it is not such a mystery to find an artist who has tremendous talent and vision. No, they always wait till the artist is already on his or her way up.

C: *What was the opera in which you felt you got your biggest ovation?* Rigoletto*?*

L: Oh yes . . . *Rigoletto. Rigoletto* was the opera where I had the biggest ovations.

C: *And where would that be?*

L: Well, for instance, in Moscow when I did it they didn't applaud. When I went to Moscow, it was a time when they shot down the U2 spy plane.

C: *So it would be about the early 1960s.*

L: About that, yes. I finished the first act of *Rigoletto* and (I tell you one thing, it was crazy) they opened up the curtain for at least one minute and there was not one applause. The curtain is open, the chorus is there, the orchestra is in the orchestra pit, the public is there and I'm wondering, well, what is happening? What am I going to do? I must have sung badly. I became very panicky, but all of a sudden one person started to clap. Oh my God! It became so powerful and it was the first time I could hear boom, boom, boom, Russian style rhythmic clapping. Somebody came and pushed me in the back and I fell on the floor to my knees and I cried. It was quite an experience. One of my greatest.

C: *Tell me about Covent Garden and the incredible ovation you had in* Lucia.

L: I sang only one performance of *Lucia* at Covent Garden. They had already done something like 25–30 performances and there was always another baritone or tenor. But that night the soprano was Joan Sutherland, and myself. We started the performance and it seems that according to what I heard afterwards there was something very special about that evening. God knows why. But they told us that the three voices matched so beautifully that it was incredible. Anyway, we came to the sextet and after we finished, the public started to applaud tremendously. The conductor, seeing this, wanted to keep on going and he started the orchestra. The public started to scream even louder, bravo, bravo, bravo! And it went on and on. I don't know how many times, but there were quite a few that he tried to start but the public started to scream, "We want a bis!" (encore) At Covent Garden in those years it was against the tradition to do an encore in the middle of an opera. But that night there was nothing we could do. The conductor, Sir John Pritchard looked at Joan and said, "Well, what are we going to do?" She looked at him, turned towards the tenor, then towards me. When it came to my turn I said, "Please, don't ask me. Do what you want. If you want to make an encore we'll do it!" Finally, we had to repeat the sextet of *Lucia*. And in the history of Covent Garden, only twice was there a bis. Ten years before, Callas sang *Norma* with the same conductor, Pritchard, and had to repeat the duet with Mme Stignani, the mezzo.

After we finished, there must have been about a thousand people outside waiting for us to sign autographs. Well, just to give you an idea, I would say we were still taking curtain bows after 45 minutes. The longest act we had done that night was taking the curtain bows. I asked a lot of people, "Why did you make us repeat the sextet?" They said, "Listen, when God is on the stage, you ask him to repeat himself and that's what we did tonight." I have to say, it was incredible. But the funniest thing about it, for me it was one of the greatest evenings in my life, and I don't want to brag about it or anything like that, but it was one of the greatest evenings from the point of the view of the public. However there was not even one mention of it in the newspaper. I think there was one gentleman who wrote a book on Covent Garden and he mentioned that evening. But there was no mention anywhere else about that famous performance.

𝒞: *What about contemporary opera which is so popular right now? There are many smaller opera companies that are very successful now.*

ℒ: Well, I'm going to tell you the reason why contemporary opera will survive. For one reason. Some of it is good and I think the good might survive. But still, when you come to a Verdi there isn't much contemporary music that can come close to that.

𝒞: *Do you ever get sick and tired of singing in opera?*

ℒ: Definitely not. Because real masters wrote them.

𝒞: *Even the famous arias? Do you ever get tired of singing "Eri tu"?*

ℒ: No! Definitely, never in your life can you, because it's so beautifully written. Who are we to judge? You know, it's like when you pick a rose once, and you go another time and pick a rose, and it's exactly the beautiful rose that you want but it's a little different. Do you get tired, to pick a rose? That's exactly the same thing. It makes your life much more wonderful. It's something that is very spiritual.

𝒞: *It had been an astounding performance of Scarpia the last night at the Met Performance in the Park but one of the classic moments of that performance that's going to go down in history for me was when the soprano Tosca had the famous line . . . you say it.*

ℒ: The famous line is "E avant' a lui tremava tutta Roma."

𝒞: *And what's the translation?*

ℒ: "In front of him (lui)." It's not 'me', it's 'him'. "In front of him all Rome trembles." Because Scarpia was a very, very nasty chief of police. He was an evil man. To get what he wanted he would do anything.

𝒞: *Can you explain what happened with Tosca's line?*

ℒ: Some sopranos sing it, some others speak it. It could be said or sung. And she did the first part, "E avant a lui . . ." She spoke it. But the funniest thing about it, I remember very clearly, she was humming. I think, and she said after we asked her, she was not sure if she was going to do the end of the line speaking or singing. And that was the indecision. And everybody, even the conductor, thought she had a blank.

𝒞: *It seemed from the audience's point of view that she had completely frozen and forgotten the famous line.*

ℒ: Well, I made a joke out of it, you know. What can you do? She says, "Avant a lui." (Sounds like 'Louis'.)

𝒞: *That's right . . .*

ℒ: . . . right in front of me, and she was speechless after that.

𝒞: *That's right . . .*

ℒ: My feeling is that she wanted to sing it but then she changed her mind, because she started to say the line and she spoke it.

𝒞: *Well, in Tosca, I find that some of the wonderful music that's not spoken enough about is the aria for the baritone, "Te deum." Everyone talks about the one soprano aria "Vissi d'arte" and the two tenor arias that are so famous. Can you explain in your words what makes the "Te deum" such a fabulous piece of music?*

ℒ: First of all, if you think about it, the words are incredible. You have this orchestration that is tremendous, you have a chorus that's so tremendous and Scarpia that is so tremendous. Musically, I think it's practically one of the most perfect passages that has ever been written. Puccini was really an inspiration, a tremendous inspiration for singers.

𝒞: *The character of Scarpia seems familiar even in today's society when we hear about all sorts of violence. How do you feel about him?*

ℒ: *Tosca* is a drama that could very well be lived today. But at the same time, unless you are in an oppressed country where there's not much supervision in government, it's very difficult to imagine. Scarpia, I don't know whether it could happen again.

𝒞: *No. But as a personality, here you have the classic triangle: man loves girl, girl loves other man. And you have Scarpia completely obsessed with jealousy and with . . .*

ℒ: Wait, wait, wait . . . not jealousy. Because his problem is that he wants Tosca. He wants her for one thing alone. Give me an hour, then you can do what you want. That means, let's make love and that's all. That's the only thing he's interested in. Except one thing he doesn't say to her. It's very possible that after she would have given herself he would have to kill her. He had no remorse, no shame or anything like that. For him, a human being was a piece of meat. There was nothing much more than that. Scarpia is a very treacherous man. He's a man that has, how can I say, no soul. Simple as that.

𝒞: *And yet the aria is so emotional.*

ℒ: But this is the beauty of the composer. They'll give you the most beautiful music to show the most evil part of a character. Like Scarpia, for example, sings an aria, but at the same time it's not an aria, like "E Lucevan le stelle." It's the opposite when you start to hear the music it's the most divine music. When I first started to do Scarpia, hearing this music and being caught by it, I would sing it so sentimentally. The conductor would say, "But Louis, you are making a mistake!" "Oh, no, it's such a beautiful music!" But I did not realize that it is the opposite. Verdi's exactly the same, the villains get the most beautiful music.

𝒞: *How do you compare this with Iago?*

ℒ: Well, Iago would like to arrive where Scarpia was. And I'm sure that if you compare the two personalities, Scarpia going for power and Iago wanting power, Scarpia could have also sung Iago's "Credo." They are almost the same kind of personality. Scarpia has power and at the same time he likes to torture people and to manipulate others for his own motives. For instance, when he's torturing Cavaradossi, Tosca is there. And he feels that inside of her, she's screaming and there's nothing that he loves better. For him, it's his triumph! The suffering of a person makes him joyful.

He thrives on that. That's his way of living. He wants to get certain things from people but at the same time he's a sadist.

𝒞: *So in a sense Scarpia is more sadistic than Iago because Iago is doing it to gain power rather than to enjoy cruelty?*

ℒ: Scarpia is worse, but there's one thing that you have to understand. One has arrived, the other one wants to arrive. You have to be very careful when you want the power, but when you succeed you can do what you want. That is the point. Both of them have a very, very evil undercurrent in themselves.

𝒞: *Scarpia still lusts for Tosca, but does Iago lust for Desdemona?*

ℒ: Oh, no! Not at all. Iago doesn't care about her. What he wants is the palace and the power. That's all he's interested in and he'll use anything if he has to. In fact he used Desdemona for that reason. But in reality he hates Desdemona. He hates everything that has to do with humans. You see, Scarpia is also a man who doesn't love human beings. They're very similar. But one is a man that has arrived and uses all kinds of evil things to be able to achieve what he wants. In this case he wants Tosca. With how many other Toscas did he do exactly the same thing? Iago has to be careful and even more subtle than Scarpia. Scarpia, when he's interrogating Tosca, has to show that he's a nice man. The voice has to change. There's one phrase when he gets frustrated, you feel it, and all of a sudden there it is. Not only frustration but his calculation, his true evilness. Tosca comes to the point where she cannot stand that kind of torture. She hears Cavaradossi scream. There's nothing she can do about it. The only thing she can do is to give up or give herself to Scarpia.

𝒞: *Which part do you prefer to sing? Iago or Scarpia?*

ℒ: Ah! Both are so incredible, but Scarpia has something that is so incredible: the entrance. You ask any singer and they'll tell you that they would like to be Scarpia just for one minute.

𝒞: *The "Te deum"?*

ℒ: Not the "Te deum," the entrance, when the orchestra plays so loudly. Where else do you have an entrance like this? There's nothing! I still listen to that music and before I start to sing I get goosebumps. You are saturated from an incredible orchestration that is so strong in your mind that it creates a tremendous satisfaction physically and mentally.

𝒞: *Are there any other roles that are equal in evil to these two, Iago and Scarpia, or can you talk about some other baritone roles where you're the villain?*

ℒ: I think these two are very special. Maybe some Wagner but for the rest, no. You do have a role that is not at all like that, but that is very, very dramatic and at one point as great as a Iago or Scarpia. In Debussy's *Pelléas et Mélisande*, Golaud comes in and talks to his wife. All of a sudden he looks at her hands and says, "These beautiful little hands I could destroy like flowers." Then he notices that she's supposed to have a ring and the ring is not there. "Where is the ring I gave you?" The orchestra plays one chord. The music reaches a peak. Beauty, love, and all of a sudden not seeing the ring there. It's downhill after that, never to stop.

𝒞: *The other famous baritone role is Renato in* Un Ballo in Maschera *with the famous aria "Eri tu."*

ℒ: Not only the aria but the whole opera is very interesting. In this opera too, for instance, it is during the orchestral chord that Renato notices it is his wife with the King and the whole tragedy starts from there.

𝒞: *The opera is a triangle again, with political overtones, the same as in* Tosca *and* Otello.

ℒ: That's exactly right, you're always in politics. What is more cruel than politics? Nothing!

𝒞: *That and the eternal triangle. Can you talk a bit about your role as Renato and some of your performances in* Un Ballo in Maschera. *You've made a video with Luciano Pavarotti.*

L: Live from the Met, yes. You talk about *Otello*, you talk about Scarpia, but *Un Ballo in Maschera* is an incredible opera. Renato in the opera has an incredible part. First of all, Verdi was a baritone, and I don't know if he cherished every baritone part but I have to consider myself maybe one of the luckiest men in the world to have sung Verdi, Verdi, and Verdi! For baritones there is the famous aria "Eri Tu" in *Un Ballo in Maschera*, and I feel very sorry for the tenor and the soprano, because with that simple aria you put the opera in your pocket and you go home. That aria always lay perfectly in my cords, and the success I had!! You can name all the tenors in the world that I sang with. Not one tenor could steal the show from me. I'm not saying this to brag, it's because the opera is so incredible! It's a little bit like *Rigoletto*. Renato in *Un Ballo in Maschera* is a very beautiful character. At first he's the most beautiful character you can think of. But, when you realize he's been betrayed by his friend, the count or the king, well, now there's no more friendship, especially because it concerns his wife.

C: *However, he still remains the sympathetic character, so you can't hate him like you do Scarpia.*

L: Well you cannot, because you are taken by him, because you know that he has been betrayed and, well, when a person has been betrayed, he is the underdog and people don't like that.

C: *Can you talk a bit about* Don Carlos*? You had an experience in Madrid that you've spoken about to me several times.*

L: I was leaving to go to Buenos Aires, South America, to sing Iago. The night before, at the Paris Opera, I had sung *Don Carlos*. The plane we were taking had to stop in Madrid because of mechanical trouble and to pick up some people. It didn't leave for Buenos Aires until 7 o'clock the next night. We had to sleep in the airport until the bus came to take us into Madrid for the night. I got on the bus with the other passengers and we finally arrived in the city. The bus driver got out, went to our hotel, came back and said "There's no place here. We have to go to L'escurial."

We arrived in L'escurial and where do you think we went to sleep? At the old hotel 'Philip the Second'. Good! In about an hour I woke up and decided to sightsee. Somebody said that there is a great cathedral to visit. And I went to visit the church, which was beautiful but it's an average church like any other. When they closed the church, I walked out but a guy on my side selling postcards said, "Want to buy some postcards? How did you enjoy it?" I said, "Well it's a church." But he said, "Didn't you see the chambers of the king?" "No, I didn't see anything." It still didn't dawn on me, you know. There I am at L'escurial at the hotel Philip the Second, and he's talking about the king. Nothing registered in my brain. He then said, "Come back at 2 o'clock, it's going to be open. You can visit the chamber of the king!"

I went back at 2 o'clock. Still nothing dawned on me. Imagine singing *Don Carlos* the night before and here I am, realizing nothing. The guide started to talk, "L'escurial, L'escurial, the chamber of the king, the chamber of the king . . . Philip the Second." Nothing registered. Nothing, nothing, nothing. All of a sudden he said one word. And it's so funny because the name I recognize appears at the beginning of the opera and at the end of the opera when I'm not there anymore, but I heard the name of that famous man at the beginning of the opera. He's called Carlos Quinto, Charles the Fifth. I said, wait a minute, Carlos Quinto . . . Philip the Second, L'Infante, L'escurial . . . what am I doing here? I'm right in the middle of the story of *Don Carlos*. I became frantic like a child because it was so funny. I went through it and looked at the chair of the king. He must have been a very, very small man. And his suit on the bed and everything else. Boy, it was so funny to see. I always thought that Philip the Second would be a tall, tall man, but no, he was a very small man. But that was my adventure with *Don Carlos*. It was very funny. I felt so stupid not to have understood at the very beginning when they said L'escurial, because Philip the Second sings 'L'escurial' in his big aria.

𝒞: *Can you talk about your part?*

ℒ: In *Don Carlos*? My role is Rodrigo but Philip the Second calls him the Marchese di Posa. It's a sad story, because he is the only really sympathetic man in the opera. He's a good man and he dies as a good man. Loyalty and honour are important to him. When a man would swear allegiance to the crown he would be true to the crown, even if it meant he had to die for it. And that's what happened with *Don Carlos*. He's a man who realized that the only one who would become king after Philip the Second would be the Infante. However, he has to try to protect him against himself. But the big problem with the Infante is that he's somewhat mad. In fact he also had epilepsy. But at the end he gets killed.

𝒞: Don Carlos *has a lot of interesting political and religious aspects.*

ℒ: The Freemasons existed in the time of the Inquisition. In this way people could help each other. It seems that the Catholic religion was after everybody that would say anything against them. Even the power of the king was not as strong as the Inquisition. And this is why Posa, in a certain way, became an offender, helping a man who was against the Inquisition. But at the same time, when you think about the Infante, he was not a bad person. He was trying to help people but it was against the Inquisition and the king. That's why they try to kill him. But Posa dies instead. It's a beautiful opera. The music is some of the greatest music that has ever been written. And it's funny to think that Verdi would have written a good honest character like Posa and then created music for Iago after that!

𝒞: *What's the famous aria for baritone in* Don Carlos*?*

ℒ: "Per me giunto." In fact it's not only one, it's two arias in one. It's not a cabaletta, because usually a cabaletta goes very fast. But there's a part which gives another side of Posa. He's singing the aria after he has been shot. And it's more or less his last words to Don Carlos. It's a wonderful aria.

𝒞: *We've been talking about Verdi and his political overtones. Wasn't he asked to seek political office?*

ℒ: Yes. He could have become President of Italy.

𝒞: *So he was very much concerned with politics, and his operas seem to be relevant today. The emotional triangles and the political overtones seem familiar. Could you see these operas being done in modern costume?*

ℒ: I think that, spiritually, they are operas which could be relevant today. But for me the only problem is to try to modernize this kind of opera. I think to give the public something that they can see in their own backyard is not very interesting. I think it's much more interesting to give them something of the past and not of today or even the future.

𝒞: *So they can compare the two. This happened in the past, the same as it's happening now.*

ℒ: I think the public wants to go see an opera, sit in their seat and dream, and see something that is not in their time. Some people create in their mind any kind of situation in any way, because they are used to it. They read about history, current events and they can, in their own mind, envision things, but people in general don't see that. They are not aware of a transition, and that is the problem that I feel today. We're trying to put too much into the eyes of the public. Let them dream about something and try not to make them understand every little nuance. Opera isn't a class at the university. They're not there to study. They are there to let their mind and spirit absorb the evolution in time and not to bring them down to earth where they belong and where they are.

𝒞: *You made your point very well. Another opera, Verdi's* La Traviata *has one of the great baritone arias, "di Provenza." Isn't Germont a very sympathetic character?*

ℒ: Ah! Now let's not push the thing too, too far, because he is sympathetic but at the same time he is not. He came to see Violetta for only one thing, to get this woman to give up his son, because she's a libertine, a call-girl in those times. Violetta herself is the kind of person that doesn't belong in his social circles. But the funniest thing about it, especially when you do the role, at the very beginning of his entrance the old man realizes how noble this woman really is. She's a libertine, but at the same time the greatest soul he ever met. However, he says, I'm sorry, you may be the greatest person in the world, but you have to give up my son because I have a daughter who's going to marry. There can't be a flaw in the family. You have to sacrifice yourself. And she does. And when you look at it, it's not that he's an evil man, but he cannot accept the fact that his son loves this kind of person.

𝒞: *Well, he sounds like an interesting character then, which must make him wonderful to portray.*

ℒ: I find him very difficult to portray.

𝒞: *You do?*

ℒ: Yes, because the thing is, he's a very straightforward person. If you just listen to the words that he says: I know that the sacrifice I'm asking you to do will make you feel more noble in later years. And at the end he really repents, himself, because he realized what kind of person she really is. It's very, very wonderful to be in this opera because of the interplay between Violetta and Germont. Germont is the drama of the whole opera.

𝒞: *That's right, he's the pivotal character.*

ℒ: Absolutely! That's one thing Verdi did with all the baritones. And this is why I feel I was very privileged to have sung Verdi all my life. I think it is one of the greatest honors that could be given to anybody, because his baritones are always the key of the opera. The tenor has the beautiful aria and gets the girl, but the key role in the opera is the baritone, and that is why it makes it very interesting to perform. You can create a tremendous personality in these kinds of roles. The tenor, is always straightforward. He has to accept what the baritone tells him and he's always at the mercy of the baritone. And the soprano has practically the same thing. But the baritone is the one who guides the whole thing, and it's beautiful for that reason. Somebody was asking me, aren't you tired of doing this role or aren't you tired of doing that role of Verdi. You cannot! Because you're the one who pushes the whole opera.

𝒞: *As you're doing these roles, the depth of characterization is so enormous that it makes you want to do them over and over. Do you find your character and your interpretation developing?*

ℒ: You never finish to discover new things. I don't know how much Verdi thought about these things but the genius is that he did. What is amazing is that you practically don't have to try to do anything with Verdi. We think it's only beautiful singing, yes! When I started to do Verdi I thought of only one thing: make a beautiful sound! But started to notice that there was much more to it. For instance, I've done 510 performances of *Rigoletto*, and let's say about 510 dress rehearsals and a thousand or more rehearsals maybe. Altogether I don't know how many performances that would make because I haven't calculated. But the thing is that each time you do it, from one dress rehearsal to the performance, you find something different.

𝒞: *And Verdi seems to be such a fabulous composer that you don't need a completely beautiful voice.*

ℒ: You are touching on a very delicate subject. Verdi is very treacherous for that. It's not only a matter of a beautiful voice but to be able to translate in your voice the drama of the opera. Verdi, oh boy! It's so exposed that every single role is always treacherous for that reason. But if you learn how to do Verdi well, it's the best medicine for any voice in the repertoire of opera that exists.

Puccini was also very treacherous for the voice. Maybe he gets too dramatic at certain moments. You can do drama without reversing your vocal technique but sometimes you have people that don't exactly understand that. Drama is not making a false sound. No, you have to find a sound, but without ever creating a problem for your voice. That is the thing that is very dangerous. That's why I always say if I would be a soprano, Tosca or Butterfly, I would wait till I'm maybe 40, 45 before I would do it. You need a certain maturity to be able to cope with these kind of roles, because they're so demanding and in the wrong way. If you're not a well-schooled person or your mind is not up to the situation you might do something bad, technically, for your voice. I saw more sopranos being betrayed vocally by an opera like *Tosca* or *Butterfly* than any other opera in the world.

For instance, if I were a tenor I would wait until about 40 years old to start singing Cavaradossi. You need somebody with a certain understanding. Some people sang Butterfly at the age of 25 years old. I do not say you cannot sing it, but you have to have a knowledge and technical vocal skill so that you will not create a vocal problem.

C: *How do you compare* Traviata *(Verdi) to* Tosca *(Puccini).*

L: The soprano in Verdi never had as many dramatic moments as in Puccini's *Tosca*, because *Tosca* has many different levels. There's a moment of love, a moment of rage, a moment of sorrow, a moment of torture. That is very difficult and people don't realize that they think more of the drama than the vocal sense. You always have to be in control in these kinds of opera. You always have to be in control of your vocal approach.

For instance, if I were a tenor, I would wait until I was 50 years old to sing *Carmen*. Because it's always been said that to sing *Carmen* you need four different kinds of tenors. And it is true; it's a very simple thing. Some operas lie a certain way. And what happens, it's easy at that point to let yourself go. But when you have to start to sing higher again it's practically impossible.

C: *One of my favorite stories you told was about a San Francisco director who asked you to do* Il Trovatore *at the last minute. Can you explain?*

L: I arrived on Thursday from Europe about 4:30 in the afternoon. About 6 o'clock I got a phone call from Mr. Kurt Adler, director of the theatre. "Louis Quilico, I need your services because my baritone is sick and I want you to come and do *Il Trovatore*." I said, "Fine, when do you need me?" He said, "You take the plane tonight." I said, "No, Mr. Adler, I am deeply sorry, I am too tired. There is no way that I can leave tonight! And another thing, if you want me to come, do me a favour. Call me back. Good-bye!" and I closed the line.

Well, about half an hour later he calls back and he says, "Alright. Please, when could you leave?" I said, "I could leave only tomorrow morning." He says, "No, please . . ." I said, "Mr. Adler, don't insist, because I'm going to close the line and I'm not coming." He said, "That's fine. But *Il Trovatore* is very complicated." I said, "Mr. Adler, the staging of *Il Trovatore* is a very simple one. When I walk in, I'm alone. Now, that means I can go on the left, I can go on the right, I can go in the middle, I can go in the back, I can do what I want. Then the soprano is going to come in. Well, I find out where she is going to come in from. If she comes from the right, I go to the left. If she comes from the left, I go on the right. After that the tenor comes in. Now, if the tenor is on the left, she's on the right, I go in the middle. If they're both on the left, I go on the right. And if they're both in the middle, I go either on the right or the left." I said, "That is the staging of *Il Trovatore*." It's a singer's opera and that's what you have to do. Deliver, as well as possible, your music, your voice, because that's all that counts. And if you're not very good at it, people know, and *Il Trovatore* is very treacherous for that reason. And that was the famous *Il Trovatore* of San Francisco.

𝒞: *I wanted you to talk for a minute about* Il Trovatore. *Here we have a quartet.*

ℒ: Well, I don't think you can call it quartet because it's quartet, duets, solo, it's a mixture of everything. This is why I say it's a singer's opera. Because you get a fantastic aria, and then when you finish that you get a big ensemble. It's a singing opera, and it's very difficult to be able to turn towards your partner when you have to sing forward.

𝒞: *So it's not an actor's opera. How would you compare it, say, to the characterization of a Renato, Iago or a Scarpia?*

Is the role of Count di Luna as deep psychologically or not?

ℒ: I would say it's deep, but maybe not as deep. The only thing he wants is to kill the tenor. In fact, he loved Leonora too. It's a bizarre scenario because the tenor and the baritone are brothers from birth. But one was abducted and the other one stayed. The idea of the whole plot is simple. The old gypsy wants revenge and she finally gets it, even though she loves the Trovatore she brought up as her own son because her own son was killed by the father of Luna and Manrico.

𝒞: *So, in other words, in this particular opera, the pivotal or main character that unites all the leading roles is the gypsy.*

ℒ: I would say yes and no. I think the baritone is still the central figure. The gypsy creates the atmosphere, yes, and she is a pivot too but the real great pivot of the opera is Count di Luna.

𝒞: *Tell me about Count di Luna's big aria.*

ℒ: "Il balen"? He talks about how much love he has for Leonora.

𝒞: *Who have you done this opera with? Who were the tenors?*

ℒ: The first time I sang it was in 1956. My first season in opera was with Leontyne Price. And it was the first time for Leontyne Price too. They still talk about that famous performance because she was impeccable vocally, Jussi Björling was impeccable vocally and I was impeccable vocally. The public was completely mesmerized by these three singers.

𝒞: *What are other operas in which you felt this magic happened? You spoke about the sextet of* Lucia *in Covent Garden. Are there other examples where you felt the ensemble was so wonderful that it stayed in your memory?* I Puritani*?*

ℒ: *I Puritani*? Yes. Definitely. It was incredible. And it's not an opera that I have done a lot. The thing that is most memorable in my mind is when I did the recording with Beverly Sills, Nicolai Gedda and Paul Plishka.

𝒞: *Didn't you record it with Pavarotti?*

ℒ: Yes, I have done it with Pavarotti, and again with Plishka. But in the professional recording, I'm not going to brag about it, but for me the duet between the bass and me, is maybe one of the most perfect male duets I ever heard in my life. Julius Rudel was conducting and there was magic in the air. It's funny that you find it in the recording; usually it's during a performance. Julius had the perfect rhythm, and he had the exact speed of this duet.

𝒞: *Can you name some other operas which you feel reached similar levels?*

ℒ: I would say *Otello* and *La Traviata.*

𝒞: *What about "Credo" from* Otello*?*

ℒ: "Credo" is not the kind of aria that will really transport the public. It's wonderful but it's not an aria that finishes with a tremendous ovation but ends calmly and cynically. The public is taken, yes. But it is taken the other way. The aria "Di Quella Pira" for tenor is so incredible because of the speed, the resolution and the delivery.

𝒞: *One of the famous baritone arias, of course, is from Carmen.*

ℒ: I have to say that there's probably not a soul who doesn't know the Toreador's aria. In the context of the opera the aria is placed extremely well because there are so many other things that are wonderful for the rest of the singers. But as a piece by itself, to do in concert, it's one of the greatest arias. It's like the aria from the *Barber of Seville.*

𝒞: *The "Largo al Factotum."*

ℒ: You can raise the people from their seats with this kind of aria.

𝒞: *What about* La Forza del Destino*?*

ℒ: *La Forza* is a low-key opera. The arias are very beautiful. For instance the aria of the baritone, "Urna fatale," is maybe one of the greatest arias. My sorrow about this opera is that it killed my favorite baritone.

𝒞: *What about* L'Elisir d'Amore*?*

ℒ: It's a fun opera for baritones that you can enjoy as a singer. It's a comic opera and that is beautiful for me, but when you start to understand the drama of the music this kind of opera doesn't satisfy you. For instance, I sang so many *La Bohèmes* it used to come out of my ears. And I used to love it, but when I started to do a character role, like Rigoletto or Scarpia, the others pale by comparison.

𝒞: *But* L'Elisir d'Amore *is not a baritone's opera.*

ℒ: No. it is not. It's a tenor's opera. Even though the soprano has an aria which is more difficult, when the tenor comes in with "Una Furtiva Lagrima," she never has success like the tenor because the tenor aria is so incredible.

𝒞: *What are some of the other roles you feel are wonderful for the baritone? You've mentioned Scarpia, Iago and Rigoletto, and of course Renato.*

ℒ: I've said *Pelléas and Mélisande*. One other role that is not very well-known but very interesting because it has a lot of character is *Faust*'s Valentine. It's a very short role and he doesn't have the greatest aria but he has a scene that stops the show. The music is so powerful, and very often the craziest thing in opera is to have an aria that falls on the laps of the public at the right moment in the opera. For instance, "di Provenza" from *Traviata* falls right there on the laps of the public. The public expects it, and if you do well it's worth its weight in gold.

𝒞: *We missed one of the main roles that I'd like you to talk about, Falstaff.*

ℒ: Good, now *Falstaff* is everybody's opera. It's not an opera that you can say Falstaff is the key role because he's always there, but without the rest of the people around him it wouldn't be as wonderful. The interplay among all the characters makes the opera so strong.

𝒞: *The fabulous Fugue in the end culminates Verdi's masterpiece.*

𝓛: Falstaff is a wonderful role for that reason. You have all kinds of emotions in it. It doesn't have the same kind of emotion as Rigoletto but it has one place towards the last act, after he was thrown in the water, when Falstaff has a monologue by himself. This old man starts to reminisce and all of a sudden he sees exactly what is happening to him. He even feels foolish about it, because he feels the drama that he was part of and he realizes that people are laughing at him.

The amazing thing about Falstaff is that when the man from the tavern comes with the glass of wine he says, "But it's the past, the past is gone!" It's finished. And he goes towards another adventure. One thing he says that is incredible is, "I make people laugh. Without me who are they? Nothing. Thanks to me there is life." And that is beautiful. Because it's really very deep, the way it's written.

When Toscanini conducted *Falstaff* for the first time it was the original score of Verdi, and right in the middle of the third act there were maybe 10 pages glued together. He said to Verdi, "Maestro, why is this . . ." Verdi said, "It's just a little thing of mine, forget about it." Anyway, Toscanini, not to displease Verdi, left it like this. But after Verdi died, Toscanini went to get the score and opened up these 10 pages and in one of the pages there was something very curious. There was a long bar of music with the notes which were exactly what he says in the third act, "Va, Vecchio John, Va." And everybody was asking what was meant by this.

But Verdi was an old wizard. It meant only one thing: John was Verdi! Meaning, what's going to happen after I'm dead? And when you think about it, after Verdi died there were a lot of other operas written, but not like his masterpieces.

𝓒: *I would have liked to see Verdi do all the Shakespeare plays. King Lear would have been a fantastic role.*

𝓛: Verdi's librettist was incredible as well. If I remember well *Falstaff* is a combination of *Henry IV Part I* and the *Merry*

Wives of Windsor. The librettist took the two plays and made one.

𝒞: *Tell me how you envisage Falstaff?*

ℒ: You have to think of Falstaff in a certain way, as a caricature. Shakespeare always said that Falstaff was a heavy man and once upon a time at the court he was, more or less, very well-respected by the King. But his way of looking at life made him understand that what is more important than court is maybe a glass of wine. And, in fact, in one of the acts he started to explain what that glass of wine represented in all these little words. It's a jewel of an opera. It may be one of the only operas I've done that when I come to the third act, I really want to cry. If I have a conductor that has the sense to do it at the right speed and doesn't go according to the score, it's like the palpitation of the heart, and I think this is the beauty of it. For me, *Falstaff* is a great opera because it's very human, very witty. It shows a man that loves life. What more can you want in life than to love life?

𝒞: *Is there a lot of Verdi in Falstaff, himself?*

ℒ: I don't think so because I think Verdi was the opposite and, very often, it's sometimes easier to write about something that is your opposite. For example, I always had difficulty doing Germont, because Germont is a little bit my type. But a Falstaff, no. Falstaff is the opposite of my nature. But maybe I became Falstaff in my life, because he cares. You have to say to yourself, I love life. People have to love life. Let's stay down to earth, and that is the big problem. People sometimes try for too much.

𝒞: *Another opera, which you have done with Mirella Freni at the Met recently, is* Adriana Lecouvreur.

ℒ: There's one thing with Michonnet, the role I sing, that I found very wonderful to do. I never expected that the man could have such love, but it's not sensuous love, it's the opposite. It's like the love for a daughter. Michonnet has transformed this little girl, Adriana, to become a great diva. And I think when you succeed in creating this kind of personality it's very satisfying. It's not the most rewarding role there is, but it's a role that's so humanly close to a person, and that's why I love it so much.

𝒞: *It's like* My Fair Lady, *or* Pygmalion.

ℒ: Well, I'm not sure, because I saw Pygmalion done by a great actor, but I never felt the drama or the real love between the creator and his pupil. I never really studied this play. You see, I don't think Michonnet was a Pygmalion. He was the opposite. Pygmalion said: "I'm going to make something out of this woman. You're going to see I'm going to succeed with it and show the world." But that was not the intention of Michonnet. He discovered a talent and said to himself, I want to help this woman become a great artist. It was for the heart. With Pygmalion it was to make her become a great lady of court.

𝒞: *What about Zeffirelli and his opulent sets? Do they inspire you? Or do they dwarf you sometimes?*

ℒ: Well, there are a lot of people who like to see his sets. I have to say that his sets are the closest thing to being appropriate to the era of the opera. But at the same time, sometimes it becomes overpowering, because there's so much to be seen with the chorus and the sets that people get lost in the shuffle. The set of *Tosca* didn't irritate me at all. In fact, I did his *Tosca*, and I think it was very beautiful. It was a very, very beautiful church for the first scene, then the studio of Scarpia was very opulent. In fact, instead of having a door for the torture chamber it was a trap in the stage. And I think that was very brilliant, to show that the torture was done in the depths of the castle.

𝒞: *What about Macbeth as a role? Tell me about it.*

ℒ: *Macbeth* is quite something. Now you're talking about a role that is completely the opposite of my nature. Lady Macbeth is the instigator of everything he does. In fact, she's the one urging him to go and kill the king. But at the same time, for him to achieve power, he will defy anything. And that is very interesting. As a role, it's monumental.

𝒞: *It's not done enough,* Macbeth *the opera. Why?*

ℒ: It's difficult to do, because to find a real Macbeth is very difficult. You need somebody who has a very special voice and is a marvelous actor. Also, this is not a play; it is an opera. You need somebody who can transform himself vocally and still not betray his technique. But at the same time you must be able to make drama.

For instance, there's one place in the banquet scene when everything has become calm. Macbeth must add some portamento in the voice to create a mood. And this is the beauty of that kind of role, to be able to act with your voice. For me, Sir Laurence Olivier was one of the greatest Shakespearean actors I ever saw in my life, because he had that temperament of not only acting with the face but with the voice.

I saw other singers doing the role Macbeth and I realize what the difficulty is in interpreting it. You must have a director who understands the person working for him especially. You should have a person who does the role the Shakespearean way, stressing the dialogue that one must deliver with the least movement. When you have the music of Verdi and a Shakespeare play you have to be very careful, because the music is so suggestive. For example, fear has to be shown. You cannot simply talk about it, it's not enough, because the music excites and incites action and above all you must have the kind of commitment to do what Verdi wanted.

𝒞: *Do most stage directors think of these operas as plays rather than as music?*

ℒ: Sometimes they try to create the kind of atmosphere that is wrong, because it is too much from the plays. You cannot do that because it becomes very monotonous. Something must happen in the music. For instance, you have an apparition, a ghost. Instead of standing up, go down on your knees to show fear. In Shakespeare you might explain, but in music, Verdi wrote certain things that have to be followed more in actions than the words of Shakespeare.

𝒞: *After all, if you want to see a play, go see a play. Don't go to the opera. Is there any other major role for baritone that we're missing that you haven't talked about?*

ℒ: I would like to do Tchaikovsky's *Eugene Onegin* but I don't know if I'm ever going to do it. There's a bass aria at the end that is so gorgeous. Oh God, it's incredible. There's another role I would have liked to do before the end of my career, Arkel from Debussy's *Pelléas et Mélisande*. And when you think of the words that he says, "You know, when you're old your lips still have to feel the freshness of the skin of someone to feel love," it's difficult to explain these things, because they're too subtle, they're too delicate. Unless you do it they're too difficult to explain.

𝒞: *You mentioned modern times. What about modern opera? Tell me the operas that you've done. I know you did* Wozzeck *by Alban Berg, now a classic.*

ℒ: Well, it's a classic for the ones who like it. You really have to like *Wozzeck*.

𝒞: *Well, compared to Lulu I believe it's easier for the audience.*

ℒ: I think so too.

𝒞: *And Wozzeck, there's another character for whom the human emotions can be completely overwhelming and emotionally draining.*

ℒ: I did *Wozzeck* only once in my life, for CBC television in 1959. When I finished I swore never to do it again because I was completely drained. I had become Wozzeck.

𝒞: *You have to murder your girlfriend.*

ℒ: That's right, but he doesn't realize that he killed her. It's a man who is born in an era that he doesn't belong in. Everybody is picking on the poor man. Wozzeck was not a rebel, could not be a rebel, because he did not understand. It's not because he was retarded, but if somebody were to spit at him he asked, "Why do you spit at me?" He could not reason because he felt that he did nothing wrong. But everybody knew the way he was and they picked on him.

So when he killed Maria he didn't even know that he killed her.

The libretto took a little bit of time to learn. It was very interesting, but I found it very difficult at first because the music was so different from anything that I had ever done before. It was a challenge for me, but at the same time I felt that it was a glorious part that has a musical line that carries you. But unlike Verdi or Puccini you have to do it by yourself. You must show the music, you can't be carried away by it. You cannot touch it physically. Wozzeck cannot understand anything that is happening to him, and that I found very fascinating. For the first time in my life I was so overpowered by a drama that I was a case for the hospital. No, this kind of opera I'm not interested in for that reason.

C: *What was it about the character that so overpowered you?*

L: This role is so contrary to my own personality that it was very difficult to bring myself to feel the role. You have to put the character under your skin. The day we did the show, we had to do it five times. That means five times through the opera. We had done a few cuts in it but to have to do it five times was extraordinary.

We started that morning at 9 o'clock and we finished that night at 11 o'clock. You needed nerves of steel to get through it. In fact the producer said to me: Louis, if you refuse it I would not keep a grudge against you, because it's a very treacherous role. He was right but I wanted to feel the challenge, and I conquered the challenge but with the greatest difficulty.

In the actual performance I had an army knife in my pocket. Just to show you the mind of the man: during the conversation with Maria, he takes that army knife and cuts her throat. And I remember very well opening that army knife with my teeth, then taking it and cutting her throat. The knife touches her throat and she falls down, and then I leave and go to a tavern and everybody asks me, "Where is Maria, where is Maria?" I go completely crazy. He goes back and all of a sudden his only interest is to find the knife. Where is the knife? On the knife there's blood. He comes in and falls right on top of his girlfriend and that makes him even crazier. I look for the knife and I start to look at her, and for at least, 30 to 40 seconds, if not a minute (I don't remember, it seems an eternity), I swear to God I thought I had done it. I was completely paralyzed, but the producer, Pierre Mercure, had the intelligence to stop and film the expression on my face. All of a sudden the music stopped and I realized I had not killed her, and we kept on going.

They had made a pool of water and told me to go in the water and drown. And as you go down in the water, you see a little branch, you break it and then you go under the water and we pan the camera on your hand and the branch. And then the only thing we see is the branch floating on the water. Count to 30. That's what I did. After I came out of the water I grabbed the side of the pool and I started to shake like a leaf and cry like a child.

I have to say one thing: if I had done *Wozzeck* for six months I would not be here to talk to you because I think I would have gone crazy like he did. It's such a powerful experience for me to be acquainted with someone of that nature. Naturally, the music was difficult like I said, but it made sense. Because let's face it, Alban Berg didn't write that kind of opera just for fun. It was beautifully done. It was incredible. I had a fabulous conductor as well, Otto Werner Mueller. It was a great privilege to do this kind of opera. But I swore to God never to do it again because I was scared of it. And I think that maybe another modern opera could have created the same problem for me.

𝒞: *How did you find the role vocally?*

ℒ: Wozzeck? I have to say that I did not find it very difficult. If you know how to cope with it, it's not a very difficult role. The way it's written is that there are seven notes. However, the voice during a Verdi opera practically never has to jump to a fifth or to a seventh or a sixth, to jump on the fourth; the voice is not accustomed to it. If you are used to doing that kind of work it's different. It's very demanding for that reason. But when you get accustomed to it and you know it very well, these extensions in the music don't make any difference because the voice knows how to do it. I always say you know a role only when you know it by memory. At that point the mind has time to give the extension in the voice. The thing that is very dangerous is when you don't know the extensions in the voice and you have to go too fast. It's like the violin. The violin will not have the right note, you have to go to the exact spot on the string. That is the ability of the greatest violinists. Even on the piano if your fingers are not ready for it, and you go too fast and hard, very often it can be dangerous.

𝒞: *Yes. I'm sure this is the same for voice. There's the tactile memory — tactile, aural and visual.*

ℒ: I would say it would be more treacherous for the voice. Because let's face it, we have two little vocal cords and we don't exactly understand them sometimes. Let's say the length of your vocal cord is one inch and you go from one octave to two octaves and a half, which is generally what people have. Your extension in your vocal cord might be a sixteenth of an inch and because you don't know exactly what you're doing, the first thing you know it's not a sixteenth anymore. It might extend a half-inch and the first thing you know you have overextended. Why do you think people have nodes? Because they don't know what to do with the voice. A person who knows what to do with the voice will not usually have trouble with nodes. It's the person who doesn't know what to do with the voice, or they're too tired or not convinced of what they are doing.

𝒞: *Can you tell me a bit more about your experience with Darius Milhaud? He sent you a score to do a world premiere.*

ℒ: I have a very funny experience with Darius because he had the habit of writing music and not finishing it before the performance. And reading his music was also treacherous, and difficult to do at the last minute. Because, like I said, I have to know the work by memory and then I'm confident that I know it.

At first he called me up and he said, "I'm writing a new opera and I would like you to sing it." "Fine," I said. "When is it?" "Well, you still have time to learn it." I said, "When?" and at that time it was the 4th of December. He says, "The 8th of December." (Laughter) I said, "You're out of your mind!" "No, no, Mr. Quilico!" he says, "I just heard about you, and I would like you to do it because I think you have the right voice for it." And I, like a crazy nut, accepted.

But the thing is, I went through hell for four days and four nights to study that music. I did not have a printed score; it was in manuscript. And sometimes these composers, the way they scribble their music. The new composers are much better than the old composers. It made it very difficult for me to read. I had two pianists. One was accustomed to the music of Milhaud. All of a sudden she would stop and say, "Is this an F sharp or an F natural?" And she would play it . . . "It sounds very good with the F natural, let me erase the sharp . . . Oh, I think the sharp sounds even better!"

Anyway, we went through the opera, and it was wonderful. After I premiered it we had to record it. It was a great experience. But the second time he asked for me I should have said, "No way!" He called me in October, and said, "Mr. Quilico, I thought of you because I'm doing an opera called *La Mère Coupable*, from Beaumarchais. The first is the *Barber of Seville*, *Marriage of Figaro* and then *La Mère Coupable*." He said, "I would like you to premiere this for me in Geneva." I said, "Fine. When is it?" I think he said it's the 14th of May the following year. Well, I said, "Good! Only one thing Maestro. I need the music right away!" "Oh you'll get it right away!"

Later I forgot about it. Then all of a sudden the month of October passed, the month of November passed, and by January I was going to America to do some concerts and I was going to be in America until April 26th. It occurred to me to ask for the score. I called him, I said, "Maestro, what happened to the score?" He said, "You didn't get it?" I said, "I didn't get anything. I'm leaving for America the

2nd of January and I need the music before. I have to have at least a little idea about the opera." He said, "I'll send you a score." The score never got here. I called and said, "I did not receive your score. It's off!" "No, no, no!" he said, "I don't understand. Ricordi was supposed to send it to you. What can we do?" I said, "Well, here are a few addresses where I'm going to be. Send me the score there. But," I said, "send it not later than the 15th of January." "Oh no! You'll get it, you'll get it!" "Okay. Good!" I leave for America.

The 25th of April came and went and no score. I took the plane back to Paris and on the 26th in the afternoon I get a call. Madame Milhaud called to tell me they expected me at rehearsal the next day in Geneva. I said, "I don't know anything about this opera." She said, "The maestro will be upset." I said, "I don't care about that. He can be very upset, but I'm not interested in doing it. Tell him to forget about me. Tell him to get somebody else. I don't have time to learn this kind of music because it's too hard for me. It's not my kind of music. Goodbye, I'm so sorry for all this."

Ten minutes later I got another call. He said, "You cannot do this. What do you think you're doing?" I said, "You did it to me. I don't have the score." "Mr. Quilico, I'm deeply sorry about this but you really have to do it for me." I said, "Maestro, I don't want to do it. I don't want to do it for anybody because I'm going to break my neck. I'm a quick enough learner but I'm not accustomed to doing it." He said, "Please come to my house tomorrow." I said, "Alright. We'll start to work on it."

So I went to his house the next day and we started to work on it. My God, if you are accustomed to doing new music it's alright, but when you're not used to it, it's not easy. When you sing Verdi, he gives you a line that keeps on going and feeds you until the end. Anyway, we finally went through the first act. And I said, "You see where we are?" He said, "It makes no difference. You come with me tomorrow on the train and we'll see." I said, "Alright." Finally, when we arrived in Geneva he gave me the schedule and I said, "Listen, I don't know it. You get somebody else." "Well," he said, "we have somebody else." "When did he get the score?" He said, "He got the score in December." I said, "Thank you very much. I am one of the principle singers and I didn't get a score until now." Anyway, until I did the performance, 14–17 days every morning 8 o'clock — till noon, one — till six, seven — till midnight, every single day I stayed in the studio and worked on it.

On the fifth day I arrived on the stage and was shaking like a leaf. I was scared because we were getting close to the performance. I said to myself it's no use. I cannot do it. Around 5 o'clock in the afternoon Milhaud was there with everybody. I started to make a mistake here, a mistake there. Although I had the score in front of me, I could not read it. I was so panicky and my mind said, don't stop Louis, don't stop! It's funny that way. All of a sudden José van Dam arrived and he had the score since December. I became so very angry that I took the score and threw it at Milhaud's feet. I said, "Maestro, you know what you can do with your opera? I am going home and that is the end of me here. I don't know this opera. Goodbye, I'm going home," and I started to walkoff stage.

When I reached the stage door I heard, "Mr. Quilico, please come here." All of a sudden there was a stop. I listened. I said, "Maestro." Then I heard an old man crying. "Mr. Quilico, please come back here. I want to talk to you." I said to myself, "Well, it won't kill me to talk to him. Let me apologize to him a little bit more." I went to him and I said, "Maestro, you saw yourself I don't know the opera. José van Dam knows it so well, give it to him please." He said, "No! When I wrote this opera I had you in mind." And I told him, "I wish you would have forgotten about me." Anyway he said to me, "I know if you want to do it you can do it Mr. Quilico." "Well, that's very beautiful, Maestro, to have such faith in me. But I don't have such faith in myself." He said, "Don't worry, you can do it if you want." "No," I said, "I'm so sorry. I would like to . . ." He said, "If you don't do it . . ." Oh, and that was a line that I wanted to shove down his throat: "I'm going to stop all rehearsals. We won't do it." He would cancel the performance and I would be responsible.

If I didn't do it, everybody else would hate me. He said, "You do me a favour. The night of the performance if you have to do it with the score in your hand you do it with the score in your hand. I don't mind. But you're doing it. If you want to, Mr. Quilico, you can." "I don't understand that. How is it that you have so much faith in me and I don't have one bit of faith in myself. I just plainly don't want to do it." He said, "Please, do it."

And believe it or not I did it. And I was the star of the show. When I lose patience for myself, nothing works. But if I challenge myself I can do it. That's what happened. But it's one of these things with modern music. You have to hear it more than once. If you hear it more, all of a sudden you hear certain things. I surprised myself and premiered two works for Milhaud.

I also changed some parts of the opera. One portion I felt we had to cut the tempo in half. I told Milhaud, "It's too beautiful. You don't have any idea what you have written there." He said, "Well, do me a favour. Do it at your speed and do it at my speed." He started to think and then said, "Give me the score and give me a pencil." And where it was written 120 he scratched it out and put 60. You know, very often that is the problem with modern music. The composers don't hear their own music.

C: *Well, it's the same for piano music. The great piano concertos were written by people who could play the piano: Mozart, Beethoven, Rachmaninoff. And with voice it must be difficult unless they really know how far to extend the voice for modern opera.*

L: When I'm having complications with a conductor: "Well, Mr. Verdi wrote that at this speed or Mr. Puccini wrote it at that speed." Even with them, you could have done it in front of them and they would have said, yes I like it that way! But you see that is the point. People must argue their point of view, their feelings.

C: *Verdi knew the voice well.*

L: Yes. Of all the composers I think Verdi was the only one who knew how to write for the voice, because Verdi was a gentleman who also had a beautiful baritone voice. That's why all his operas were sensitive to the baritone. And when you listen to all his operas the baritone parts are very, very wonderful. The greatest reward of my entire career was to have sung so much Verdi, and to be treated like a king by a composer like this. Jon Vickers said once, "Verdi is medicine for the voice." And it is true! Because if you can sing Verdi and you have in your mind the interpretation of the voice, what you get back is incredible. But you cannot come with an ugly voice and try to do Verdi. Because Verdi has to be beautiful.

𝒞: *I wanted to ask you about your favorite house, which you have told me is the Metropolitan Opera. This is where you have done most of your singing.*

ℒ: Well, if we talk about my opera house I had quite a few of them, but the Met was really the one I call home. I've been with the Met now for 25 years. And I think it's very important in my career. But it's not only the importance to my career, it is the importance of being happy in a house. When I was at Covent Garden it was very interesting but there was too much political underground. It made it very complicated in a certain way. Paris, well, I was not French. But in New York, at the Met, I felt like I was home. Plus, since I was born and since the day I could hear opera and I knew about opera, I think for me the Metropolitan was the greatest theatre in the world. I sang in Vienna and all the major houses in Europe. But the Met has a certain policy that was very wonderful for me. I did not feel like a foreigner. In the other houses, I always had that feeling of not being completely accepted.

When I was in London, my agent was the agent of another baritone. That created a problem. I remember when I was trying to get to and finally went to Vienna it took a number of years. And I used to ask him, "When are you going to do something?" And he said, "Well, listen Louis, I have to give a little bit more to the other baritone." But the other baritone was not successful like I was, and it created tremendous problems for that reason.

𝒞: *Would you say that the conductors employed by the Met also make a difference? For example, James Levine as music director?*

ℒ: Well, I don't exactly know how I can say this . . . that thanks to James Levine and a few other directors, the Met was very important for me. I was proud that these kind of people had not only respect but tremendous admiration for my art.

𝒞: *I find from my own experience, having studied in New York (James Levine studied with my piano teacher Rosina Lhévinne, who encouraged him to conduct), I always felt that New York did not strait-jacket you into a certain formula. And perhaps that's what happens in opera houses in other countries where you have, for example, the French school or the German school or the Russian school. New York seems to embrace all the ideals or the best of all schools of thought.*

ℒ: Let's put it this way, the Metropolitan in New York is an international house. That means you don't say, well he's Canadian, German, or the other one is Portuguese. It doesn't work like this. No. I think the thing that's very important for the Met is the performance. If you go to the other cities you sometimes feel a tremendous undercurrent of inequality and unfairness. It is more restrictive than the Met would be, for instance.

𝒞: *So you agree with me that New York, from a performer's point of view, embodies that ideal where the best is the best no matter where you're from.*

ℒ: Exactly, yes.

𝒞: *. . . and I always felt that about the Met. It didn't matter what country the singer was from, but if they sang well they would be embraced by the audience and by the house.*

ℒ: Oh yes! It's a policy that has been existing for so many years. You take, for instance, Caruso, who was well received at the Met but at other places was not that well received. I remember that he had to practically turn down Buenos

Aires. Finally they made him an offer he couldn't refuse and he went back for that reason. But at the Met, if you are a good artist the public accepts you and the management will have sensitivity about that.

𝒞: *I remember that there was a time when American singers were frowned upon in houses throughout Europe. If you weren't an Italian singer La Scala didn't want to take you. I feel that is changing now for the young artists. There seem to be a lot of Americans all over the world. Can you elaborate on that? Do you agree with me?*

ℒ: Well, I will agree to a certain point because Germany was much more open for the American singers than America. Since a decade now, I think it's different for the American artists. But with the Met, if an American is very good, well, he will be the favourite. But if somebody is better very often they will consider that too. And it is very important, because after all a performance is a performance. It's to make it as good as possible. Naturally, there are a lot of people who will say, well, there are bad performances at the Met. Naturally, you do find that, yes. But when you think how many performances they do every week, it's incredible.

𝒞: *Would you be interested in a job as music director of an opera company?*

ℒ: Well, I don't know about that. I think it's becoming too infected. Especially if you're Canadian you're not good enough, you know. They say, why don't you sing in Toronto? I say, "My big problem is I don't sing in Toronto because I'm not good enough for Toronto, just good enough for the Met." Singing at the Met is very satisfying.

𝒞: *Do you think the Met has benefited an enormous amount from the Texaco broadcast every Saturday? That's how I began listening to opera. Now videos on TV are doing the same thing.*

ℒ: Just look at yourself, don't go further than that. We should put up a monument for Texaco for what Texaco has done for opera. They made an artistic endeavour that was very difficult for people to understand. But to have opera transported to them so they could listen without paying a penny, I think that was a marvelous thing.

𝒞: *We now have 'Live from Lincoln Center' which is presented on public television telecasts from the Met.*

ℒ: TV is maybe the biggest of all, because London, Vienna and all these big theatres all over the world have 'Live from their theatres' on TV now. And I think the propaganda that was given to opera through TV is great, because it was a kind of art that people were always afraid of. TV created a tremendous desire to know more about it. And as long as you create an interest for people to watch opera, I think it's incredible. As for myself, as a performer it's very rewarding, because when you do a live telecast from the Met about 10 million people look at it. And it's becoming even bigger now because it's telecast all over the world. Once upon a time it was broadcast only in the United States.

𝒞: *Can you tell me about the performances that you did for 'Live from the Met'? I know that you did* Un Ballo in Maschera *and* Don Carlo *because those videos are still being sold.*

ℒ: Yes, I have to say one thing: it's a nerve-wracking thing to do one of these performances.

𝒞: *I was going to ask if you're aware of the significance as you're doing it.*

ℒ: Yes. But you have an idea that all of a sudden you're going to open your mouth and there are millions of people listening to you. I went to sing in Montreal for the baseball game during the world series, and when they said to me that there would be about 120 million people listening I just wanted to go six feet under the ground. Mistakes are so magnified and I wasn't doing anything much much more than singing the national anthem. But I was so scared that I wrote down all the words that I had to sing. I thought that if I made a mistake everyone would start to boo! It was exactly the same for the performances from the Met.

Not that you were scared of forgetting something, but you were, how can I say, you were aware that it was live. And that is quite a challenge.

𝒞: *What were your best roles, do you think, in those telecasts?*

ℒ: I would have to say *Un Ballo* and *Rigoletto*. I wish I would have done *Don Carlos* sooner. It's not because I was passé or anything like that, but I felt when I saw the telecast of *Don Carlo* that I was not exactly as dashing as I was for *Un Ballo in Maschera* or *Rigoletto*.

𝒞: *What others did you do?*

ℒ: I did the Centennial from the Met and that was very interesting. I enjoyed it but it was a long, long day! We started at 10 o'clock in the morning and went way past midnight. And, you did not know exactly when you were singing.

𝒞: *Can you talk about* I Due Foscari*? It's an opera that's not well-known but you seem to like to sing it. Can you explain why?*

ℒ: I have to say that I have not done many performances, maybe three. First of all, it's great Verdi, and the character of Foscari is a very interesting one. In those years, the Doge of Venice was a kind of a honourary title but he had no power. The chamber and the government had the power. The Doge was a public figure. To give you an idea, in Venice you will never find a monument or a bust of any Doge of Venice because even that was against the constitution. But the only one who left his mark on Venice was Foscari. In the main entrance of the Palace in Venice there are the two big doors and the sculpture of Foscari.

In fact, I had something wonderful happen to me when I did it in Hamilton. The Board of the Opera had invited one of the great-grandchildren of Foscari to the performance and it was funny to be in the presence of an actual member of the Foscari family. Everything else in the opera is fictional. The names never resemble anybody who was alive. However, it was kind of a true story. The Doge would have liked to be able to use his power but the chamber is always thwarting him. For instance, he has to send his son into exile and he doesn't want to. This is the reason I found it very fascinating to perform, because it's completely against my nature.

As a person he's very good but realizes that certain things are not right, and because he cannot do anything about it this makes him very frustrated. In fact, at the end of the opera he loses his mind and that's how he dies, losing his mind. But the thing that is so incredible about *Foscari* is that the music at the end is glorious: the chorus, the orchestra, the Doge and all the soloists. It should be performed more often so that the people get used to it. However, it's not an opera that has great arias. There are some arias in it, but they're not the greatest. But as a whole, *Due Foscari* is a fabulous opera and it has to be seen at least once to really appreciate it. When you see it you understand why this kind of opera should have been performed more often than it was done.

𝒞: *Do you prefer* Foscari *to* Stiffelio *and* I Lombardi*? Which do you feel has the better music and why are* I Lombardi *and* Stiffelio *recorded and done more?*

ℒ: *Due Foscari* is not a tenor's opera. And there is only a little for the soprano. Mainly it's the baritone and the bass. And it seems that the recording company has a policy to sell an opera with a big-name tenor and soprano rather than basses and baritones. And I think that is the reason why *Due Foscari* was always eliminated. They have done *Stiffelio.* But I prefer *I Due Foscari.*

𝒞: *You told me told me a funny story about* Macbeth, *something about what not to do if a stage director tells you to do it. Can you describe that incident?*

ℒ: Sometimes stage directors should give a certain freedom to the artist. I remember very, very vividly when I was doing *Macbeth.* I will not name the theatre or the person, but it was one of these performances which the director wanted to do as a Shakespearean play rather than opera. And I'm sorry to say, Shakespeare is Shakespeare! Verdi is Verdi!

That means you cannot be at the mercy of doing a recitativo instead of an aria.

In Shakespeare there are monologues. And in Shakespeare people expect that a monologue should be done a certain way because of the words. If the artist moves too much it disturbs the essence of the monologue. But when you come to opera and you have a recitativo, it has to be suggested not only by voice but by action, because very often the action will enhance the meaning of the word. This is the big problem sometimes with staging.

I remember very vividly the artist who was doing Macbeth. I don't know if he was in trouble or if he didn't want to do it. But he had put into his mind that this should be a Shakespeare play. And it was completely wrong. At certain moments, it was really funny. But when I came to the sixth performance of it, it was completely different. The public did not laugh. And I felt very sorry because I even said to the other artists when doing the rehearsal, please, why don't you give some of yourself and don't do only what the director asks you to do.

You have artists, however, who feel that if they are placid, it's easy for them. You have some other artists who need a tremendous drive. Direction and gesture means a lot and is very important. When you impair artists to do that, you are inhibiting a beautiful performance. When I saw the director I asked him, "Are we having any rehearsal?" He said no, because after the fifth performance it is not his job anymore. I was very happy about it because then the sixth performance was going to be my performance, and I did exactly what I wanted. I feel that very often the directors don't put enough faith in the artists. If the artist is not free very often he or she will freeze. You're not going to give a full and complete interpretation of what you're supposed to do.

𝒞: *What was the visual image that made it laughable? Because it's hard to understand just by words what would set off that mood. What should be happening at that dramatic moment that didn't happen? And visually what was it that set the audience off?*

L: I think what set the audience off at first was the artists themselves, who should have been strong enough from the very beginning, from the very first word they sang. And this is why I reproached the director. He should have left the artists to do what they felt was right because they were very powerful in a certain way. The director had the brilliant idea that the soloists should go up and down on the stage and the first thing you know, it was laughable. I was laughing myself. All of a sudden, somebody went, "whooo." And that was funny. Then, a little bit later somebody screamed "Peter Pan, Peter Pan," because of what was happening. Things were flying across the stage.

C: *Are there any other examples that you can give of your own experiences with stage directors?*

L: Well, for instance, I remember doing *La Traviata* once and the director came to me and he said, "Louis, you know that in the opera you have to treat Violetta not as a plain person, but you have had an affair with her." And I said, "How could I have an affair with a woman I don't even know when I walked in?" Sometimes the director will make a mistake.

I remember, for instance, doing *Madama Butterfly*. The director asked me to do something that was completely against my will because it was not possible. In the last act there's a big recitativo between the tenor and the baritone. The baritone starts to explain to the tenor, "You are playing with something that is very frail. You are creating a tremendous problem for a gentle woman." It's not gentle the way he says it. It's very, very powerful and forceful. The stage director came to me and said, "No, Louis, you cannot do that. You have to have pity for the tenor. I said, "Over my dead body I'm going to have pity!" Because the words don't mean that, you know. And this is why sometimes I feel sorry that the stage directors have funny ideas. They should read a little bit more of what is happening within the libretto.

C: *Do you find that sometimes in their search for a new interpretation they go beyond the limits of the libretto? Is it just to enhance the opera or is it to create a new production that might be more exciting? Do you discuss this with the stage director? How close is the relationship between the opera stars and the stage directors?*

ℒ: It depends on the stage directors. Sometimes you have a stage director who has a tremendous flair for the theatre. You know, for instance, when you listen to the actors in Hollywood. They talk about a director and they say, this one was fabulous, this one was no good. Why do you think they're going to say this one was no good? Because he wasn't.

I remember that I did *Rigoletto* with Frank Corsaro. With Frank, somebody told me, you're going to have a big fight. I was ready to fight when I first met him. But the first thing he said to me was, "Louis, listen to me very carefully. I'm going to give you some ideas. If you don't like them let's discuss it."

Sometimes you think your own ideas are great or wonderful but somebody else's might be better. And this is the tremendous rapport I had with Frank. Frank was a man you could talk to if you did not feel what he wanted you to do was right for you. When I did *Rigoletto* he had his ideas, I had my idea. It was the first time I came across a stage director who would not do the usual. If I could have talked to Verdi, I would have asked about the end of the first act in *Rigoletto* where the old man cursed me.

𝒞: *So a stage director is there to get the best out of the actors rather than impose his or her idea on the audience. They need the actors the same way the composers need the instrumentalists.*

ℒ: I think the stage director is like the camera. He's the one that sees your action, he's the one that feels what you are going to do. When you have four or five different people or you have the whole stage full of chorus and you have to give direction it's difficult. I still think the interpretation should be left a little bit to the interpreter. What makes a great stage director is not the stage director as much as the artists who are able to do what the stage director wanted.

𝒞: *So you need to leave a little bit to the singers or actors for spontaneous reactions among them. This gives that extra spark and magic to the performance. A little bit of the unexpected is needed; otherwise it becomes a stylized production.*

ℒ: If you're going to buy five different recordings of an overture, for example, one by Bruno Walter or von Karajan, etc. Each one has his own special taste so who is to say which performance is valid? What can be brought to the audience that's wonderful? A director should be more, excuse the expression, like a policeman. He's the one who tells us where to go and what to do. At the same time, his greatest asset is to be able to see what we can bring on our own.

𝒞: *You mentioned the word validity in productions. You've been in so many productions for so many years, do you find that they change? Certain styles are popular at a certain times.*

ℒ: They're trying to change the style. Sometime you're listening and looking and you say to yourself, what is it that they want? Because it makes no sense. In the *Barber of Seville* that I'm doing right now there is a lot of mime. This is not a dramatic opera, it is a commedia dell'arte. You could do many innovative things without disturbing the opera. *Rigoletto* or other heavy dramas are more difficult to alter. Why try to? I always say to myself, does the director want to distract from the actual composition or the opera itself? To give themselves self-glorification? And for me, I'm sorry to say, it doesn't work that way.

𝒞: *Do you find comedy more difficult to do than the dramatic roles? For instance Rigoletto versus Dr. Bartolo?*

ℒ: I don't think one or the other is more difficult to do because if you're really sincere in your approach, the *Barber* or *Rigoletto* will be the same. You have one way to look at *Rigoletto* and another way to look at the *Barber*. If you are intelligent and you understand, don't try to make a lot of it. What you have to create is what you feel inside. Don't try to do it from the outside.

𝒞: *You don't want to create one-dimensional characters like slapstick comedy routines. Is that what you mean? These comic figures from* Barber, *for example, should still have an element of humanity that makes the audience identify with them. Is that what you're saying?*

ℒ: Well, the point is, sometimes you don't need much to create an atmosphere. Just a look on your face sometimes is enough to create exactly what is needed. I did one single performance of *Gianni Schicchi* at the Met, and don't ask me why because I still don't understand it, but the moment I walked on the stage everyone laughed. I don't think I'm a comedian, just the opposite. I played Gianni Schicchi as a dramatic person but there was something that created a tremendous atmosphere. The next thing I know was that from the beginning to the end of the opera people were laughing.

𝒞: *You did the same with Falstaff, you just walked on and people laughed.*

ℒ: But why? I think it's more psychological than physical in interpretation.

𝒞: *I've been watching you do Dr. Bartolo with two different singers. I've also watched your understudy do your role. Everyone is quite different. You do a lot with just minimal movements of your face which are very, very funny but your understudy does a lot more physical activity.*

ℒ: Don't try to overdo the role. Don't try to be better than the composer. Try to be what the composer wanted.

𝒞: *Can you give us a few insights on Dr. Bartolo as you are working on him now? What are your feelings? What is he feeling?*

ℒ: Well, here is a man who is a little bit lost. He's practically a Falstaff. The thing is, he puts himself into situations that are so ridiculous. For instance, at the beginning it is said that he wants to marry Rosina for her money. But Falstaff wants to do anything that he wants, to drink and eat and chase women. That's all he wants. Just that. And this is the thing with Bartolo: don't be Quilico trying to be Bartolo, no! Be Bartolo directly. It's a marvelous feeling to be able to transport yourself. To translate yourself into a role like Bartolo. The situations were so unusual and the composers so intelligent. Be part of that creation. It's wonderful to be able to transform yourself into someone who is completely different from you.

𝒞: *I want you to talk a bit more about Bartolo. You mentioned that it was easier to talk about Falstaff and I'm wondering if it's because you become Bartolo now that you're performing him and it therefore makes it more difficult to talk about him. It's like talking about yourself because you're in the role.*

ℒ: I think the difference between Bartolo and Falstaff creates a little problem. Bartolo is a direct person. Falstaff is not as direct. There are certain things that Falstaff does in his life that he doesn't understand, he doesn't even think about it. But Bartolo, he's got a one-track mind. He wants to marry this girl, get her money and she will be his pupil. With Falstaff there is more than that. I think this is why, in a certain way it is easier for me to do Falstaff than to do Bartolo. Bartolo is very straightforward; somebody else creates the situations. But in *Falstaff,* very often it's Falstaff himself that creates the situation he's in. And that is where the challenge comes into focus. It's wonderful! When you are with Bartolo, you create one situation then you go to another situation, but it is still the same in any situation.

𝒞: *So Bartolo, in effect, doesn't develop but with Falstaff you see a development from the beginning to the end. There's a conclusion that is satisfying.*

ℒ: That's right.

𝒞: *And with Bartolo there's basically no conclusion. It's a comedy, but he doesn't develop as a character. He remains the same from the beginning to the end.*

L: Well, I would not go as far as to say that he doesn't develop as a character. He does, but the character is much less complex than Falstaff. This is what I felt. For other people it might be different. In my own personal interpretation of roles I feel that the creation of Bartolo is much more difficult.

C: *Is Bartolo more demanding vocally?*

L: The vocal approach of Bartolo is more difficult for one reason: it lies a bit too low for my own pleasure and no matter what I do the voice commands too much. At certain moments the voice creates too much weight. And that is the thing I always avoided in my life, to make the voice heavy. But I enjoy doing the role. It's wonderful, but I prefer to do Falstaff.

C: *Or Rigoletto.*

L: Oh yes, yes! That's one thing for sure.

C: *Critics and media have been known to typecast singers in various roles and operas. How do you feel about that? Is this wrong?*

L: The thing is, critics really don't have much to say about casting in a role. I remember a great artist, I won't mention the name because I don't like to mention names. But there was a famous world-renowned baritone who was a fantastic Schubert, Bach and Brahms interpreter. But to say that he was the greatest Rigoletto, the greatest Count di Luna, the greatest Don Giovanni was really appalling. When you see things like that you say to yourself, sometimes critics should let the public know that it's just their opinion. Critics want people to agree with everything they say. And I think it is wrong. They have a way to make people believe in them. And I don't think it is fair to use that tool for their own personal reasons. There are some great shows. You might say, well the show was a great show but there were mistakes, or something was badly produced, and explain a little bit. Instead of helping people make their own opinion about something they write in such way you feel that all they want is to destroy the show. And I don't think it is fair.

Because, after all, artists are people who have put years of work into their performance.

𝒞: *I'm going to rephrase my question. You are known as a Verdi baritone. I'm wondering whether it's the critics and media or whether it's the managers who hear a singer's performance of a Verdi opera and if it is good then the singer gets invited to do those roles over and over again. Are singers pigeonholed in roles for a long time? Is it good for singers or is it bad? On the one hand I suppose it's good because they get work, but does that stop their development? For example, a Mozart soprano might like to do different composers but won't get work in it. Is this good or bad?*

ℒ: I will not say that critics are responsible for that, but the critics can be a great influence. And this is where, excuse the expression, there's a very big Mafia in this. What I mean by this is that when you buy a product you buy it because you have read about it or seen it on TV. Very often critics are not responsible for that, but at the same time because they're the ones that often create these kinds of personalities. I feel that the duty of the critic should not be to rule the media. The other problem is that you have to have money to be able to put certain artists in certain repertoire, maybe where they don't have the right to be.

𝒞: *I think it's wonderful when you do get an educated critic because, as you said before, they give constructive and concrete criticism.*

ℒ: Well, if you can get an educated critic that's a wonderful thing. I saw not too long ago a new critic coming to the *New York Times* and where do you think he comes from? If I remember right, he was a writer for baseball somewhere in the States. He was very eloquent with his speech, and they said, well, why don't we make him a music critic? And you would be surprised too, that the director of a theatre will see that certain artists are well-favoured by the press. Don't let criticism be the voice of your soul, because it could be very dangerous. Instead of thinking of the one who writes badly, listen to the one that writes good reviews.

𝒞: *Good advice. In other words, if it's concrete and constructive learn from it. If it's good, keep it because you need any kind of press for your career, and if it's bad throw it out.*

ℒ: That's exactly right. Years ago I read a review where the critic complained that the singer was limping as if crippled and it ruined the show; however, the man was really handicapped. Or I saw another review when I was doing *Traviata.* The tenor was black. And the first thing the critic said was: I never saw a black person sing Alfredo in *Traviata.* What has colour got to do with it? You know, it shows how much prejudice there was with that one man. Because if you have somebody who does a good job, accept that. I spoke once with a critic and the critic said to me, no, we're not there to enjoy. But, I said, how can you criticize if you're not there to enjoy the performance?

𝒞: *Well, I hope we're not losing the intellectual and analytical writers and critics. Soon we'll be left with newsbriefs saying what took place and when.*

ℒ: Well, the big problem is that people might prefer to read that kind of review than to read well-written and analyzed reviews. If they would only understand that a bad critic is a bad critic. And that's another thing that I find very offensive. It's not for the artists as much as for the people who go and listen. You have three or four thousand people who will listen to a performance and love it and the critic comes out and destroys it completely. If I was there to listen to the performance and I really enjoyed it, who is the man to tell me what I have heard is bad? If somebody has the knack to make you forget about your dream and can go as far as to prevent you to become a singer, something is wrong.

𝒞: *Talking about criticism, how about some self-criticism for you as a pianist. Tell me how you learned to play the piano?*

ℒ: Well, that was a terrible thing. One must be careful with people that are so unsure of themselves. I was studying at the Conservatorio of Santa Cecilia in Rome. When I enrolled they said I had to study an instrument, and I said that I would like to learn piano. The first day of my class I went to the Conservatorio and I waited at the door. When I knocked a lady opened the door. I said, “My name is Louis Quilico. I am here for my lesson.” “Come on in.”

And I walked in and there were maybe 15 or 20 young children about the age of 8 to 12 years old. She was finishing a lesson and I was listening. I was amazed to see how these young children were doing at the piano. I had never taken piano in my life. Also, musically I was not yet solid.

Then she said, “Mr. Quilico, it’s your turn. Please sit down.” I sat down and the first thing I know all these children surrounded the piano. I became red like a tomato because I knew that I did not know anything about the piano. She said to me, “Do you know where Do (C) is?” And I looked at the keyboard trying to find the Do or middle C.

There was a little boy right next to me who noticed that I did not even know where the C is on the piano. He came to me and said, “You see the two black notes: there’s a white note in between, and what’s before these two black notes is the C, stupid!” And when I heard “stupid,” that was the end of my career as a pianist. I became so panicky that I got up and I said, “Madame, dear lady, I’m deeply sorry but today I am very, very sick,” and that was the end of my piano career.

𝒞: *In retrospect, do you think it’s important to be able to sit down and accompany yourself? Would you have liked to do that?*

ℒ: It’s one thing that would be very nice to be able to do, but we become singers much later in life. The career comes quickly if it comes and then you don’t really have the time to become an instrumentalist. But I would say that it is very important for a voice career that the person should be able to play the piano, so that they could accompany themselves. It doesn’t have to be great but at least that they have a notion, for instance, of the rhythm of the piano and maybe the right chord here or there.

Prince Igor, Montreal TV, 1958
(Photo by Henri Paul)

Il Trovatore, La Fenice, Italy 1958

Duca d'Alba, Spoleto 1959

La Traviata with Joan Sutherland and Mary Collier
at Covent Garden, 1960

Louis Quilico as Enrico in
Lucia di Lammermoor at
Covent Garden, 1960

Queen of Spades
Covent Garden, 1961

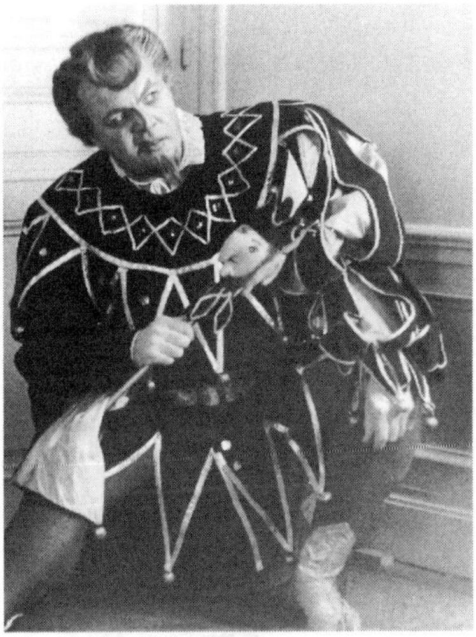

Rigoletto
Paris Opera, 1962
(Photo by Satar)

Fanciulla del West
Strasbourg 1964

With Margherita Wallmann,
Jerome Hines in *Don Carlo*,
Palermo 1964

La Mère Coupable by Darius Milhaud,
Geneva 1964 (Photo by Canera-Nell)

With Leontyne Price in *Aida*, Paris 1968 (Photo by Satar)

Meeting Prime Minister Pierre Elliot Trudeau after *Aida*, 1968 Toronto (Photo by Boris Spremo)

Otello in Minsk, Russia 1969

With Patricia Brooks in *Rigoletto*
at City Opera NYC, 1969
(Photo by Beth Bergman)

Roberto Devereux with Beverly Wolf
at New York City Opera, 1970
(Photo by Beth Bergman)

Roberto Devereux
New York City Opera, 1970 with
Beverly Sills, Placido Domingo and
Beverly Wolf (Photo by Fred Fehl)

Roberto Devereux
New York City Opera, 1970
(Photo by Beth Bergman)

With Patricia Brooks in *Pélleas et Mélisande* at
New York City Opera, 1970
(Photo by Beth Bergman)

Pélleas et Mélisande debut at
the Metropolitan Opera, 1972
(Photo by Louis Mélancon.
© Winnie Klotz.)

With Jon Vickers in *Otello* at the Metropolitan Opera, 1972
(Photo by J. Heffernan. © Winnie Klotz.)

Falstaff with Clarice Carson, Montreal 1974

Il Trovatore at
the Metropolitan Opera, 1977

I Pagliacci at
the Metropolitan Opera, 1979
(Photo by Winnie Klotz)

With Luciano Pavarotti in *Rigoletto* at
the Metropolitan Opera 1980 (Photo by Winnie Klotz)

Portrait as *Renato* in *Un Ballo in Maschera* from *Opera Illustrated* by Christina Petrowska (North York: Captus Press, 1994)

As Renato in
Un Ballo in Maschera,
the Metropolitan Opera, 1980
(Photo by J. Heffernan.
© Winnie Klotz)

Tosca, with Teresa Zylis-Gara
at the Metropolitan Opera, 1981
(Photo by Beth Bergman)

Adriana Lecouvreur at the Metropolitan Opera 1981 (Photo by J. Heffernan. © Winnie Klotz)

Luciano Pavarotti and Louis Quilico after *Un Ballo in Maschera* at the Metropolitan Opera, 1982 (Photo by Walter Karling)

Meeting Andy Warhol after *Un Ballo in Maschera* at the Metropolitan Opera, 1982 (Photo by Walter Karling)

Il Trovatore with Leontyne Price at the Metropolitan Opera, 1982 (Photo by Beth Bergman)

Gianni Schicchi at the Metropolitan Opera, 1983

Queen Elizabeth and Prince Philip, Ottawa 1982

With Olivia Stapp in *Macbeth* at
the Metropolitan Opera 1983 (Photo by Winnie Klotz)

With Placido Domingo in *Don Carlo* at
the Metropolitan Opera 1983 (Photo by Winnie Klotz)

With Mirella Freni in *Don Carlo*
at the Metropolitan Opera 1983
(Photo by Beth Bergman)

As Macbeth in *Macbeth*
at the Metropolitan Opera, 1983
(Photo by Winnie Klotz)

Portrait as *Michonnet* in *Adriana Lecouvreur* from *Opera Illustrated* by Christina Petrowska
(North York: Captus Press, 1994)

Rigoletto, Montreal 1984 (Photo by J. André Lecoz)

Louis Quilico as Germont in *La Traviata* at L'Opera de Montreal, 1984 (Photo by Photographex)

Rigoletto at the Metropolitan Opera, 1984 (Photo by J. Heffernan. © Winnie Klotz.)

Portrait as Rigoletto from
Opera Illustrated by Christina Petrowska
(North York: Captus Press, 1994)

Portrait as Rigoletto from *Opera Illustrated*
by Christina Petrowska
(North York: Captus Press, 1994)

Portrait as Falstaff from *Opera Illustrated* by Christina Petrowska
(North York: Captus Press, 1994)

Samson et Dalila, Louis Quilico as the High Priest and Marilyn Horne as Dalila, at the Metropolitan Opera, 1986 (Photo by William Acheson)

Portrait as Il Doge in *I Due Foscari* from *Opera Illustrated* by Christina Petrowska (North York: Captus Press, 1994)

With Thomas Hampson in *Barber of Seville* at
the Metropolitan Opera 1989
(Photo by Winnie Klotz)

With Patricia Neal after *I Pagliacci* at the Metropolitan Opera (Photo by John King)

Rigoletto at the Kennedy Center Opera House, 1991 (Photo by Joan Marcus)

In his last Rigoletto, 510th at Opera Lyra, Ottawa 1994 (Photo by André Pierre Leduc)

On Rigoletto

𝒞: *Why do people call you Mr. Rigoletto?*

ℒ: When I was singing *Luisa Miller* with Pavarotti in San Francisco, the Italian stage director insisted on calling me "Mr. Rigoletto". With 16 pirated recordings of Rigoletto the name stuck.

𝒞: *What was your first* Rigoletto *and how did you mentally prepare for the role of Rigoletto?*

ℒ: Well, my first *Rigoletto* was done with the New York City Opera in 1959. It was after the season in New York and we were going to Burlington, Vermont. I had promised to drive the tenor who was singing the Duke in *Rigoletto*. His name was Gismondo. In fact my first soprano who sang Gilda in *Rigoletto* was Lisa di Julio. We did a dress rehearsal in New York the day before.

When we arrived in Burlington, I delivered the tenor and at that moment he decided to go see a performance of *Madama Butterfly*. By 9 o'clock I had just finished eating in the restaurant and I was going to go home when all of a sudden the tenor ran towards me. "Louis, you have to come to the theatre! You have to finish the opera because the baritone is sick and they cannot finish the performance of *Butterfly*. You have done *Butterfly* so please come and help them." I decided that I would stay and I did the performance. I finished the second and the third acts of *Butterfly*. What I should have done that day is stay in Burlington and sleep there, but what I did was drive all the way to Montreal. That was about 125 miles or more.

The next day I came back and in the afternoon there was the other dress rehearsal of *Rigoletto* with orchestra, chorus and scenery. That night I had to do the performance, but at the dress rehearsal that afternoon I sang like a maniac. I really sang as though it was the final performance. In fact, Julius Rudel, the conductor, walked into my dressing room and said, "Louis, please shut up!" I said, "You see the door, take it and get out. Either I'll be able to master this opera or it's going to master me." Anyway, we finished the dress rehearsal in the afternoon and that night I did the performance. 50 performances after that night, I still felt that the first time I sang it was still the best performance. I was like a real racehorse. It was incredible.

𝒞: *You must have been inspired by the challenge of doing such a role. What makes it so difficult for baritones?*

ℒ: Dramatically it's a very difficult opera because there are a lot of demands physically and mentally. That is my big problem. I'm mentally always stressed out in doing a performance of *Rigoletto*. I always say that when I do a performance, it's like my last performance. And that is why it is difficult to do that kind of role. I needed to see whether I am the master of this opera or the opera is the master of me. And **that** I discovered the first time I sang it.

𝒞: *What makes the role so difficult vocally?*

ℒ: Because it lies in a tessitura that is extremely high. It's as if a tenor would sing G, A, B and C natural all evening. And that's why it's very, very, very difficult and, like I said, physically it demands a lot. Mentally, also, *Rigoletto* is a complete drama and it's very dangerous.

𝒞: *Why?*

ℒ: Because you can become overwhelmed by the role.

𝒞: *What about vocalizing for* Rigoletto*?*

ℒ: I sing as little as possible because there is so much singing to be done in *Rigoletto*. I think that for me, what is most important is to condition the mind for this role. Because if I don't condition my mind I can't go through this kind of opera. There is no way.

𝒞: *By conditioning your mind to a role such as Rigoletto do you avoid being overwhelmed by it?*

ℒ: Well, the point is to be able to come to where you are just by yourself. Nothing in this world can disturb you. Your mind has to be conditioned to be alone in a world by yourself. For me, *Rigoletto* is one of the greatest operas that has ever been written, because it has all kinds of emotions, and vocally it's demanding, never to finish. And technically, oh boy, it's a toughie!

𝒞: *Tell me how it feels to be Rigoletto?*

ℒ: Well, in those years to be handicapped physically was terrifying. Nobody had pity for these kind of people, and that was already a struggle for a man like Rigoletto. But at the same time, this handicap created the monster that he became, because in court in those years the buffoons like Rigoletto were in general the most powerful people in court.

𝒞: *Why was that?*

ℒ: They were powerful because they were very close to either the king or the duke. On top of that they had a mind that was always investigating, not the beauty of life but the opposite, to see if they could harm or blackmail anybody.

𝒞: *Rigoletto was a jester. How do you compare him to the other great clowns, for example, Pagliacci and The Hunchback of Notre Dame?*

ℒ: Well, Rigoletto was at the court and used to be the confidant of the king. That was the difference. In *Pagliacci* there's no court. In fact he's a buffoon with the circus.

𝒞: *But as a character, can you define the differences between the clowns?*

ℒ: There is something similar about the characters of Rigoletto and Pagliacci but one is much broader than the other one. Tonio in *Pagliacci* is more dimensional, although in reality he is the one that brings Canio to discover the infidelity of his wife. And what happened with Rigoletto was the opposite.

𝒞: *For what reason?*

ℒ: In the court he liked to find the person whom he was able to make suffer, because with that he felt glorified.

𝒞: *In other words it gave him power.*

ℒ: Yes, and the king would also glorify Rigoletto. He was thrilled to have found this kind of a character because most of the court people were also trying to instigate something against one another.

𝒞: *They were gossipmongers, 'spin doctors', manipulators. Sounds like the government today. How do you like to play Rigoletto? For example, do you like the audience to feel sympathy for him?*

ℒ: I tell you frankly, I never try to have sympathy for him. On the contrary, I think sympathy is not exactly right. I think it is the opposite. Well, yes, there is a moment of sympathy, yes. The public knows the opera and very often they will feel that there must be sympathy for this man. But in reality it's not really sympathy that they should have. He doesn't let anybody know who the girl is (his daughter), not even the courtiers. The courtiers abducted the girl thinking she was Rigoletto's lover. And this is the point. Rigoletto was the kind of person who manipulated all the time and this time it backfired. For instance, at the beginning Monterone comes in and Rigoletto insults him. When Monterone starts to talk about his own daughter, Rigoletto takes over and ridicules the daughter completely. And this is where Rigoletto shows his kind of personality. Naturally he's afraid of the vendetta or curse that Monterone shouted at him.

𝒞: *Who are your favorite Rigoletto's other than yourself?*

ℒ: Well, I did not see many many Rigoletto's. I saw very few of them. There's one that I was really very satisfied with when I saw it: Leonard Warren. And I think another one, when I saw him for the very first time, was vocally very, very good but after that it was not possible to listen to him in it: Tito Gobbi. For the rest, I don't know. I saw many, many, many Rigoletto's and they don't really play Rigoletto the way I see him.

𝒞: *How many times have you played Rigoletto?*

ℒ: I think about 510 times. That's getting to be quite a few of them.

𝒞: *Now add that to the dress rehearsals and music rehearsals and other run-throughs.*

ℒ: It comes to many more than 1,000 times that I've performed it.

𝒞: *Before you step on the stage, how do you prepare yourself for the role?*

ℒ: I never prepare myself, for one reason: I'm a man who works on instinct and if I have to prepare and think this is how I'm going to do this phrase and that phrase I cannot do that, it is just not possible. That's how a lot of people do it. I never do it the same way.

𝒞: *How do you manage with the stage directors in a difficult and major role like this where you have very strong ideas about your role and the character's portrayal?*

ℒ: I have to say one thing: I never really had a problem with the stage director, because most of the stage directors are intelligent. They also know how many times I've done *Rigoletto* and they saw me do it many times, so that if they know I've also done the productions they leave me alone to my role.

𝒞: *Tell me who you sang with, the conductors, the stage directors . . .*

L: Oh my God! There are so many of them! I remember Julius Rudel at the New York City Opera and director Frank Corsaro.

C: *For example, who was your Gilda, who was the Duke?*

L: There was Gail Robinson, Colette Boky. I did it in Russia but I don't remember the names of the Russian women.

C: *But is there one particular* Rigoletto *that stands out for you more than any other?*

L: There is one, but I still don't know who the Gilda was because I came and replaced the second act at the Metropolitan Opera in New York.

C: *That was with Giuseppe Patané, conductor at the Metropolitan Opera.*

L: Yes, and that was the greatest *Rigoletto* I have done in my life. There was an excitement, a sense of drama that was so incredible I never felt it with others as much as I felt it that night.

C: *Do you attribute that to Patané?*

L: Oh yes! In fact I'm sorry to say it's not my doing, although my performance was a hit for the public. For me on the stage it's the conductor who has to give "it" to me.

C: *The "it" refers to that magical indescribable tempo, excitement, drive and push . . . the ensemble and the moment. What was it about his conducting that night?*

L: He was like a racehorse, ah . . . it was like you're out of breath, the mind spins so fast. The way he conducted that night, my mind was spinning like never before. It was incredible. And not only for me. Patané was responsible for that.

C: *You're talking about your famous aria "Cortigiani" that Rigoletto sings, but with opera it's the whole ensemble that has to work together.*

L: Yes. But sometimes you might have somebody that can stand out. Like for instance with Placido Domingo, Luciano

Pavarotti, you know there is something, there is a charisma about these two men that is so important. And this is what happened with Patané, and it was incredible.

𝒞: *Explain how the performance with Patané came about at the Metropolitan?*

ℒ: Fifteen minutes before the performance I called the Met and they said "Don't worry, Mr. Quilico you don't really have to be at the Met." But that night I said to myself, being that I'm only covering, and it's Cornell MacNeil who was doing the performance, I thought that nothing would go wrong and he would finish the performance. About five past nine the phone rang. I was supposed to go to dinner with friends about 9:30 p.m. I heard the voice of Larry Stair, who worked at the Met. I said, "Oh Shit!" He says, "Oh no, Louis it's not Oh Shit. Bring your carcass around here. We need you tonight!"

And I rushed as much as I could so as not to make the people wait too long. But I should have done something that night, I should have made them wait, because that would have been nice. Anyway, I started to sing. I came on in the second act of *Rigoletto*, in the "Cortigiani" and the vendetta, and when I finished the vendetta (in fact, I have that written in black and white in the *New York Times*), although it's never been seen at the Met I had a standing ovation that night, right after the "Cortigiani". I was responsible for it, yes, but at the same time, I have to say, Patané was incredible. Before we started the performance I said, "Maestro, remember one thing: I'm going to watch you. Watch me and we're going to try to do a good performance. He said, "Don't worry. I'm there." And he was there. And that's the beautiful thing about this performance that I'll remember for the rest of my life.

𝒞: *After the Met production what was another favorite production of* Rigoletto *for you?*

ℒ: Maybe the *Rigoletto* for the New York City Opera might be the production that I enjoyed the most in my entire career. Maybe not as a performance, because I think the one of Patané mentioned before is the greatest performance of any opera that I have done in my life, but I would say the production of the City Opera with Frank Corsaro was superb. And the reason I liked it so much is because of all the detail. You see, before I met Frank I was doing my own Rigoletto, a Rigoletto who was always scared but always threatening.

But when I met Frank, he said to me, "Louis, it's not because you're afraid." Just a simple thing. For instance, in the first act the only man that doesn't believe in the vendetta, although he's cursed by the old Monterone, is Rigoletto. Frank said, "Louis, listen to me very carefully. You're the only one who doesn't believe in the curse. In the second scene, the first thing you say is, 'Qual vecchio maledivami,' the phrase the old man curses me with. You say it three times. Verdi did not write with piano (soft), more piano, even more piano or change the rhythm. He didn't put exactly what he wanted, but if you say one phrase three times, there's got to be a difference. I'm not Verdi but my feeling was that in the first scene Rigoletto was the only one who didn't believe in the curse. And in the second scene he starts to talk about the curse and doesn't believe it. He then starts to talk about the duke and the court and they make him believe the curse and they make him what he becomes. Then after that he says again, 'The old man cursed me,' and then the tone of your voice has to change. It's not the same anymore. You're starting to believe it, and before you reach the third one you say in so many words that you are deformed and you are cursed by the court and everything. The third curse, you believe in it, it's you!"

And I tell you one thing, it was hair-raising. At the end of the last act Gilda is begging for herself and the duke, and what I used to do was to grab her from the floor and shake her, with the meaning that I don't want you to die, I want you to stay with me. And even worse, Sparafucile used to bring the bag containing the body of Gilda out of the house. They put it on the floor and I would come around and kick that bag and you could hear the public gasp. It was so incredible. Some moments towards the end of the last act I would be very nasty with her, and I could hear people in the hall crying.

𝒞: *Who was the unfortunate soprano that got kicked?*

ℒ: For me she was very famous. She was fantastic, Pat Brooks.

𝒞: *What was one of your worst performances of* Rigoletto*?*

ℒ: One of the worst was in Paris. And the soprano was a mean-tempered soprano with a beautiful voice. I'm not going to name her, but she didn't realize that this opera is not called *Lucia* or *Traviata*, it's called *Rigoletto*, and suddenly I was not supposed to do this and I was not supposed to do that. I said, "Madame, when you sing *Traviata* and when you sing *Lucia* do I come and command you to do what I want?" I had told her that in the ending of the vendetta the note has to be held for so long. After the performance she came up and said, "Why couldn't you tell me before!" Sopranos!

𝒞: *What do you mean? Can you explain it further?*

ℒ: In the end of the act you take a high note and you hold it maybe seven or eight beats. She cut at the fifth beat, I went on to the eighth beat. I'm sorry to say it, but I'm supposed to go to the eighth beat; she didn't. But she got really mad and I wanted to give up the performance, and then I came back to myself and I said, uhn uhn, that's all she would like me to do because her husband used to sing Rigoletto. But thank God, when I was there he didn't sing it.

One of the worst times ever . . . San Diego, California. I had a conductor who was so full of himself that he believed there was only one way to conduct *Rigoletto*. But there's only one way to sing *Rigoletto*, the way Verdi intended it. I know that in the score the "Si vendetta" is written in four, and the conductor wanted to conduct it in four. I said, "Maestro there's no human being that can do that." He said, "But Verdi intended that." I replied, "Don't beat it in four but in two." When we did the dress rehearsal he beat it in four. I stopped and said, "Maestro, not in four." Finally I went to see the director of the theatre and I said, "You better tell him not to beat it in four because I'm going to finish much sooner than him. Plus, he's going to finish the opera by himself because, after all, I'm Rigoletto. It's already difficult enough the way it is."

𝒞: *It starts in four but with the accelerando you must conduct it in two. Verdi intended the emotion and the music, not the black and white notes. Having worked with a lot of composers I know that quite a lot of things are left up to the performer. There is a give and take for performance. Tell me, when you're doing Rigoletto with a company, how many rehearsals do you get?*

ℒ: It depends where you go. If you go into smaller houses in the United States, let's call it 'provincial' you will have roughly about 10 to 12 days of rehearsal. And, in fact, it came to a point where I was so renowned for my Rigoletto that before I would go down to rehearse, the director would call me and say, "Louis would you mind coming only six days before the performance, because we know exactly what you want to do and that's what we want to do too." That was the point! You see, my Rigoletto became so known by these people, and it was the closest role for me.

𝒞: *Was Rigoletto your favorite role?*

ℒ: I have to say yes. Because *Rigoletto* is one of the greatest operas and I repeat what I said before: it is one of the greatest roles that's ever been written. My big sorrow about *Rigoletto* is that very often the theatre doesn't do anything special for it. And it is true. *Rigoletto* bad, good, or terrible is still going to come out a real winner.

𝒞: *Is that because of the story or the music?*

ℒ: I think it's a fusion of both of them. Actually, the fusion is incredible, because even if you get somebody who doesn't sing the part right it's still going to come out successfully.

𝒞: *It has one of the most famous tenor arias as well.*

ℒ: "La Donna e' mobile"

𝒞: *And the soprano aria.*

ℒ: "Caro Nome". Well they are, and I have to say that sometimes I wish I could be a tenor to be able to sing, and show the rest of the tenors in the world how to sing, "La Donna e' mobile". I don't recall hearing many tenors that really give me satisfaction in that aria. As for "Caro Nome" I think it's more easy to be satisfied. Maybe there are more sopranos and fewer good tenors.

𝒞: *There is also the famous quartet.*

ℒ: That is a masterpiece. You don't have to hear the words or anything like that, you just listen to it. It's beautiful music, a masterpiece, and it has it's own impact. It has everything in it.

𝒞: *What about costuming for* Rigoletto*? What are your thoughts on some of the modern productions? For example, Rigoletto in a wheelchair. Are you in favour of redesigning opera and putting it in modern-day clothes?*

ℒ: There are certain things you can do. But do it with other operas rather than *Rigoletto.* When the public goes to the theatre, they want to forget, they want to see something that is not part of their life. And you give them exactly what is happening every single day of their life, violence and everything else. I'm sorry to say the director, very often, makes a mistake in changing the opera.

𝒞: *How important are the costumes and the sets for you in* Rigoletto*? Do you feel comfortable only in one costume or are you willing to change?*

ℒ: You can change. But you know when it comes to modern costume, I'm a little bit against that. When you go to a theatre, would you go and see Shakespeare in just plain clothes? Like when I saw *Don Giovanni*, Donna Anna was wearing just a brassiere and there was somebody else who was completely nude. I don't think it's what the public wants to see. I think that the public wants to be engaged in something of the past. They want to forget today. Maybe a few operas can be given a new look. I'm not against that.

𝒞: *But some productions can be done in a very interesting way with a contemporary style or edge. Are you saying not to touch* Rigoletto *at all?*

ℒ: I would not say that, but don't bring me *Rigoletto* in a Cadillac. For instance, I did the role of Scarpia in *Tosca* once in very modern dress but it was still not today. It represented Italy in, I think it was 1935, the time of Mussolini. I was dressed like Mussolini, and it worked very beautifully. But when you come up with things that I don't recognize — for example, Aida and the tenor have to die in the gas chamber, or be electrocuted . . . No . . . leave a little bit to the imagination of the public. There was a *Rigoletto* that was done in a Mafia style, and the Mafia killed the daughter . . . No . . . you know, I think the glamour is important. There are a lot of things you can do, other things. But an opera like *Rigoletto*, leave it with the original flavour, that's the way to do it. It's dangerous to come up with something else. Like *Manon*. If you don't do *Manon* with the period dresses it's not *Manon* any more. You know, they did that! Nudity doesn't belong in those operas. It makes me think it's just for publicity. What about the music?

𝒞: *So you think it takes away from the beauty of the words and the music and leaves a little bit less to the imagination of the public?*

ℒ: I don't think it takes away from the words or anything like that. No. But it takes away from the imagination of the people that are there paying $60, $70, $110 up to $175 (at 1996 prices) for a ticket.

𝒞: *Did you do* Rigoletto *with Luciano Pavarotti?*

ℒ: Oh yes! Many times at the Metropolitan Opera.

𝒞: *And Placido Domingo?*

ℒ: Domingo, no. I'm not sure if Domingo ever sang *Rigoletto* with me.

𝒞: *You have a CD with José Carreras.*

ℒ: Yes. That was the very first CD Carreras ever did in the role in America. In fact, when he came to America that was his debut at the New York City Opera.

𝒞: *And how old was he? He must have been pretty young.*

ℒ: Well, I think he had about three year's of career.

𝒞: *Can you tell me a bit about that performance?*

ℒ: Well, we heard that we would have a new tenor, but there was not much said about him because the publicity machine was not yet on the go for him. Everybody was wondering how he would sound. Boy, when he opened his mouth, that was it. He sang very beautifully. He knew how to sing.

𝒞: *And how was it singing with Luciano?*

ℒ: Well, I'm going to say one thing: Luciano is a great, great, great, great man. And to be with him in an opera is something very special. I feel that we are very sincere about our roles. And I have a funny feeling that he is exactly like me: that the performance he does seems to be his last performance. And it is beautiful to see that, you know. In his dressing room, before a performance we did of *Ballo in Maschera* Luciano said to me that the day he would die, he hopes that God will place him next to me in heaven. It really touched me.

𝒞: *It's wonderful to hear this rather than the stories of the prima donnas that seem to be plaguing opera today.*

ℒ: Well, prima donnas, it is a little bit of the past, you know. There are maybe one or two here or there, but in general there is not much of that anymore. Everyone is there to work and to cooperate with one another.

𝒞: *Who were some of the other sopranos and tenors that you sang* Rigolettos *with?*

ℒ: Well, I had the opportunity and I was very glad about it, of singing with Carreras in his first performance in the United States. In fact there is a pirate recording with both of us. But when you have sung 510 performances of *Rigoletto*, there are too many of them to remember.

𝒞: *What else was there about this particular production at New York City Opera that made it so memorable for you?*

ℒ: Well, it was wonderful for a single reason: the simplicity. Sometimes we believe that we have to make a big, big thing with scenery and production, but this one was the opposite. Simplicity leaves a tremendous amount of freedom for people to imagine. I thought it was very interesting.

𝒞: *What about the Covent Garden production?*

ℒ: Ah, Covent Garden, that was very funny because first of all, I don't know about now, but then I was the only male operatic singer who had ever received flowers on the stage. And it was after a performance of *Rigoletto*. I received a wreath and I was very proud of it. The only thing is that at Covent Garden you were not allowed to have a claque. And we had an Italian tenor that came in, and he said to me, "I've got to get myself a claque." I said, "It's the worst thing you can do!" Anyway, he didn't listen to what I said, and what happened was exactly what I knew was going to happen. If he had a claque, the audience would know it and would boo him. I was maybe the only one in the whole performance who was not booed. The soprano was booed, the tenor was booed, the conductor was booed. I took it as a great compliment.

𝒞: *Getting back to* Rigoletto. *What happened in Russia that had something to do with scenery?*

ℒ: That was very funny, I've got to say, because it was something that I didn't expect at all. Each time we rehearsed in Russia there was no time to really do anything with the scenery. We were rehearsing in a hall and they would tell me a few things, but I would forget certain things. But you do what you can. And in general what happens with the other artists is that if you're a guest, they abide by what you want. Anyway, they had said something that I did not completely understand. When I finished the first act wondering where I'm supposed to go, I could hear everybody screaming at me in Russian. I could not understand anything until all of a sudden I look on one side, and I look on the other side, and there are two walls coming towards me and I was going to be caught like a sandwich in between.

That was very funny. I got out of that 'bloody' thing as fast as I could.

And there was another thing, while I'm thinking about it. I was doing *Rigoletto*, and during a tour you would arrive the night before and the next day you would go to the theatre. Most of the theatres would have a group of singers there, the ones that usually do the role of *Rigoletto*. They would watch and learn from the 'guest' artists. We started the rehearsal. The soprano was there, with a tall gentlemen who usually sang Rigoletto in the house. And as I'm singing I could see that this man was always smiling. At first it was OK and nice, but after a while it got to be ridiculous. I looked at him a little bit more and I could see one shoulder lower than the other and he's smiling again. I turned towards my interpreter and I said, "Please, would you tell this gentleman not to laugh and smile." The man also said the words at the same time I sang. Naturally I felt a little bit distracted by the man.

We finished the rehearsal and my interpreter called me and said, "Mr. Quilico, would you mind coming into another room?" I went there, and who's in the room but this tall man and my soprano. I walked in and I said to the soprano, "Bravo, bravo, bravo" and all of a sudden she started to talk in Russian. My interpreter said, "Mr. Quilico, she wants you to know that she's the wife of that gentleman and she wants you to know why this gentleman is smiling and why he's got a shoulder lower." I thought he was trying to be fresh or something like that. She said, "This young man, when he finished the conservatoire, did a concert, and in the constitution of the conservatoire there were certain songs he was not supposed to do. He did them just the same, and right after his concert he was arrested and they sent him away for seven years into the salt mines to carry bags of salt. And she would like you to know that he was not trying to imitate you or laugh at you." I looked at her and I said, "I feel so sorry because I didn't expect it. For me, for a moment it was . . ." She says "It's understandable. Don't worry about it."

𝒞: *What about the constant smile?*

ℒ: I'm very happy you ask about it. His wife said, "If you had been in the salt mines for 7 years, wouldn't you be smiling to be here today?" I said, "I would be smiling for the rest of my life I can tell you that!" It was true! He was happy to be liberated.

𝒞: *What happened in Baku?*

ℒ: A very funny experience happened there. I was doing *Rigoletto*, always *Rigoletto*, and I finished my famous aria "Cortigiani" and I could hear the public going boo, boo. I assumed that I didn't sing that well that night. What can you do? You cannot sing well all the time. Anyway I finished that act and we took our curtain bow. The soprano is with me, and all of a sudden I could see all the instrumentalists going bang, bang, bang. And I could see the public screaming like mad but the only thing I could hear was: Boo, Boo. My God, I said, this is a crazy schizophrenic country. I don't have the foggiest idea what they're doing. I said, "I'm going home!" and I walked out. All of a sudden the soprano came right after me and the public is still screaming: Boo, Boo. She grabbed me and we went out again for our curtain calls. I said to her, "What's the matter?" She doesn't know because she spoke only Russian. She said only "Vendetta." Finally I understood what she meant. They wanted an encore. I felt so stupid because after the "Cortigiani" that's what happened. I didn't know. You're not used to these things you know. That was Baku, dear old Baku.

𝒞: *Can you tell me about some of the* Rigoletto *performances at the Paris Opera?*

ℒ: During the time I was in Paris I did nine performances only, because I refused to do *Rigoletto* in French. I hated the French translation and I like to do *Rigoletto* in Italian. I told the French Opera, "If you want to do it in French get somebody else." And that's what they did, they always tried to get somebody else. One day, the management at the Paris Opera said, "Mr. Quilico, we have a very special guest that's coming from Moscow, Mr. Gromyko." "Oh," I said, "the Premier?" They said yes. He says, "We would like you to sing *Rigoletto*." I said, "Only in Italian." He said, "In Italian. We are going to do an Italian performance." I finished the whole performance, and there were a lot of people.

You know what used to drive me insane with the Paris Opera? When they would do it with a French baritone, he had one curtain call, or maybe two curtain calls. When I did my nine performances, each time there were 15, up to 20 and some performances up to 25 curtain calls. I used to say to myself, but don't they understand what they have in the house? I mean, I didn't want to brag about it, but I'm a hell of a good Rigoletto. The management at the opera didn't care about that. They're coo-coo about that you know.

Anyway, I agreed to do that performance for Premier Gromyko. It was a great success. I knew that I was going to Russia a month later. And when I saw Mr. Gromyko I said, "Mr. Gromyko, I want you to know that I'm very happy to have sung for you tonight. It's a kind of audition." We were joking about it. And I said, "I'm going to be in your country in exactly one month. I'm coming to do *Rigoletto* over there too." "Ah," he says, "I'm very happy that you're coming, it's very nice, I love what you did tonight. If you ever need me, call me."

I didn't want to disturb him for that, but I should have taken it because a month later when I went to Russia I didn't have my visa. I had forgotten to make my visa in Ottawa because I had no time. When I came to Rumania, I thought I was going to find a Russian Consulate there but there was no Russian Consulate there. So there was no way I could make my visa. They shipped me out and I arrived in Moscow on Saturday about 1:30 p.m. At the airport I saw an officer, I gave him my passport, and he started to go through the passport trying to find the visa. He says, "Visa." I said "Sir, I don't have a visa! Make me one." I had a bad day that day and when I have a bad day, don't push me around too much.

Anyway, while I was talking to him two girls came right up next to me and one said "Mr. Quilico? I want you to know that I'm your interpreter and this is the Canadian Ambassador's secretary. "Oh!" I said, "Wonderful, wonderful! But we have a little problem here, I did not make my visa." The Canadian Ambassador's secretary said, "Mr. Quilico, you cannot come into Russia if you do not have your visa." I said, "Listen, I'm here, let's do something. I know that in Russia you work 7 days a week, 24 hours a day." She said, "Oh no, Mr. Quilico." The interpreter said to me, "Oh no, we have the English week!" It was very funny to hear this from the Russian.

About an hour later I called the girls and I said, "Listen, what is happening?" They said, "Mr. Quilico, we won't be able to make the visa. You'll have to stay here for the weekend, here, at the hotel." I said, "Can you show me the hotel?" I don't know why I asked that, but I had a premonition of something strange. She showed me a building that had bars in the windows. I said, "This is a prison! This is not a hotel! You find me a visa because if you don't get me a visa I'm going right back to Canada and that's it! You'll have to answer for it."

She went on the phone again and blah, blah, blah. Finally she came back and said, "Listen, Mr. Quilico, there is no way. We don't know what to do." I said, "You do me a favour. You are my interpreter. Call the officer and tell him exactly what I'm going to tell you. You're going to translate." She went and got the officer. "Would you ask him the private number of Mr. Gromyko?" "But," she said, "Mr. Quilico, you're not allowed to call our Premier." I said, "I am not asking you a question. I want you to ask this gentleman for his private number." She turned around, she started to talk to him . . . Mr. Gromyko . . . Oh my God! And all of a sudden she said, "I don't know what to do." I said, "It's very simple. Get me in." The officer said to leave my passport at the airport.

When the Ambassador's secretary heard this, she said "Oh no, Mr. Quilico, you don't leave your passport." I said "Listen, I'm going to give him my passport, he's going to give me a receipt. I'm giving you the receipt. Every night at 6 o'clock I'm going to call you. If I don't call you, start to search for me. That's all I can tell you." When I told the Canadian Ambassador that I was in Russia for two weeks without a visa, he couldn't believe it. He said, "Mr. Quilico, it is not possible in this country. You don't get in." "Dear Ambassador," I said, "I've gotten in. It's not a visa; I've got something better."

Three days or four days later my interpreter came to me and said, "Mr. Quilico, you must have been joking about Mr. Gromyko!" I said, "No, I never joke about these things, you know." But she said, "You know, he's our Premier and you are not allowed to call him." "You're not allowed to call him! But," I said, "I'm allowed." She says, "Who gives you the permission?" I said, "It's very simple, it's him." She says, "What do you mean by that?" I said, "Well, a month ago he came to Paris. I sang for him at the Paris Opera and after the performance we were introduced and I told him I was coming to Russia. He told me if I needed anything to call him." She could not understand that. It was quite something.

C: *What was your worst performance and why?*

L: The one in San Diego, California we already talked about might be not one of the worst but it's not far to be one of the worst.

C: *You have another production that was close to being as bad as that? What made it bad?*

L: When you give me pupils from school to be prima donnas it doesn't work. It's not because I have anything against the kids, because they were wonderful, but that's not the way to do it. When you sing with the bass, Sparafucile (he's the guy with a long sword and he can kill you any moment), he must frighten you, but when you have to scare yourself it's no good. It was said to me, "Louis, cancel, you're going to be very unhappy." The thing is, I need reaction from my cast members. I had no reaction. Gilda sang very beautifully. She had a beautiful voice, was the right size and everything, but my God, she was talking about her mother like she was talking about "Let's go to the corner tavern." I need cooperation, and after doing so many performances of it and coming down to that, I was disappointed.

𝒞: *So, lack of depth, lack of energy?*

ℒ: Oh, everything.

𝒞: *Can a stage director help with that type of situation?*

ℒ: No way! The conductor, director, no way! If your partner across from you cannot help you! In Texas once the soprano was twenty-four years old and felt that she was becoming a superstar at the Met. I was not with the Met at that time. You could feel it in the way she would look at me: "Who do you think you are, I'm from the Met! You're not from the Met." She was so remote, she was never with me, so I stopped the rehearsal and grabbed her and said, "You know how powerful Rigoletto is?" She said, "I know!" I said, "My dear girl, if I get mad I'm going to finish my performance right now. People will not even remember your performance. Let's play together, let's be together, and you're going to thank me for it." After that, she thanked me every single performance and said, "Mr. Quilico, it was wonderful what you did, and I'm very happy that you brought me back to earth." I'm not alone, she's not alone, everybody is there, you know? And that is terrible, to fear that you're by yourself. Who wants that? You don't need that, you know.

𝒞: *What about doing* Rigoletto *in English? Have you done that?*

ℒ: Yes, I've done it in English for CBC television. And I have to say, it was really torture for a simple reason: the English language especially for an opera like *Rigoletto* doesn't work. The English language is so anti-dramatic. For instance, just to give you an idea, the aria starts, "Cortigiani, vil razza, dannata." In English the words are terrible: "Race of courtiers, vile rabble, detested." The words are great, but dramatically and musically they don't sound right because the translation is "Court of lepers, debased and corrupted". What are you going to do with this? There's nothing you can do and this is why translations are not so well received. Because there is an edge that is not there. And that is the big problem with putting *Rigoletto* in English. I hated the French translation. It was absolutely impossible.

𝒞: *Tell me some more* Rigoletto *experiences.*

ℒ: Well, for instance, in the United States it came to a point where I was practically the only one who was doing *Rigoletto.* A lot of producers knew exactly my kind of production and what I wanted to do on stage. I remember one producer said, "Listen, Louis, your *Rigoletto* is in a certain way in my mind, so perfect that I don't want to add anything to it. I know exactly what you do and I want to have everybody around you." I don't take that as a compliment, except that it proves that some people are so well aware of the people they're working with they give these people what they really need to do their best on the stage.

𝒞: *Do you find that roles affect you? You told me you almost became a Falstaff. How do you feel about Rigoletto?*

ℒ: Rigoletto is so, so out of my nature, that in a certain way for me it's easy to understand, because it's the opposite of what I would be. Rigoletto is a personality that life made bitter, ah . . . all of a sudden he cannot cope with life. It's very difficult for him because he is lost. He said to his daughter, "The most beautiful thing I had was my wife! And I lost her! Now the only thing I have left is you."

And, you know, it's sad. I think in a certain way, Rigoletto has a sadness in his life and that is not me. I can be sad sometimes. But for me, Rigoletto was sad all the time. He said, "The court made me a jester. They want me to make them laugh! You know that I'm a man that kills with words." Imagine, he has a little daughter that he loves and there he is explaining to the public who he is, what he is and in one sentence will explain exactly who Rigoletto is, and that is not me.

He says at the beginning of the second scene, "The old man cursed me . . ." the second phrase about Sparafucile, "We are equal. He has the dagger and I have the tongue." With words he can kill anybody he wants. But at the same time, it's very interesting to see the difference between this kind of character and yourself. And I think that in a certain way, it was not difficult for me to do these kind of roles because they were something I could get my teeth into. And I like to discover the undercurrents in these roles.

𝒞: *You're doing* Rigoletto *again. Is it going to be a fresh experience for you? Do you approach it as a comfortable old shoe or are you looking at it as a new adventure?*

ℒ: I don't think I'll approach it as a new adventure because it has been an adventure during my entire life. But there's always something unexpected that I don't anticipate and I like to do these kinds of operas with spontaneity. All of a sudden, I'm doing a phrase one week and I will feel it one way and another week I will feel it another way. This opera is very mysterious for the interpreter and I never get tired of it.

𝒞: *Tell me about Rigoletto's relationship with Gilda, especially in the third scene.*

ℒ: It's a very special relationship and very unusual in fact, because Rigoletto, being such a complicated character, makes it very difficult. But at the same time, if you can comprehend the love of Rigoletto, who is handicapped physically and mentally, you might realize that he's also evil. In the second scene he explains who he is, and he's as evil as Sparafucile. Sparafucile has the dagger but Rigoletto has a verbal dagger that's even worse.

Very often people have difficulty understanding his complexity. For instance, after Gilda has been abducted and she comes out of the duke's room, Rigoletto meets her. At that point I think it is incredible, because he wants her to speak to him, to tell him what really happened, but at the same time although she wants to speak, she cannot because of shame and sorrow. I say sorrow because I think Gilda was tremendously in love with the duke, even though he dishonoured her. Rigoletto wants her to explain but she cannot. This is why very often people feel he should comfort her. No! It's the opposite. I think it arrived to a point where she herself has no way to explain.

It's an aria for Gilda, where Rigoletto sees her but she doesn't want him to. Then there's a second verse of the aria, where she starts to tell him about who it was, and at that point Rigoletto doesn't want to hear anything. She keeps on telling him but it feels like listening to something that comes from somewhere but you don't understand it. It doesn't feed your mind, it feeds your emotions, but your mind is suddenly taken by that conversation. This conversation then makes you realize who you are, rather than the subject of that conversation! Rigoletto at that point says, "Only infamy for me." Do you understand what it means? Not Gilda, not the world, nothing else matters but himself. It's funny to think about it that way.

C: *How do you see it in the second act? You actually throw her down.*

L: Well, she sings the first part of that aria by herself. Rigoletto has been moved by everything she has explained to him and he turns towards her and wants to listen. All of a sudden she takes a step towards him and he turns away from her. He doesn't want to listen. What happens at the end of this moment is tremendous. The words are incredible but at the same time the soul, the inside of Rigoletto, becomes so involved in bitterness, in vengeance, that Gilda does not exist anymore. When she comes towards him to be comforted at the end of this aria Rigoletto throws her on the floor. "No, I'm the only one and everything is happening to me, it's me, it's me!" It's wonderful, because she doesn't exist for him. There he is, talking to God, "Why do you do this to me? You know, this infamy, why do you . . ." and the infamy, it's his daughter. But in reality it's not his daughter. It is the action that happened. I don't know if I make myself clear but that is exactly why he throws her down.

At the end of his little passage there is a kind of a recitative. He hears her and that's why he asks Gilda, "Please let me hear you cry." Very often the Gilda will look at him and they will want to laugh, but it's nothing to laugh about. They're both taken in by such drama. And Gilda, feeling that her father has, more or less, rejected her because he threw her on the floor, suddenly feels alone. She believes that there is nothing else for her and she doesn't become hysterical, she cries. The father is not there to help comfort her, but he will help her only in a certain way. She feels that she's lost and starts to cry. Rigoletto hears that cry and what happens is incredible. All of a sudden, the whole world just crumbles and there are only two human beings remaining in the middle of that stage. The father is trying to comfort his daughter. *Rigoletto* is an opera that is more powerful than life, because unless you are dragged in that kind of situation it's practically impossible to understand. You have to be not the character of Rigoletto, but in his shoes. You have to be him.

This is the thing that I found so incredible about Rigoletto, to be able to transport yourself inside that man and to understand what he thinks, how he feels, what he sees, what he wants to do, and what he does. It's amazing. If you just think of words, yes, they are very dramatic. But you have to go further than that. Verdi was incredible, because in Verdi, as in Puccini, you really have to work to read between the lines because of what they imply. It's not what it seems to be, it's more than that. And today we change the whole opera, sometimes spoiling it with too many strange ideas. For me, in a role, the thing is not costuming but going deep into the mind of the man. And that is very difficult in *Rigoletto* because there's so much spontaneity in this role, but it is also wonderful for that reason.

𝒞: *What about the relationship of Gilda with her mother and Rigoletto? Can you go into that?*

ℒ: Well, she said, "Tell me about my mother because I don't know anything about my mother." He says to her, "Don't talk to me about that. I don't want to hear about this." He doesn't want to explain to her, because he feels the mother was only his. And he's jealous of that. You see, in everything that he does he's a man of extremes. For instance, he doesn't want to confide in his daughter, although he depends on her. He doesn't want to confide in anybody else either. It's only her, like it was only the mother. When it comes to the courtier, it's only the courtier. There's not one moment that you can say that one passes to the other, no. It's always something very different. He does explain to his daughter about her mother, but not that it was a woman who was your mother, only she was my wife. Then he changes. All of a sudden, he turns around and says to her, "But there's only one thing left for me . . . you." I just get goosebumps thinking about it, you know. It's so intense, focused one on one.

𝒞: *In this opera, for me at least, Gilda comes off as the only one with a pure love. In today's society, especially concerning women's issues, I see Rigoletto as a tyrant of a father with an obsessive relationship with his daughter. The duke is a womanizer with no morals or scruples. How do you see this opera today concerning these issues?*

ℒ: Well, I think that if you look at it very carefully today there's not much change from the past, except you might not find someone as emotional or temperamental as Rigoletto.

𝒞: *I disagree. You find a lot of Rigoletto's today. Just look at the news.*

ℒ: What did you say about Gilda?

𝒞: *She was the only one with a pure love for the duke and her father.*

ℒ: I disagree with this. Gilda has a true love, but at the same time the father has a completely true love for her. He's so afraid to lose her, and for her, the same. Today, you love your daughter but it comes to a point where you're wondering how difficult it is for young people to go through life because it's so dangerous.

𝒞: *I see Rigoletto as having an obsessive, suffocating love for his daughter. Even if you say you're afraid to let her out for her own safety, it isn't love keeping a daughter trapped in the house. He was afraid to let her fall in love, to experience life. And I find that Verdi often made the women characters very shallow. It's not the opera singer's fault but Gilda does not have a great role in relation to Rigoletto and the duke, although she gets a lovely aria "Care nome" and duets. But in regard to the relationship I find that Rigoletto did not have a normal life and he did, as you said yourself, not what was best for his daughter but what was best for himself. That reflects on the morals of that period of society where virginity was considered a prize rather than a passage of time. He refused to give information to his daughter regarding her mother. He did not treat her as a woman, he treated her as an infant by not giving her information about her background and never having an adult conversation with her and not letting her experience knowledge and life.*

ℒ: There's a lot of controversy about this kind of opera. First of all it's not the libretto that Mr. Verdi wrote. Mr. Verdi wrote the music, but the plot itself was done by Alexandre Dumas. And that is the reason he took only what could be used from the play and put it in the opera.

𝒞: *Society then treated women shabbily — the 'madonna or whore syndrome'. Gilda/Maddalena. The music is wonderful, of course, but the libretto! I think if it were changed or written today it would have to accommodate women of today. I would certainly hope that women today would not put up with a Rigoletto and would certainly not put up with the Duke of Mantua. I find these operas historical pieces with glorious music but a sad reflection of women's times in that period of history.*

ℒ: In those years women did not have the liberty that they have today. The protection was not there. Women were there to service the man. Today it's not exactly the same thing: all this has been changed. But thank God that even in this kind of environment and play, let's face it, there was still a romanticism in those days more than today. There was always that mystery between the man and the woman and it made for exquisite music.

𝒞: *How do you play the scene with the daughter, then, when she asks about the mother?*

ℒ: This is the point that I never understood. Sometimes directors want Gilda to play it like, "Well, what about my mother?"

Rigoletto should say, "Oh, well your mother was . . ." No! It's just the opposite. This is the beauty of *Rigoletto*. It's up and down, up and down. And if you play it down, down, down, naturally . . . Verdi wrote such beautiful music that you are caught by this music. And the first thing you know, you are so caught by it, as well as the public, that you don't have to do anything with it. But if you can put a little bit of yourself into the role and try to understand the personality of Rigoletto you have a much greater interpretation than you could ever imagine. It was said to me so many times, "Mr. Quilico, I saw your Rigoletto. I never saw any other Rigoletto doing it that way." And I would ask, "Why do you say that?" The person would answer, "There is such a different mood. How do you manage to carry this off in this kind of a way?" The mood is very simple, it's written right there. Words, words mean everything.

𝒞: *So you've based your interpretation on the words and on what the music makes you feel.*

ℒ: It's very surprising that the words will give you an education, but Verdi's such a master that he gives you the inspiration through the music too. And this I don't understand when I see other people doing Rigoletto. I feel very sad for that reason. I don't see anything new or unique coming out of the role. They sing it very beautifully, some of them, they have beautiful voices and everything, but I would rather hear a man that has an ugly voice do it than to hear a man that has a beautiful voice and sings without meaning. I heard a lot of great ones. But there was not much interaction between their own souls, Verdi and the words.

𝒞: *That's what really makes the role then, a combination of all of it. Otherwise you just have the voice or you can read the text, but it's the interaction between the three aspects.*

ℒ: That's exactly right.

𝒞: *Now that you've identified yourself with the role, do you see yourself changing or is it just like a second skin, this role of Rigoletto?*

ℒ: Oh, no! With a role like Rigoletto you start the performance and you feel it a certain way. During the evening you don't feel too good or your mind has something that disturbs you — you'd be surprised how the interpretation of Rigoletto will change. But you have some people for whom it makes no difference. That is, they feel good, they don't feel good, they feel this sensation, they feel nothing. It's always the same thing and the same interpretation.

𝒞: *Does the character Rigoletto and the way that he feels about Gilda change? Is there sometimes a new feeling or perspective that you try to infuse into the role?*

ℒ: Absolutely, it changes. It's difficult to explain the change. You go according to the drama of the music. The big change, very often, is not a big change. It's a change of maybe one phrase. You did a phrase one way and all of a sudden you feel it differently. When you learn an opera you think you know it, but you never possess it because the man who wrote that opera was a master. You are not the master. There's always something that escapes you a little bit. Yes, sometimes maybe your performance is better than anybody else's. Your own thoughts about the opera itself are personal, yes, but at the same time they are given to you by the music and words.

𝒞: *If a stage director comes in and tells you to change your character, how do you feel about that?*

ℒ: I want to kill him. (laughter) You heard me the other day during a rehearsal of *Rigoletto.*

𝒞: *That's right. But you are in control of the role. You're not going to change your concept unless you feel it absolutely necessary. It' dictated to you by what you feel, not somebody else.*

ℒ: Well, that is the point, especially with *Rigoletto.* I've done so many productions, you come to a point where there is one conception of it. You have different moods, but not different conceptions of the role. For instance, the other day when I had an argument on the set and we were discussing the role, you have to understand what the person sees from the other side. They see Gilda, poor soul, but to study the role of Gilda is not living it.

For example, why does Rigoletto know about life? You know, we have children, and there are certain things you will not permit them, because something might have happened to you and you now have your way of looking at it. For instance, the other day when I was having the argument, it doesn't matter that I know Gilda at that point. She wants to explain to her father. But what creates a tremendous impact is that she wants to explain to him, at first, but she cannot. Because what she has been part of, what makes her guilty, is that Gilda was in love with the duke. She must also have had a great affinity for the more physical aspects of love as well. At that moment she doesn't want to say it and Rigoletto would like her to come to him, but she won't because she feels it's too terrible. She knows she's going to insult him.

Then for the second half, it's the opposite. When he says "Solo . . . ," "Only for me, the infamy . . ." How can you say this with your daughter in your arms? It's not possible. Something similar happened between my father and me, and my father practically killed me. They stopped my father. This happened because I swore at him. In those years you didn't swear at your parents. Imagine an altercation in Rigoletto's time. I feel these things very strongly: pain, sorrow, intensity and passion. This is why I have many people tell me, "When we see your *Rigoletto* we cry all the time, Mr. Quilico." I don't want to make them cry. But the thing is, he is that kind of a personality. And that is the beauty of that kind of role. I always enjoyed it: I always loved it.

I remember the first time I performed it I didn't understand anything. I was like the audience, completely 'gone' with the music. But when I started to understand Rigoletto, it became such a treasure. Like I always say, if I really love a person I wish I could transmit them one thing: to be able to have the chance to sing Rigoletto once in their life. The emotions are so powerful. If someone doesn't understand that, I'm sorry for them. Actually, maybe I was lucky to have sung it so many times.

𝒞: *What makes the vendetta so difficult to sing?*

ℒ: Because the music is so powerful. Just imagine that you're going to get killed and you cannot stop it. And the vendetta, that's what it is. It's something that starts, it's like a train, and it's coming and you cannot stop it. It's like scaring yourself.

𝒞: *So the intensity of the music is so overwhelming that you can almost lose it. One side of you has to keep control of the technical aspects of actually producing vocal sound without having your emotions completely overtake you.*

ℒ: Like I said before, I saw many other singers singing Rigoletto. But the problem with them is that maybe the music overpowered them.

𝒞: *Which is harder to sing: "Cortigiani" the aria, or the vendetta?*

ℒ: The vendetta! The "Cortigiani" is not easy, but the vendetta is tremendous. First you had the "Cortigiani," and that is a tremendous confrontation with the chorus. Then after that comes Gilda, and right in the middle before the vendetta the old man, Monterone, comes in and he curses the portrait of the duke. While you are his vengeance, he has the power. And then you have to sing the vendetta. And all this is such a hurricane of thought, a hurricane of interpretation that is incredibly intense, you get caught by it. That is the thing with Rigoletto. You have to come to a point where you can control it, because you cannot let yourself go.

I got caught quite a few times, especially in the duet with Gilda. I don't know now if it will happen but I sang many, many performances crying like a baby when she sings explaining to him what has happened. Not the duet with her, but after she's been abducted. I go through hell sometimes. And this is why, very often, it came to the point where I used to say to myself, I'm not going to sing it any more, because it used to overpower me. And you cannot be overpowered with a role like Rigoletto. People always say, Oh well, I'm completely in the role . . . no way! That's very dangerous. You're the one who has to control it. But at the same time this emotion is a fight in you; it's quite something. You need a very special kind of mind to do these kinds of opera.

𝒞: *These are such deep emotions that we don't normally see in everyday life and that's why, in fact, I think that there's such an avid curiosity for live courtroom drama. People thrive on what they don't have in their own lives. Opera makes use of these deep, secret emotions — the killing, the love, and the overpowering passion that people have for each other and for their principles. Somebody suggested that Gilda committed suicide.*

ℒ: Well, at the end it became a suicide. She says, "My father, he wants a corpse, he's going to have my corpse and that's it."

𝒞: *She dies for love.*

ℒ: You just said it, she dies for love. Because, even while she's dying at the end she asks for forgiveness for the duke. How much forgiveness can you give for someone that helps you to die? He's not exactly the one that kills her, but thanks to him she dies.

𝒞: *What do you think the relationship was between Rigoletto and his wife?*

ℒ: That was never really clear, was it? Maybe she was not beautiful, God knows! But for him she was completely beautiful. That's the temperament of Rigoletto. Things happen and he cannot control them. For instance, he said, "The courtiers, I make them laugh." He's too intense about everything. He's too involved with many different situations and that is the big problem with his kind of character. It's so immense that you are completely overpowered with something that you cannot control.

Highlights and Reviews

What the Critics Said of the Quilico Voice

"Quilico seems to have everything a big-time baritone needs, a great rich controlled voice that inspires opera buffs to rush worshipfully to the footlights."

— *Maclean's Magazine*

"Mr. Quilico sang in a golden-age manner, making easily the finest vocal impression of the night."

— *The New York Times*

"A voice of glorious quality. Louis Quilico dominated the vocal scene. He seemed to be in the top of his great vocal form for not only was his voice robustly beautiful, but it was also a superb interpretive instrument."

— *The Globe and Mail, Toronto*

"Splendid Quilico Voice"

— *Toronto Telegram*

"Quilico in opulent voice finds no difficulty in dominating the stage."

— *Toronto Star*

"Louis Quilico was an example of well-focused, smooth vocalism."

— *The New York Times*

"The Quilico voice, always attractive, seemed even more beautiful. As an interpretative instrument it ranks with the past great baritone voices heard."

— *Toronto Telegram*

"Blessed with a gorgeous voice, Quilico showed the splendor of his vocalism."

— *New York Post*

"His baritone voice proved of splendid quality."

— *San Francisco News*

"Louis Quilico...I believe him to be the best all-round baritone in opera."

— *Newsday, Houston*

"[T]empered steel-voice in a velvet glove. Louis Quilico, shades of Tito Gobbi and the young Leonard Warren. A glorious voice."

— *Honolulu Star — Bulletin*

"Louis Quilico...gave us a demonstration of powerful, controlled singing, he soared above the stave in ringing fashion. His voice possesses that Italianate quality so important in Verdi. An evening of beautiful singing."

— *New York Post*

Highlights from Opera Reviews

Adriana Lecouvreur — The Met
with Montserrat Caballé and José Carreras

"Louis Quilico made a strong and sympathetic Michonnet."
— *Opera, London, May 1978*

"As Michonnet, Louis Quilico...has a gorgeous baritone which he uses expertly."
— *New York Post, February 6, 1978*

Adriana Lecouvreur — Montreal

"Il fait soulinger l'exceptionnelle participation du baryton Louis Quilico. Il a se rapport avec Michonnet — le régisseur de la Comedie-Française, l'amoureux transi et fidèle ami d'Adriana — une superbe dignité vocale."
— *La Presse, September 13, 1990*

Aida — Covent Garden
with Galina Vishnevskaya

"The most interesting thing in the performance is Louis Quilico's sonorous, dignified Amonasro."

— *David Cairns, London Times, 1961*

Aida — Covent Garden
with Gloria Davy and Rita Gorr

"Mr. Quilico made a terrific impression with his opening cry of 'Suo padre'. One sensed an electric thrill around the house."

— *Andrew Porter, London Times, July 1960*

"The new Amonasro, Mr. Louis Quilico is another excellent acquisition to the cast, with a vibrant yet muscular and incisive vocal delivery and a vivid appreciation of words."

— *The Times, July 1, 1960*

Aida — with Mario del Monaco,
Lucine Amara and Giorgio Tozzi

"Louis Quilico was a splendid majestic Amonasro perfectly immersed in his role and its outstanding music. And he was wonderfully team minded rather than competitive in his duets with Miss Amara."

— *San Francisco Bulletin, October 3, 1959*

"Louis Quilico sang beautifully with big tone and fine understanding of the role."

— *San Francisco Chronicle, October 4, 1959*

Aida — Paris Opera
with Leontyne Price

"Il faudra la superbe autorité de roi Amonasro, M. Quilico pour éviter le désastre."

— *L'Express, Paris, February 12–18, 1968*

Aida — with Leontyne Price

"Quilico donne à Amonasro un puissant relief vocal; il a été trés applaudit."

— Le Figaro, Paris, Fevrier 2, 1964

Aida — Centre Filled for Trudeau (Prime Minister) . . .

"Louis Quilico, from the time he appeared in the 2nd act to the end of the 3rd he dominated the vocal scene. He seemed to be in the top of his great vocal form for not only was his voice robustly beautiful, but it was also a superb interpretive instrument, that conveyed tenderness and remorse as effectively as it communicated anger and stormy passion."

— The Globe and Mail, September 14, 1968

Aida — with Carol Neblett, Vladimir Popov and José Garcia

"Canadian baritone Louis Quilico was great as Amonasro, Aida's formidable papa; he's simply a crowd-pleasing charmer with loads of charisma."

— The Edmonton Journal, May 6, 1989

Alzira — Carnegie Hall with Elinor Ross

"Among those who stood out was the Gusmano, Louis Quilico, a superb Canadian baritone, whom I had not previously heard and who showed himself to be not only the possessor of a fine voice with ringing upper tones but also the possessor of a mind capable of infusing color and dramatic tension into that voice. His death scene, at the end, was magnificently done. With reliance purely on sound, Mr. Quilico is a find."

— The New Yorker, January 27, 1968

"It turned out to be the baritone's evening, however, not only because Verdi gave him the best tune but because Louis Quilico (Gusmano) proved stylish as well as stalwart."

— *Opera News, February 17, 1968*

The Barber of Seville — Florida

"Baritone, Louis Quilico as Rosina's guardian Dr. Bartolo, possessed the most exciting voice of the evening. His rich and powerful voice here made him a leading baritone with the Metropolitan Opera. Quilico commanded numerous laughs with his comic antics as the jealous Dr. Bartolo, demonstrating an acting ability to match his voice."

— *Palm Beach Daily News, January 24, 1994*

"The center of gravity was not the conniving barber, Figaro but the crusty old goat, Dr. Bartolo. That's because veteran Louis Quilico had quite a romp with the Bartolo role, bringing the character to life in one colourful, even delightfully hammy, gesture after another...Quilico's generally robust, cleanly articulated tones left little to be desired musically."

— *Sun-Sentinel, January 24, 1994*

"In this Barber he was the focal Dr. Bartolo...he displayed a deft touch for the fatuous old doctor and the voice. Quilico knows how to be amusingly exasperated without resorting to blatant burlesque...the performance struck a nice balance in comedy."

— *Miami Herald, January 24, 1994*

Cavalleria Rusticana and I Pagliacci — The Met

"Louis Quilico has perhaps never sounded better than he did in the prologue."

— *The New York Times, January 26, 1978*

Don Carlos — Paris Opera

"De toute la distribution, seul le baryton canadien, Louis Quilico est tout à fait digne de son rôle celin du marquis di Posa."

— *France-Soir, March 11, 1963*

"M. Quilico nous a donné une interpretation très musicale."

— *Le Parisien, November 3, 1963*

Don Carlo — Philadelphia Lyric Opera with Franco Corelli, Nicolai Ghiaurov and Raina Kabavianska

"Louis Quilico, as Rodrigo singing with unflagging zeal and beautiful round tones. His big moment came in the prison scene. He has rarely appeared to such advantage here."

— *Philadelphia Evening Bulletin*
October 26, 1966

Don Carlo — with Jerome Hines

"Luigi Quilico ha prestato un note volissimo temperamento et la sua bella voce a suggestita figura de Marchese di Posa."

— *Palermo, Italy, June 13, 1964*

Esclarmonde — with Joan Sutherland and Richard Bonynge

"Louis Quilico, dramatically and vocally the star of the opera."

— *Long Island Press, 1976*

Falstaff — Montreal with Clarice Carson

"Louis Quilico sings the title role most impressively. Quilico's voice seems ideally suited to the part of

Falstaff and when he gives his impersonation of the role more depth, adds several dimensions to it, this may well become one of the most important performances of our time."

— *Montreal Gazette, October 9, 1974*

"Louis Quilico is excellent in the part, not only for his singing, but for his acting. He manages to put across the fat knight's rapid changes of mood, his natural authority, his self delusions and also the pathetic side of the man."

— *Eric McLean, Montreal Star, October 9, 1974*

Admirable Falstaff Upstages Stratford . . .

"Quilico, in opulent voice, finds no difficulty in dominating the stage during the great monologues."

— *William Littler, Toronto Star, September 17, 1982*

Faust — Debut at the Met

"Singing Valentine for the first time at the Met was Louis Quilico. Best of all Mr. Quilico sang in a golden-age manner, too, making easily the finest vocal impression of the night."

— *The New York Times, January 20, 1973*

I Due Foscari — Hamilton, Ontario

"Louis Quilico anchored the action, his impassioned baritone and tired dignity filling the elder Foscari with the faded splendor of a powerless doge."

— *Opera Canada, December 23, 1989*

Opera Hamilton Overcomes Verdi's Warning of Boredom . . .

"Canadian baritone, Louis Quilico, sang the part of Francesco Foscari with warmth, compassion and suffering. The production offered...in the Canadian baritone

Louis Quilico, a Francesco Foscari with the warmth, compassion and suffering in his voice of a great man rendered impotent."

— *Toronto Star, September 25, 1989*

"The elder Foscari is sung by baritone Louis Quilico. His is a much warmer voice filled with pathos which he effectively makes sound more feeble as the crunching hopelessness of his position becomes apparent."

— *The Buffalo News, September 22, 1989*

Bravo! Opera Hamilton Triumphs with Verdi's I Due Foscari Louis Quilico Said It All . . .

"Not the least of the treasures they dug up was a superb dramatic performance from Quilico himself. His voice, huge, noble and perfectly cast in the role of the aging Doge, Quilico cracked and roared his grief in superb style.... Last night he was magnificent."

— *The Spectator, September 22, 1989*

I Puritani — with Beverly Sills and Luciano Pavarotti

"Louis Quilico confirmed the belief that for all the coloratura fireworks, Bellini wrote best for low voices."

— *Philadelphia Inquirer, January 20, 1972*

I Puritani — London Philharmonic with Beverly Sills and Nicolai Gedda

"Louis Quilico infuses it with life."

— *Records, Opera News, Winter 1972*

Il Duca d'Alba — Spoleto

"The really cultivated singing of the evening is supplied by the Canadian baritone, Louis Quilico."

— *The New York Times, July 12, 1959*

Il Trovatore — San Francisco with Leontyne Price and Jussi Björling

"Louis Quilico turned in a flawless interpretation of Count di Luna. Coloratura baritones are perhaps the hardest of all to find and a baritone as silky-suave and big in sound as Quilico is greatly to be cherished."

— *San Francisco Examiner, October 19, 1958*

Substitute Baritone a Hit in Opera . . .

"As di Luna (Quilico) he was again a true Verdian baritone of high order. His voice has dark, broad power perfectly suited to Italian melodrama. In addition to his dramatic impact, he sang his big aria 'Il balen' with a fine, expressive, melodic flow. He had the top tones to bring the aria, and his other prime moments to grand climax. As a stage figure, Quilico takes a simple approach. His voice was able to make full effect without subtle histrionics, and he was a major reason why the sell-out audience let fly with cheers."

— *San Francisco Examiner, November 4, 1968*

Quilico Stops Show . . .

"Also cheered was Quilico, Canadian-born baritone who has sung several roles here, but none better than this. In a few short years, Quilico has become one of the top baritones of today. His straightforward, rousingly sung 'Il balen' won an ovation that stopped the show."

— *Philadelphia Inquirer, November 1, 1962*

Il Trovatore — with Franco Corelli

"Mr. Quilico, a Canadian baritone with a very forward, resonant voice and admirable style in its employment had a great success and scored an ovation after the aria 'Il balen' encompassed with complete ease and brought down the house."

— *Philadelphia Evening Chronicle, November 1, 1962*

Il Trovatore — The Met with Leontyne Price

"Louis Quilico's burly baritone and performing style, to say nothing of his brilliant top notes were superbly suited to the one of Count di Luna."

— *New York Daily News, January 18, 1982*

"Count di Luna was superbly sung and acted by Louis Quilico."

— *New York Post, January 18, 1982*

Iphigénie en Tauride — Carnegie Hall with Gloria Davy, Martial Singher and Martina Arroyo

"Louis Quilico, a mellow baritone was impressive as Thoas."

— *The New York Times, January 20, 1959*

"The surprise of the evening however, was baritone Louis Quilico, whose vibrant quality and dynamic interpretation as Thoas, King of Tauris, made a remarkable impression."

— *New York Post, January 20, 1959*

La Fanciulla del West — Strasbourg

"As Jack Rance, Louis Quilico was the best of a very good team. Both in voice and in acting he was the dominating presence on stage."

— *Opera, October 1964*

La Gioconda — The Met with Renata Scotto

"Baritone Louis Quilico quite impressive in his first Barnaba."

— *New York Daily News, 1979*

La Parisina d'Este — Carnegie Hall
with Montserrat Caballé and James Morris

"The role of Azzo was sung very well by Louis Quilico. His voice is both big and rich and he was never less than impressive."

— *New York Post, March 8, 1974*

"Louis Quilico and James Morris, had commanding voices and styles which provided some exciting, resonating moments."

— *The New York Times, March 8, 1974*

La Traviata — Debut at the Met
with Gilda Cruz-Romo

"Louis Quilico sang his first Germont with the company. He gave a vocally robust account of the notes and filled out the part with small but telling characterizational niceties."

— *The New York Times, January 3, 1973*

La Traviata — Covent Garden
with Mary Costa

"It was the Canadian baritone, Louis Quilico who scored the vocal honors. He made the stern father of Alfredo a compelling figure and his passionate singing gave more character to the music than all the others."

— *London Times, January 1962*

La Traviata — Covent Garden
with Joan Sutherland and Alfredo Kraus

"Quilico, a magnificent baritone too long absent and a grand stage presence, capped the scene with a beautifully paced di Provenza (Verdi's greatest hurdle)."

— *Arts Guardian, January 7, 1975*

"Il peut se comporter en très grand artiste. La voix hier soir avait une rondeur, une force, une expression, une justesse admirables, et son jeu avait tour à tour la tendresse et la sévérité voulues."

— *La Presse, May 3, 1972*

La Traviata: Warm Welcome for Louis Quilico in L'opera du Quebec's Production . . .

"The fact that Louis Quilico is a Montrealer had something to do with the warmth of his reception from last night's audience, but there were more important factors involved. There was no question but that he offered the surest characterization and the most beautiful singing of the evening. Germont père all but stole the show."

— *Montreal Star, May 3, 1972*

"Digne et imposant dans son rôle de père, pureté de style et opulence de la voix étaient constamment au service de l'expression."

— *Le Devoir, May 4, 1972*

La Traviata
— with Barbara Daniels and Enrico di Giuseppe

"Top honors of the evening go to Louis Quilico, another Met regular, who played the Elder Germont. He is a big man with a big voice of house-filling capacity."

— *Pittsburgh Press, January 19, 1977*

Elder Germont of Louis Quilico Saves La Traviata . . .

"It is worthwhile to attend the opera, just for Louis Quilico's interpretation of the elder Germont. His was the only valid interpretation of the role."

— *The Globe and Mail, September 5, 1966*

Traviata Rolled Out Again to Be Saved by Quilico . . .

"Fortunately for the salvation of this act and of the production as a whole, Louis Quilico as the elder Germont came looking for the Violetta of the evening. The Canadian baritone is in superb form these days, able to spin out the almost too-honeyed tones of 'di Provenza il mar' in a rich legato rivaled by few of his contemporaries. Both in voice and carriage he simply is Germont."

— William Littler, Toronto Star, September 21, 1970

Another Triumph for Louis Quilico . . .

"In this act, baritone Louis Quilico gives us a Germont, as good on its very different terms, as the Macbeth he gave us last week — marvelously sung and full of the dignity one needs from Germont. Quilico sings in tune with unfailing musicality. His voice is beautiful too, but more important than its beauty is its obedience and flexibility, its way of exploring the moods and underlying the contour of the phrase. Indeed, if last night's Germont and last week's Macbeth are typical of his current work, Quilico must surely take a place with Gobbi and Fischer-Dieskau among the foremost operatic baritones of our time."

— Toronto Telegram, September 21, 1966

Les Troyens — The Met
with Jon Vickers, Judith Blegen and Shirley Verrett

"Louis Quilico made a stalwart Choroebus."

— Opera in Canada

Lucia di Lammermoor — Covent Garden
with Joan Sutherland and Luciano Pavarotti

"We have Louis Quilico, welcome back as the villainous Lord Henry, warm and wooing of voice, no rasping or brawling rascal but dignified and firm, a calculating, diplomatic scoundrel — utterly convincing."

— The Times, May 17, 1973

"Lucia's brother was played by Louis Quilico, a splendid Canadian baritone from the New York Metropolitan and for far too long absent from the Royal Opera House."

— *Evening Standard, May 17, 1973*

Lucrezia Borgia — Vancouver Opera with Joan Sutherland

"Another great pleasure was hearing Louis Quilico's Don Alfonso which was sonorously energetic without being swashbuckling and successfully projected varying degrees of malice and vehemence."

— *The Province, October 27, 1972*

Luisa Miller — San Francisco with Luciano Pavarotti and Katia Ricciarelli

Some Opera Singing to Melt Your Spumoni . . .

"Miller has others marvelously exploited by Louis Quilico's Rigolettan voice which also dramatized the brilliant letter-reading sequence brilliantly."

— *San Francisco Herald-Tribune, November 1974*

Canadian Opera's Macbeth a Marvel by Any Yardstick . . .

"Louis Quilico is a baritone with few peers and couples this with a stage presence that rivets you to your seat."

— *Toronto Telegram, September 29, 1971*

Macbeth — CBC TV Telecast

"Louis Quilico is known today as one of the finest Rigolettos to be heard on the operatic stage. He may also be the best Macbeth. His is one of the most powerful baritone voices Canada has produced."

— *Eric McLean, Montreal Star, November 17, 1973*

Macbeth — with Marisa Galvany

"Vocally, Louis Quilico as Macbeth dominated the opera."

— *The Tulsa Tribune, March 11, 1977*

Macbeth — The Met with James Levine

"Louis Quilico, this solid baritone did not disappoint. He gave us a demonstration of powerful, controlled singing, especially in 'Pieta' where he soared above the stave in ringing fashion. His voice possesses that Italianate quality so important in Verdi. The straightforward, musical approach brought an evening of beautiful singing — probably his best ever — from Quilico as Macbeth."

— *New York Post, December 10, 1982*

Quilico a Memorable Macbeth . . .

"In this one, it is Macbeth himself who dominates the production, and the memories that are likely to last longest are of Quilico's performance."

— *The Gazette, June 2, 1983*

Le "Macbeth" de verdi . . . et de Quilico . . .

"Reste Quilico. Il s'impose sans conteste come le héros de ce spectacle. Voix puissante, richement timbrée, plus nuancée que d'ordinaire chez lui.... En pleine possession du rôle, il le chante avec une autorité sans faille et une musicalité à l'avenant. Au point de conférer à son Macbeth une dimension que Verdi et son librettiste Piave n'ont pas su lui apporter."

— *Le Soleil, June 4, 1983*

Macbeth: Quilico Triomphe

"Dès son entrée; Quilico s'est révélé dans une forme remarquable et tout au long des quatre actes, il a littéralement rempli sans arrêt la vaste enceinte de sa voix d'or. À tous moments, l'expression atteignait des sommets, tant dans les passages ou il doit affirmer une autorité aveugle que dans ceux plus pathétiques quand il reconnait l'absurdité et l'inutilité des gestes qu'il a proféré sous l'influence démoniaque de sa femme. À cet égard, son grand air final, 'Pietà, rispetto, amore' fut une démonstration de grand art et lui a valu une véritable ovation. On n'en finirait plus de détailler une interprétation qui n'a probablement pas son pareil nulle part."

— *Le Devoir, June 1, 1983*

Un Macbeth magnifiquement rendu à la place des arts . . .

"Louis Quilico reçoit une ovation debout au rideau final, pour une interprétation magistrale du rôle-titre."

— *Le Nouvelliste, June 11, 1983*

"Louis Quilico in the title role gave a characteristically assured performance, honorably acted and strongly sung."

— *The New York Times, December 10, 1982*

"Baritone Louis Quilico sang Macbeth with his customary tonal resplendence."

— *Daily News, December 9, 1982*

Madama Butterfly — Vancouver with Teresa Stratas

"Louis Quilico endowed the role of the American Consul Sharpless, with considerable depth and sincerity."

— *Victoria Daily Times, July 23, 1960*

Madama Butterfly — Los Angeles with Dorothy Kirsten

"Mr. Quilico again demonstrated the smoothness of his voice."

— *Los Angeles Times, November 5, 1956*

Madama Butterfly — San Francisco with Licia Albanese

"The new Sharpless was Louis Quilico, who gave a good account of the role."

— *San Francisco News, October 8, 1956*

Manon Lescaut — San Francisco with Jussi Björling and Dorothy Kirsten

"Louis Quilico made a gratifying debut as Lescaut. His baritone voice proved of splendid quality, and he was eminently stageworthy."

— *San Francisco News, September 14, 1956*

"A new baritone, Louis Quilico was introduced in the role of Lescaut and proved to be one of the most interesting singers we have ever heard. He has a big, velvety extremely colorful voice, seems to know how to act and should be one of the company's most valuable members."

— *San Francisco Chronicle, September 9, 1956*

"Lescaut, sergeant of the King's Guards, was sung by newcomer, the baritone Louis Quilico, who gave an excellent portrayal and sang in a lusty pleasing voice."

— *San Francisco Bulletin, September 11, 1956*

Most Happy Fella — New York City Opera

"Louis Quilico's Tony, at the center of the production, skilfully and often touchingly manoeuvred his way through a role that spans high drama and low sentimentality. His accent was unaffected and convincing; he was able to give 'Happy to Make Your Acquaintance' an infectious charm, and use his focused baritone to suggest an ecstatic anticipation of pleasure that the plot always went out of its way to frustrate."

— *The New York Times, September 6, 1991*

Oedipus Rex — Toronto
with Igor Stravinsky, Marilyn Horne and Robert Kraft

"Louis Quilico, the best of the excellent soloists. Mr. Quilico as Creon, Ernst Hoefliger as Oedipus and Marilyn Horne as Jocasta contributed superbly."

— *Toronto Telegram, May 16, 1961*

Opera Gala — with Luciano Pavarotti, Jess Thomas, Claramae Turner, Giorgio Tozzi, Anna Tomova-Sintow, James King, Katia Ricciarelli, Hugette Tourangeau

"Louis Quilico just great in the Barber's aria 'Largo al factotum'."

— *San Francisco Chronicle, November 23, 1974*

Otello — The Met
with Jon Vickers and Teresa Zylis-Gara

"His 'Credo' was expounded with subtle attention to the shading of its clauses."

— *The New Yorker, December 16, 1972*

"Louis Quilico singing Iago for the first time was impressively sinister."

— *New York Daily News, December 6, 1972*

"Louis Quilico, blessed with a gorgeous voice sang his first Met Iago...and showed the splendour of his vocalism."

— *New York Post, December 6, 1972*

"The new Iago revealed no surprises. In his previous work around town, Mr. Quilico has shown himself to be an imposing vocalist with an imposing presence. His is a big well-trained voice capable of impressive bursts of sound."

— *Harold Schönberg, The New York Times, December 7, 1972*

Otello — Philadelphia with Renata Tebaldi and Jon Vickers

"Louis Quilico brought with him excellent notation of Iago. He quite dominated the early scenes with an enveloping presence."

— *Philadelphia Evening Bulletin*
December 6, 1967

Otello — Cincinnati with Mary Costa

"Louis Quilico displayed the vital spark that brings this taxing role to life."

— *The Post, July 23, 1970*

"Louis Quilico evoked one burst of applause after another. In Iago's 'Credo' Quilico evoked an ovation. He sang it with all the wickedness the original Shakesperean villain meant."

— *The Cincinnati Enquirer, July 23, 1970*

Pelléas et Mélisande — New York City Opera

"The hero of the stage however, was Louis Quilico as Golaud. He was magnificent as the husband, driven mad by suspicion and misplaced love. His diction was superb, his voice vibrant. Altogether, he made a towering figure. In himself he was an evening of histrionic excitement."

— *New York Post, March 19, 1970*

Pelléas et Mélisande — Debut at the Met

"A baritone long familiar to the American scene Louis Quilico made an unexpected debut with the Metropolitan in Pelleas et Mélisande on February 10. His characterization of Golaud has been admired at the New York City Opera, but in the glowing musical-dramatic framework provided by the Heeley, Deiber-Davis team his portrayal reached even greater distinction. And it should be noted that his voice filled the house nobly."

— *Opera News, March 18, 1972*

Louis Quilico, Hero of the Evening . . .

"By far the best work of the evening was done by Louis Quilico as Golaud.... Mr. Quilico sang with a good deal of style, with clear enunciation and with a constant threat in his burly figure. Here was a real artist at work."

— *Harold Schönberg, The New York Times*
March 20, 1970

"Louis Quilico is among the finest Golauds I have ever heard with every word of his role distinct and understandable."

— *Winthrop Sargeant, The New Yorker,*
October 31, 1970

"The hero of the evening was that splendid baritone Louis Quilico, one of the finest Golauds I have ever heard or seen."

— *The New Yorker, March 28, 1970*

The Queen of Spades — Covent Garden with Marie Collier

"Louis Quilico lifted up his splendid baritone to good effect in the solo for Prince Yeletsky."

— *The Guardian, December 4, 1961*

"Mr. Louis Quilico fully deserved the ovation his second-act aria won."

— *The Times, December 4, 1961*

Roberto Devereux — with Beverly Sills and Placido Domingo

"Louis Quilico, as the Duke of Nottingham, had an imposing presence and sang powerfully."

— *The New Yorker, October 24, 1970*

Roberto Devereux
— with Beverly Sills and Placido Domingo

"Louis Quilico sang with huge, beautiful tone...his contribution was enormous."

— *Dallas Times-Herald, October 18, 1970*

"Mr. Quilico was strong in every department."

— *The New York Times, October 16, 1970*

Samson et Dalila — San Francisco
with Marilyn Horne

"Louis Quilico turned in a commanding performance as the high priest. In his invocation to the god Dagon (a marvellous duet with Dalila) in the final act, the effect and the excitement of the music was enough to make pagans of at least half the audience."

— *Sacramento Union, October 22, 1983*

"Louis Quilico as the High Priest of Dagon appears in some outfits that are beyond spectacular. His singing, by the way is some of the best work he's done — impressive from top to bottom. He commands the stage completely."

— *San Francisco Examiner, October 21, 1983*

"Louis Quilico, as the High Priest of Dagon was quite another story, the firebrand of the affair. His baritone voice, with its natural wealth of overtones and direct penetration, was stirring, his performance inflammatory."

— *San Francisco Chronicle, October 22, 1983*

Tales of Hoffmann — Strasbourg

"M. Louis Quilico efface tous ceux qui l'ont précedé dans les quatre emplois de Lindorf, Coppeluis, Dapertutto et du Dr. Miracle. Une voix multiforme dira-t-on. Oui, et qui monte encore plus facilerment qu'elle ne descend. Mais elle est d'une qualité rare de plus le comédien et le chanteur sont pareillement remarquables."

— *Strasbourg, December 24, 1965*

Tannhäuser — Paris Opera

"Louis Quilico, très beaux Wolfram, chant la Romance à l'Etoile avec un gôut exquis."

— *Le Parisien, August 7, 1963*

Thérèse — National Arts Center, Ottawa with Mignon Dunn

"Quilico was in splendid voice throughout the evening."

— *Ottawa Citizen, July 28, 1980*

Tosca — San Francisco with Placido Domingo and Dorothy Kirsten

"Quilico should go down in the books as one of the best Scarpia's seen in Van Ness. He plays the role with relish, giving us a police chief who does things with dispatch and a barely concealed malevolence. Not a man to meet in a dark alley. But one with an impressive baritone voice, mellifluous enough and pointed in its delivery."

— *Examiner, San Francisco, November 23, 1970*

Tosca — with Renata Tebaldi and Giuseppe di Stefano

"Quilico's performance in the villain's role was worth watching. He conveyed the character strongly."

— *Philadelphia Inquirer, December 16, 1969*

Tosca — with Klara Barlow and Richard Tucker

"And Louis Quilico? I believe him to be the best all-round baritone in opera...gave a magnificent performance. The man sang beautifully and the stage crackled with excitement whenever he appeared. Quilico is everything an opera singer should be. He sings faultlessly, acts with intelligence and intensity, and generally improves every score in which he performs."

— *Newsday, Houston, December 30, 1971*

Tosca — with Dorothy Kirsten and Barry Morell

"And Louis Quilico, tempered steel voice in a velvet glove, dripping malice. Louis Quilico, shades of Tito Gobbi and the young Leonard Warren. A glorious voice and as an actor absolutely superb."

— *Honolulu Star-Bulletin, February 16, 1971*

Tosca — Met on tour at Wolf Trap with Gilda Cruz-Romo and Barry Morell

"Louis Quilico was a marvelous Scarpia in last night's Metropolitan Opera performance of Tosca."

— *Washington Post, June 9, 1977*

Tosca — Seattle Opera with Raina Kabavianska and Barry Morell

"Louis Quilico created a masterpiece of menace in his role as Scarpia. His interpretation is carefully crafted, with a score of tiny details contributing to the most sinister malevolence."

— *Seattle Times, May 6, 1977*

Tosca Came to Life with Quilico's Entrance . . .

"With Louis Quilico's entrance, dramatic tension came to an opera which cannot survive without it."

— *Toronto Star, September 23, 1968*

Tosca — Houston Opera with Teresa Kubiak

"Impressive opposite her was Louis Quilico's silkily sinister Scarpia."

— *Opera News, December 25, 1971*

Un Ballo in Maschera — The Met
with Luciano Pavarotti and Katia Ricciarelli

"Louis Quilico's sturdy baritone was likewise in fine shape for Renato, giving full Verdian sweep and dignity to every phrase — his exceptional delivery of 'Eri Tu' earned him the first real ovation of the evening."

— *New York Daily News, 1980*

"Louis Quilico — his 'Eri Tu' was an example of well-focused, smooth vocalism."

— *Harold Schönberg,*
The New York Times, 1980

Un Ballo in Maschera
— with Jon Vickers and Elinor Ross

"Mr. Quilico's voice remained his loyal and obedient servant and his 'Eri Tu' was the heart-breaker it is meant to be."

— *Houston Post, 1964*

Un Ballo in Maschera
— with Giuseppe di Stefano and Antonietta Stella
'Upstaged' Tenor Delays 'Masked Ball' . . .

"Quilico brought vocal and dramatic forthrightness to his portrayal of Renato. His singing of the famous 'Eri Tu' as usual stopped the show."

— *Philadelphia Inquirer, November 27, 1963*

Un Ballo in Maschera — with Giuseppe di Stefano

"Greatest applause of the evening was reserved for Louis Quilico with his baritone aria 'Eri Tu' by far the greatest of the score. The house applauded Mr. Quilico for several minutes after his beautiful singing of one of Verdi's finest inspirations. Even better was his first act "Alla vita che m'aride." Quilico's tone has a brilliant resonance."

— *Philadelphia Evening Bulletin,*
November 27, 1963

Un Ballo in Maschera — NY City Opera with Gilda Cruz-Romo and Enrico di Giuseppe

"Louis Quilico, as Renato is hard to fault and he rose nobly to his big moment, the 'Eri Tu'. It is not only that he has a resonant voice. He is also a first class musician with impeccable diction and superior acting ability."

— *Harold Schönberg, The New York Times, April 3, 1971*

"Louis Quilico sang the role of Renato about as well as it can be sung, with a sonorous baritone voice and considerable dramatic effect."

— *Winthrop Sargeant, The New Yorker, April 3, 1971*

William Tell — Carnegie Hall with Klara Barlow and Eve Queler

"Louis Quilico...sang as expected, with authority, resonance and skill. This fine artist never gives a bad performance...has a power, a wide range, an easy delivery. Best of all, Mr. Quilico is a superior musician."

— *Harold Schönberg, The New York Times, March 15, 1972*

"Met and New York City Opera baritone Louis Quilico, in the title role was superb, his impressive rich baritone rolling out with splendor and especially so in his most important aria in Act III."

— *New York Post, March 15, 1972*

Singer, Pianist in Fine Form, Quilico Shows He Still Has It after 25 Years . . .

"Quilico showed powers undiminished in a program of familiar operatic arias. He was partnered by his wife Christina Petrowska, who also took a solo turn in three operatic realizations by Liszt.... You need a singer capable of instantly fixing the character in the mind's eye and Quilico did just that in splendid voice with bloom and power to spare. He's a wonderful Don Giovanni — sly yet ingratiating, caressing in 'Deh Vieni al finestra' and sparkling in the Catalogue aria. 'Eri Tu' from Verdi's 'Masked Ball' was more spaciously paced than usual but the menace was there, with Quilico delivering Verdi's words as if he believed everyone. Quilico has 510 Rigoletto's to his credit, so there was no doubting an intimate rapport in 'Cortigiani'. Arias from Prince Igor, Herodiade and Tannhäuser were delivered with the most rapt line and ideal proportion."

— *James Manishen, The Winnipeg Free Press, 31 March 1995*

Baritone Delights Audiences with Golden Chords . . .

"Louis Quilico, acclaimed baritone of the Metropolitan Opera and Christina Petrowska, pianist, brought the house to a standing ovation in the final concert of the Barrie Concert Association series Saturday evening. The golden vocal cords of this 69-year old singer have the years of training and performance to offer a very seasoned recital. Supported with the relaxed accompaniment of Christina Petrowska, this couple makes beautiful music."

— *Simon Phillips, The Barrie Examiner, 3 May 1995*

Old Pro Quilico Still Knows How . . .

"The product, last night, was an agreeable display of professionalism, charm and longevity by one of Canada's greatest singers."

— *Montreal Gazette, 5 May 1995*

Louis Quilico/Christina Petrowska — Two of a Kind

"Quilico sings remarkably for a man of 70 and still commands a rich storehouse of tone."

— *Toronto Star, 10 February 1996*

"Now in his 70s, Quilico sings with the assurance of a man fully in command of his craft. His top notes are there when needed; no sign of strain affects the middle range where songs demand so much inflection. His articulation ensures each word is clear as his voice weights its meaning.

His program reminded listeners of the breadth of his singing life....

With his wife, Christina Petrowska, at the piano, he surveyed some less-than-usual Russian songs before touching songs nearer the center of the repertoire....

He was always the singer in these, even at the height of towering passion."

— *Daniel Webster, Philadelphia Inquirer, May 11, 1996*

Highlights from Rigoletto Reviews

Opera: Rigoletto at the Met . . .

"Though Luciano Pavarotti as the Duke may attract the most attention, Louis Quilico, as Rigoletto, was at the center of the drama; his passions and fears could be heard in his voice as well as seen in his face and body. His "La rà, la rà, la la" seemed sobbed out by a jester who has lived too long and seen too much."

— *The New York Times,*
December 11, 1981

Quilico, Bernardi:
The Stars of Rigoletto . . .

"Two of the greatest things to happen to the Canadian Opera Company this season happened last night when the company gave the first of six performances of Verdi's Rigoletto at O'Keefe Centre.... The one was baritone Louis Quilico in the title role; the other, conductor Mario Bernardi.... The role of Rigoletto is not new to Quilico, but last night's interpretation demonstrated that an artist who has been superb in past performances can still bring freshness and insight to a part one might suspect was beginning to pall on him after an endless number of performances.... He was not playing the role: he was Rigoletto, revealing vividly the twisted side of his character, yet commanding the audience's full sympathy.... The Quilico voice, always attractive, seemed even more beautiful. As an interpretive instrument it ranks with the past great baritone voices heard in this role.... His singing of the Cortigiani recitative and aria was enough to tear even the most blasé listener to emotional shreds."

— *The Globe and Mail, September 26, 1969*

A Base Hit at Last for Toronto Opera as Rigoletto Opens . . .

"No Rigoletto team would be right, naturally, without a singing actor of major stature in the title role. This is what the COC has in Louis Quilico, whose characterization continues to gain insights each season.... He covers the stage marvellously, darting about almost in a dance step, the kind of step a man with a limp might well cultivate to render his affliction less obvious. And he sings no less marvellously, particularly in passages charged with emotion — such as his duets with Gilda and his aria denouncing the courtiers. The notes pour out.... It has to be admitted that Louis Quilico alone among the members of the cast stood tall in an international sense."

— *Toronto Daily Star, September 26, 1969*

Best of Opera Season, Quilico's Rigoletto A Must . . .

"As for Quilico himself, his handling of Act Three alone would place him firmly among the great Rigolettos of our time. Emotionally it is vigorous, vocally it is boundless and the audience last night dissolved in bravos, and probably tears, at the end of it."

— *Toronto Telegram, September 26, 1969*

"He is a fine baritone, and his performance last night was more than good. It was distinguished. There was plenty of voice, there was strength without ham, and Mr. Quilico gave a three-dimensional portrait of the complex Verdi anti-hero."

— Harold Schönberg, The New York Times, March 21, 1969

"The Rigoletto was Louis Quilico and he was a resounding success."

— New York Daily News, March 21, 1969

"Louis Quilico is a stirring Rigoletto in tone and action."

— New York Post, March 21, 1969

"Clearly the evening belonged to Louis Quilico, for his blustering, powerful voiced portrayal of the title role."

— Raymond Ericson, The New York Times, March 28, 1969

"The principal figure was, of course, Rigoletto himself, sung by the Canadian baritone Louis Quilico. I have heard Mr. Quilico a number of times, always with pleasure, but I have never heard him go through such a gamut of moods and varied vocal inflections as he puts into this role. Altogether, he made about as fine a Rigoletto as has ever come to my attention."

— Winthrop Sargeant, The New Yorker, March 29, 1969

Well, at Least It Wasn't an Egg! . . .

"Baritone Louis Quilico, suddenly stopped in mid-aria and rushed from the stage during the performance of Rigoletto. A doctor plucked a feather from his throat which had fluttered into his mouth from a nest of pigeons in the rafters."

— Daily Mail, Santiago, Chile, August 22, 1970

Quilico a Casualty . . .

"Canadian baritone Louis Quilico fainted and fell to the floor in the second act of the opera Rigoletto here Thursday after swallowing a pigeon feather which wafted down from the roof. Quilico, the latest casualty in an accident-prone production at the Municipal Theatre, was quickly revived by a doctor but had to give up again midway through the third act. On Tuesday the producer went on stage to apologize for a previous series of on-stage mishaps, but tripped over a flowing costume and plunged into the audience. He was unhurt."

— *Reuters, Santiago, Chile, August 22, 1970*

A Ticklish Problem for Singer Quilico . . .

"Canadian baritone Louis Quilico, his voice booming to the upper balconies in mid-aria, suddenly stopped, gagged, and rushed off-stage during a performance of Rigoletto. A hastily-summoned doctor plucked a feather from his throat. It had fluttered down into his open mouth from a nest of pigeons in the rafters. Quilico is a star of the Canadian Opera Company and is on the University of Toronto's music faculty."

— *Toronto Daily Star, August 21, 1970*

Louis Quilico's Rigoletto Quite Superb . . .

"Last night's performance was ignited by Canada's greatest baritone in his greatest role. At this point having sung it more than 350 times, Louis Quilico virtually is Rigoletto.... He almost shattered the bonds of stage convention to utter a father's cries of anguish. He came as close as the lyric theatre comes to making palpable the experience of heartbreak."

— *William Littler, Toronto Star, 1973*

Quilico's Rigoletto Marvellous . . .

"Mr. Quilico's Rigoletto is quite simply, marvellous. There is no other word for him. His voice is a rich instrument and his characterization is finally honed and absolutely consistent."

— Lauretta Thistle, Ottawa Citizen, October 16, 1969

"Savage, Superb Rigoletto Captures the First Nighters."

— The Province, October 23, 1967

Rigoletto by Quilico, Original, Deeply Felt . . .

"Louis Quilico is a Rigoletto in the tradition of the late Leonard Warren, this is in dramatic impact and vocal impact, not in his approach to it, for this was a Quilico interpretation, deeply felt, understood and projected. But the miracle of Mr. Quilico's interpretation is that most of this was conveyed by vocal means. His is a great voice of impressive power and great beauty. He uses it with the sort of subtlety and musicianship that can convey bitterness and suffering."

— John Kraglund, The Globe and Mail, October 16, 1962

"Last minute — Louis Quilico went into costume and stepped into the role. The audience gave him a standing ovation during the second act."

— The New York Times, November 26, 1978

Quilico Is Magnificent in Rigoletto . . .

"Quilico takes us down this tormented path just as inexorably as Verdi."

— Hugh Fraser, Hamilton, September 18, 1983

Rigoletto Belongs to Quilico . . .

"The singers, all the audience stood in stupefaction listening to Quilico's marvelous voice — forgetting that they were on stage and had to act."

— Elma Miller, Hamilton, September 18, 1983

***Rigoletto* Standing Ovation for Quilico . . .**

"Quilico's bass baritone is cavernous in its depths and exhilerating at its heights and in its texture there is a dark chocolate quality. It is no wonder he is such a favorite at the Met."

— Toronto Sun, September 21, 1973

***Rigoletto*, Exciting, Brilliant . . .**

"Even if he had not acted as superbly as he did, Mr. Quilico's deeply emotional, yet excellently controlled singing alone would have brought to full life the tortures and agonies of a ridiculed man whose only great love is his daughter."

— Toronto Star, October 16, 1962

***Rigoletto* Enchants Boston Audiences . . .**

"Quilico has had a host of vocal triumphs at the prestigious Metropolitan Opera. Louis Quilico had the thousands hanging on the ropes by the time he finished his Rigoletto. Not only did his rich baritone display the emotional qualities necessary to a good portrayal but his acting was better than superb. It was sensational. At the end, the audience clogged the aisles at the huge Met Center, showering him with Bravos.... Quilico gives nothing but the best, of course, but this one was positively out of reach of anything. Roberta Peters was Quilico's lovely daughter and Nello Santi was at the helm, and he helped make *Rigoletto* the dazzling success it was."

— The Union Leader, Manchester, New Hampshire, June 14, 1982

A *Rigoletto* to Remember . . .

"Quilico, a leading figure on the Metropolitan and New York City Opera stages is an uncommonly powerful singer of magnetic expression."

— Milwaukee Sentinel, May 4, 1973

Rigoletto Gets Superb Rating . . .

"Louis Quilico, the Canadian baritone of the Metropolitan Opera, is a singing actor in the grand tradition of Pinza, John Charles Thomas and Lawrence Tibbett. He has a rich, strong voice, which he uses with fluent finesse and he made the title character, a compelling figure, a jester both fearsome and pathetic."

— *Milwaukee Journal, May 4, 1973*

"There may be a better Rigoletto, but it isn't likely there is a strength and quality in his portrayal that would be hard to equal."

— *Montreal Gazette, February 1, 1970*

James Levine Conducts Philharmonic in Rigoletto . . .

"The central character of Saturday's performance was Louis Quilico. He is a first-rate Verdi baritone, a singer capable of both suavity and authority. He displayed both these qualities in plenitude.... José Carreras made his West Coast debut as the Duke of Mantua. The Spanish tenor evidenced tremendous promise."

— *Los Angeles Herald-Examiner, September 12, 1972*

Rigoletto Mighty Pleasant, Both Listening and Looking . . .

"Quilico who had stepped in (at the last moment) has a baritone voice in the Leonard Warren tradition. It's big and warm but at all times it is in the service of his dramatic art. In solo work or in ensemble, especially with the Gilda, Lisa Di Julio, Quilico displayed artistry of a superlative order. His Cortigiani was chilling."

— *Burlington, Vermont, 1960*

Rigoletto Is First Class . . .

"Quilico has given many effective, dramatic performances. In this interpretation he proved that a great vocal performance can make up for even a total absence of visual props. His gloriously robust voice conveyed the mockery, the self-pity, his pure affection for Gilda, his terror of Monterone's curse and his helpless rage against the courtiers, with only a minimum of gesture. When has Cortigiani sounded more musical and more powerfully moving. As a performance of Rigoletto this was an outstanding achievement. As Seiji Ozawa's first operatic venture it was a near miracle."

— *The Globe and Mail, January 12, 1968*

Beauty of Tone Fine Debut as Rigoletto . . .

"Louis Quilico sang the name part for the first time in last night's performance of "Rigoletto" at Covent Garden. The large audience acclaimed him for his beauty of tone and for his complete understanding of the role. The inflections of his soft singing in 'Pari siamo' and the glorious ringing quality of his top notes in 'Cortigiani' showed the almost unlimited range of his voice."

— *Martin Cooper, London Times, 1960*

"But head, hump and shoulders above them all was the misshapen Rigoletto of Canadian baritone Louis Quilico. His was not a good performance, it was a great one — a towering characterization that was profound, poetic and passionate. This was not because of any vocal sorcery, though his voice was an impressive one, but because of his inner glow of conviction that could warm with tenderness or sear with hate."

— *The Vancouver Sun, October 23, 1967*

"As Rigoletto, Louis Quilico's performance is so compelling that the remainder of the cast remains in shadow."

— *Toronto Telegram, October 16, 1962*

Rigoletto Superb in TV Translation . . .

"Louis Quilico, who is an actor of range, as well as a magnificent baritone. His bitter jester and loving, broken father remained deeply moving. He dominated the production in a performance that was in every way splendid."

— *Montreal Star, February 4, 1965*

Magnificent CBC Production of Rigoletto . . .

"Enriched by fine performances by French-Canadian baritone Louis Quilico in the title role."

— *Montreal Gazette, February 4, 1965*

Festival's Rigoletto Sumptuous . . .

"Last night's 'Rigoletto' has to rate as one of the very best operatic productions ever put on visual record. Quilico's performance of the tragic court jester Rigoletto was monumental."

— *Toronto Daily Star, February 4, 1965*

Mady Mesplé Makes Bow in Met's Rigoletto . . .

"On the whole the only excitement of the evening came with Quilico's moments in the third act."

— *New York Post, September 26, 1973*

Singers, Conductor Shine in Rigoletto . . .

"Louis Quilico, in the title role, proved to be a vocalist of major stature, with a gorgeous stentorian sound and in his own way, a convincing projection of the character. Quilico moved well on stage and sang with a ring in an unmannered way that was often thrilling."

— *Pittsburgh Post-Gazette, April 22, 1977*

Quilico Triumphs in New York Production . . .

"Canadian baritone Louis Quilico is off to Russia this week with roars of 'Bravo' from a New York City Center audience still ringing in his ears. He roused a

Friday night audience to tremendous enthusiasm for his performance of Rigoletto. It was his show and his alone. His is a great performance."

— *Ottawa Citizen, November 6, 1962*

"For the recent Rigoletto, the principal stars engaged were Louis Quilico, John Alexander and Patricia Brooks. Mr. Quilico (whom we used to hear at Covent Garden, but who of late has sung principally in Paris) is also to be rated highly. In voice and demeanour he is an imposing Rigoletto, modelling his tone on Tito Gobbi's."

— *Opera Magazine, Vancouver, January 1968*

Met Stars Benita Valente, Louis Quilico Excel . . .

"Quilico's devotion and fatherly concern for his daughter were easily the most moving and convincing I have ever seen. Pittsburgh Opera has been blessed with outstanding Rigolettos, Robert Weede, Sherrill Milnes, Thomas Tipton, but Quilico's acting-singing had a wider dimension."

— *Pittsburgh Press, April 22, 1977*

Beautiful to Watch . . .

"With the exception of Louis Quilico in the title role, the CBC's production of Verdi's Rigoletto was overshadowed last night by the grandeur of the visual aspects. As Rigoletto, Louis Quilico was often superb. He looked like the court jester and he acted like him. His changes of mood clearly defined. He was the bold and imitating jester who dared to sit on the Duke's throne and laugh. He was a man weighed heavy with fear. His pretence at humor when seeking his daughter was beautifully and movingly portrayed. One was immediately aware that this is a singer of considerable depth and quality, strong in musicianship and in vocal interpretation. Jan Rubes as Sparafucile was splendid."

— *Toronto Telegram, February 4, 1965*

"With Roberta Peters as Gilda and Louis Quilico as Rigoletto, the singing was able to carry the evening. Her performance was in every way enjoyable. So was that of Louis Quilico. His robust baritone was flawless in every range and dramatic situation, his appearance and movement the perfect picture of tragedy and dire, cursed fate."

— *The Cleveland Press, June 7, 1972*

Louis Quilico Lives the Role of Rigoletto . . .

"What lends such memorability to Quilico's portrayal of that pre-verismo character, Rigoletto, is the way he makes Verdi's hunchbacked jester so painfully real in terms that go beyond what are usually regarded as the histrionic resources appropriate to mid-19th century opera. The voice is still there — big, rich and sonorous in the Verdian mould. But Quilico no longer sings the role of Rigoletto, he lives it. There is no such thing as beautiful singing for its own sake anymore. The notes wear flesh."

— *Toronto Star, September 21, 1973*

Quilico Triumphs in Toronto Opening of Rigoletto . . .

"Once again, this splendid singer drove home the fact that no one on the opera stage is better qualified to fill the shoes of the late Leonard Warren."

— *Montreal Star, September 20, 1973*

30,000 Attend Dell Opener . . .

"Quilico, a dramatic baritone, singing and pouring a dark velvety sound throughout." (with Luciano Pavarotti)

— *Philadelphia Inquirer, June 19, 1973*

Good News for a Good Baritone . . .

"Quilico seems to have everything a big-time baritone needs: a great, rich controlled voice, so emotional that it sometimes inspires opera buffs to rush worshipfully to the footlights, like Judy Garland fans; a flair for acting; a well-filled stocking."

— *Maclean's Magazine, November 17, 1962*

Washington Opera's Rigoletto . . .

"Louis Quilico has sung the part of Rigoletto more than 400 times in the world's leading opera houses, and the Washington Opera was lucky to get this master of the role's smallest nuances while his superbly controlled, subtly expressive voice is still in excellent condition. His performance was completely convincing. He was particularly masterful at bringing out the abundant pathos in his role."

— *Washington Post, February 25, 1991*

Ravishing Rigoletto . . .

"As Rigoletto, the hunchback who is pitied and despised by everyone he serves, Louis Quilico moves toward his destruction with glorious vocal expressiveness and astonishing endurance.

— *Washington Post, March 1, 1991*

. . . Operas That Dazzle and Sizzle . . .

"Replacing the ailing Alain Fondary in the title role, baritone Louis Quilico, veteran of hundreds of performances of the role, has both the voice and the experience to offer operative revelations on the pathetic, twisted jester. Quilico wastes no time in exaggerated movements or grotesque makeup; his Rigoletto's deformity is within his tormented mind and through the power and clarity of his singing this becomes palpably evident."

— *Fredericksburg, Virgina, March 2, 1991*

Cutting Loose . . .

"Though baritone Quilico has ably sung 29 mostly lead roles, this season he is concentrating on the Verdi that his *lirico spinto* was made for. Quilico is able to blend the human sound of a Verdi libretto with its music."

— *Time Magazine, October 23, 1964*

"I think Quilico came out with top honors both as an actor and as a singer."

— *New York Daily News, September 12, 1969*

"Louis Quilico, who sang the bitter Rigoletto, is nearly 70. He gave every indication of owning the role. Every note he sang was musical, and every line and gesture rich with twisted humanity. In a lifetime of going to the opera, I have never encountered a finer Rigoletto than Quilico."

— *Ottawa Citizen, September 17, 1994*

"Louis Quilico portrayed Rigoletto with dramatic strength. His rich voice brought volume and depth to this role. The quality of his singing was above that of everyone else."

— *Montreal Gazette, November 11, 1991*

Opera Performance the Whole of Canada Should Hear . . .

"It was worth braving the snow for a performance like this. Quilico dominated the opera not only by the authority of his interpretation but by the power and warmth of his glorious baritone voice. The most memorable performance last night was that of Louis Quilico. I heard him a number of years ago when he first sang the role in the old New York City Center and I said at the time that he would be Leonard Warren's successor. There is no need now to refer to Warren, because great as he was, Quilico's conception of the character is his own, and I find it even more moving and more filled with musical truth. He will be remembered as one of the great Rigoletto's."

— *Montreal Star, February 16, 1970*

Rigoletto with Flair at the Bowl . . .

"Louis Quilico, offered a performance of the title role that was massively authoritative and powerfully conceived. The Quilico voice dispsened huge amounts of baritonal sonority as well as superb qualitity of other expessive and dramatic devices. The new tenor, José Carreras turned out to be a distinct discovery...Carol Neblett as Gilda."

— *Los Angeles Times, September 11, 1972*

Cuccaro, Quilico Outstanding . . .

"One of Montreal's favorite sons, Louis Quilico, in the title role, a role he has made his own many many performances ago.... Quilico's voice has happily lost none of its lustre and he gave a fine account of the deformed court jester on opening night."

— *Sunday Express, May 27, 1984*

Rigoletto: grâce à Quilico et Rouleau . . .

"Rigoletto, Verdi, Quilico. Sur l'affiche, trois noms extrêmement populaires auprès de notre public. Il n'en faut pas davantage pour remplir la salle. Sept fois. Les sept représentations sont entièrement vendues depuis plusieurs jours.... Énorme, pathétique dans son costume et ses mouvements, Quilico se donne entièrement à ce rôle qu'il chante depuis 25 ans mais pour la première fois dans sa ville natale."

— *La Presse, May 24, 1984*

Performance inoubliable
de Quilico dans Rigoletto . . .

"Au faite de sa carrière, Quilico qui a déjà interprété ce rôle-titre plus de 400 fois, mais pour qui c'était une première à Montréal, a fait vibrer la salle entière en plus d'une occasion de par le dramatique de son jeu de scène autant que par la chaleur de sa voix. Il a tout simplement envouté les 3,000 auditeurs et spectateurs venus l'acclamer pour l'occasion.... Un spectacle de classe.... S'il ést vrai que Louis Quilico incarnait véritablement la pensée musicale de Verdi, il ne faudrait pas pour autant ignorer ceux qui l'ont magnifiquement épaulé lors de cette première."

— *Journal de Montréal, May 23, 1984*

Rigoletto n'a plus aucun secret pour Louis Quilico . . .

"Aujourd'hui au sommet d'une prestigieuse carrière, Louis Quilico a acquis avec les années une connaissance intime du rôle de Rigoletto, ce qui n'a rien d'étonnant quand on songe qu'il l'a chanté plus de 400 fois! Aucune subtilité du rôle ne lui échappe et c'est avec un art consummé qu'il sait tour à tour détailler les divers sentiments de son personage: ironie, tendresse, haine ou désespoir. À une voix admirablement conservée et conduite, riche dans tous les registres, il allie une impolication dramatique fortement projetée avec le résultat qu'aucun spectateur ne saurait demeurer indifférent au drame qui l'habite. À plus d'un moment au cours de la soirée, l'émotion était devenue si vive dans la salle qu'elle était presque palpable, chacun retenant son souffle afin de mieux communier avec ce qui se passait sur la scène."

— *Le Devoir, May 25, 1984*

Appendices

Roles and Highlights of Performances

Composer	Opera	Role
BELLINI	I Puritani	Riccardo
BERG	Wozzeck	Wozzeck
BERLIOZ	Les Troyens	Choroebus
	Romeo et Juliette	Frère Laurent
BIZET	Carmen	Escamillo
	The Pearl Fishers	Zurga
BORODIN	Prince Igor	Igor
BRITTEN	A Midsummer Night's Dream	Demetrius
CILEA	Adriana Lecouvreur	Michonnet
DEBUSSY	Pelléas et Mélisande	Golaud
DONIZETTI	Gemma di Vergy	Conte di Vergy
	Il Duca d'Alba	Duca d'Alba
	L'Elisir d'Amore	Belcore
	La Favorita	Alfonso
	Lucia di Lammermoor	Enrico Ashton

Composer	Opera	Role
DONIZETTI	Lucrezia Borgia	Alfonso
	Maria Stuarda	Leicester
	La Parisina d'Este	Azzo
	Roberto Devereux	Nottingham
GLUCK	Alcest	Herod
	Iphigénie en Aulide	Orestes
	Iphigénie en Tauride	Thoas
GOUNOD	Faust	Valentin
HANDEL	Hercules	Hercules
	Julius Caesar	Caesar
LEONCAVALLO	I Pagliacci	Tonio
LERNER & LOEWE	Paint Your Wagon	Julio
LOESSER	Most Happy Fella	Tony
MARTINU	Comedy on the Bridge	
MASCAGNI	Cavalleria Rusticana	Alfio
MASSENET	Cendrillon	Pandolphe
	Esclarmonde	Bishop de Blois
	Hérodiade	Herod
	La Navaraise	Garrido
	Manon	Lescaut
	Thaïs	Athanael
	Thérèse	André Thorel
MEYERBEER	L'Africaine	Nelusko
MILHAUD	La Mère Coupable	The Count
MOZART	Don Giovanni	Masetto, Leporello
	La Clemenza di Tito	Publeus
MUSSORGSKY	Boris Godunov	Rangoni
OFFENBACH	La Grande Duchesse de Gerolstein	Prince Paul
	Tales of Hoffmann	4 villains
PACINI	Saffo	Acardro

Composer	Opera	Role
PONCHIELLI	La Gioconda	Barnaba
POULENC	Les Mamelles de Tirésias	Monsieur Presto
PUCCINI	Gianni Schicchi	Schicchi
	Il Tabarro	Michele
	La Bohème	Marcello
	La Fanciulla del West	Rance
	Madama Butterfly	Sharpless
	Manon Lescaut	Lescaut
	Tosca	Scarpia
RAMEAU	Les Fêtes d'Hébé	Hymos
ROSENTHAL	Hop Seignor	Juréal
ROSSINI	The Barber of Seville	Dr. Bartolo
	William Tell	William Tell
SAINT-SAËNS	Samson et Dalila	High Priest
TCHAIKOWSKY	The Queen of Spades	Yeletski
VERDI	Aida	Amonasro
	Alzira	The Duke
	Don Carlo	Marchese di Posa (Rodrigo)
	Ernani	Don Carlo
	Falstaff	Falstaff
	I Due Foscari	Il Doge
	Il Trovatore	Count di Luna
	La Forza del Destino	Don Carlo
	La Traviata	Germont
	Luisa Miller	Miller
	Macbeth	Macbeth
	Nabucco	Nabucco
	Otello	Iago
	Rigoletto	Rigoletto
	Simon Boccanegra	Simon
	Un Ballo in Maschera	Renato
WAGNER	Tannhäuser	Wolfram
WILSON	The Selfish Giant	Giant

✧ Roles at the Metropolitan Opera

278	Performances	1972–97
25	Seasons	
24	Roles	

Highlights from the Metropolitan Opera Performances by Louis Quilico

1955 Wins "Met auditions"

1971–72 Makes debut February 10th in Pelléas et Mélisande (Debussy)

1972–73 *Otello* (Verdi) with Vickers, Zylis-Gara, Kraft, conductor Levine

1973–74 *Rigoletto* (Verdi) with Mesple, di Giuseppe, c. Baudo

Benefit sponsored by the Metropolitan Opera Guild for the Production Funds. Metropolitan Opera Premiere

Les Troyens (Berlioz) with Verrett, Vickers, Blegen, c. Kubelik

Il Trovatore (Verdi) with McCracken, Rankin, Arroyo, c. Levine

La Traviata (Verdi) with di Giuseppe, Cruz-Romo, c. Molinari-Pradelli

Faust (Gounod) with Boky, di Giuseppe

1974–75 Benefit sponsored by the Metropolitan Opera Guild for the Benevolent and Retirement Funds. Gala Performance

Un Ballo in Maschera (Verdi) with Ross, Pavarotti, Plishka, c. Lewis

1975–76 Met Marathon (fundraising event)

From *Un Ballo in Maschera* (Verdi)

Aida (Verdi) with Caballé, Domingo, Hines, c. Levine

Madama Butterfly (Puccini) with Scotto, Love, Theyard, c. Woitach

1976–77 Met Marathon (fundraising event)

From *Don Carlos* (Verdi)

Il Trovatore (Verdi) with Scotto, Pavarotti, Verrett, c. Gavazzeni

	Benefit sponsored by the Metropolitan Opera Guild. Metropolitan Opera Premiere
	Esclarmonde (Massenet) with Sutherland, Aragall, Tourangeau, c. Bonynge
	Tosca (Puccini) with Kubiak, Lamberti, c. Woitach
1977–78	*La Traviata* (Verdi) with Mauti-Nunziata, Aragall, Kraft, c. Woitach
	Rigoletto (Verdi) with Shicoff, Cotrubas, c. Levine
	I Pagliacci (Leoncavallo) with Domingo, Monk, Niska, c. Levine
	Adriana Lecouvreur (Cilea) with Caballe, Carreras, Cossotto, c. Lopez-Cobos
	Tosca (Puccini) with Kubiak, Carreras, Capecchi, c. Conlon
	La Favorita (Donizetti) with Berini, Alexander, Morris, c. Veltri
	Il Trovatore (Verdi) with Bello, Cruz-Romo, c. Stivender
1978–79	*Aida* (Verdi) with Cruz-Romo, Bergonzi, Dunn, Hines, c. Patané
1979–80	*La Gioconda* (Ponchielli) with Scotto, Mauro, c. Patané
	Benefit sponsored by the Metropolitan Opera Guild
	Un Ballo in Maschera (Verdi) with Ricciarelli, Pavarotti, Blegen, c. Patané
	(Available on video from Met telecast)
1980–81	*Un Ballo in Maschera* (Verdi) with Zylis-Gara, Bergonzi, Berini, Blegen, c. Veltri
	(Also with Domingo, Ricciarelli, c. Patané)
	Samson et Dalila (Saint-Saens) with Cassilly, Verrett, Meredith, c. Järvi
1981–82	*Tosca* (Puccini) with Zylis-Gara, Giacomini, Capecchi, c. Patané
	Gianni Schicchi (Puccini) with Bacquier, Craig, Berini, c. Levine
	Celebration of Carlo Bergonzi's 25th anniversary with Pavarotti, Zylis-Gara, c. Levine
	Rigoletto (Verdi) with Eda-Pierre, Pavarotti, Berberian, c. Levine
	(Available on video from Met telecast)

	Il Trovatore (Verdi) with Giacomini, Price, Cortez, c. Conlon
1982–83	*Un Ballo in Maschera* (Verdi) with Bergonzi, Savova, Berini, Robinson, c. Patané
	Adriana Lecouvreur (Cilea) with Scotto, Shicoff, Cortez, c. Fulton
	Il Trovatore (Verdi) with Cruz-Romo, Cortez, Mauro, c. Santi
	Don Carlo (Verdi) with Domingo, Freni, Bumbry, Ghiaurov, c. Levine
	(Available on video from Met telecast)
	Macbeth (Verdi) with Scotto, Plishka, Mauro, c. Levine
1983–84	Celebrating the 100th anniversary of the Metropolitan Opera
	Centennial Gala I, Arias from *Falstaff* (Quilico), c. Levine
	Macbeth (Verdi) with Scotto, Vernon, Anthony, c. Levine
1984–85	*Rigoletto* (Verdi) with Devia, di Giuseppe, Conrad, Furlanetto, c. Santi
	Also performances with Peters, Upshaw, Blegen, Jones, Raffanti
	Ernani (Verdi) with Mauro, Mitchell, Plishka, Kraft, c. Fulton
1985–86	*Falstaff* (Verdi) with Blegen, Neblett, c. Levine
1986–87	*Aida* (Verdi) with Pavarotti, Tomowa-Sintow, Cossotto, c. Levine
	Manon (Massenet) with Kraus, G. Quilico
1988–89	*Il Barbiere di Siviglia* (Rossini) with Horne, Hampson, c. Levine
1990–91	*I Pagliacci* (Leoncavallo) with Domingo, c. Levine
	Un Ballo in Maschera (Verdi) with Millo, Quivar, Leech
1991–92	*Il Barbiere di Siviglia* (Rossini) with von Stade, Hampson, Ramey, c. Weikert
	Un Ballo in Maschera (Verdi) with Millo, Leech, c. Fiore
	Rigoletto (Verdi) with Swenson, Leech, c. Santi
1992–93	*I Pagliacci* (Leoncavallo) with Domingo, Soviero, c. Levine
1994–95	*Adriana Lecouvreur* (Cilea) with Freni, Lima, Tocyska, c. Abbado

	I Pagliacci (Leoncavallo) with Atlantov, Kazarmovskaya, c. Badea
	Tosca (Puccini) with Soviero, Bartolini, c. Fulton
1995–96	James Levine 25th Anniversary Gala. Honored guest

✧ Highlights from Opera Performances

1956	Los Angeles	*Madama Butterfly* Cond. Kurt Adler Margaret Roggero
1956	Los Angeles	*La Bohème* Licia Albanese, Italo Tajo, George Cehanovsky, Alessio de Paolis
1956	New York, Town Hall	*I Puritani* Rosalind Elias, Donald Gramm, Laurel Hurley, Eugene Conley
1956	San Francisco	*Manon Lescaut* Dorothy Kirsten, Jussi Björling Cesare Curzi, Margaret Roggero Lorenzo Alvary
1956	San Francisco	*La Bohème* Licia Albanese, Jan Peerce
1956	Massachusetts	*Cavalleria Rusticana* Mija Novich, Albert da Costa
1956	San Francisco	*L'Elisir d'Amore* Patrice Munsel, Italo Tajo, Giuseppe Campora
1957	Pittsburgh	*Faust* Nicolai Gedda, George London, Eileen Faun, Barry Morell
1957	New York City Opera	*La Traviata* Cond. Arturo Basile Beverly Sills, John Alexander
1957	Montreal TV	*Faust* Cond. Wilfrid Pelletier Irving Guttman, Richard Verreau,

		Gilles Lamontagne, Marguerite Gignac
1957	Detroit	*Faust* Cond. Julius Rudel Norman Treigle, Barry Morell
1958	San Francisco	*Il Trovatore* Leontyne Price, Jussi Björling Claramae Turner
1958	New Orleans	*Manon Lescaut* Eleanor Steber, Louis Roney
1958	New York, Town Hall	*La Grande Duchesse de Gerolstein* Jennie Tourel, Leopold Simoneau, Martial Singher, Pierette Alarie
1958	Pittsburgh	*Il Trovatore*
1958	New Orleans	*L'Elisir d'Amore* Leopold Simoneau
1958	Philadelphia	*Madama Butterfly* Elaine Malbin, John Alexander
1959	Philadelphia	*Madama Butterfly* Cond. Carlo Moresco John Alexander, Elaine Malbin, Harry Theyard
1959	Philadelphia	*La Bohème* Clarice Carson, Arthur Newman, Flaviano Labo
1959	Montreal TV	*Il Tabarro*
1959	Spoleto, Italy	*Il Duca d'Alba* Cond. Thomas Schippers Prod. Luchino Visconti Dir. Gian Carlo Menotti Enzo Tei, Renato Cioni, Ivana Tossini, Franco Ventriglia
1959	San Francisco	*Aida* Cond. Francesco Molinari-Pradelli Lucine Amara, Mario del Monaco, Irene Dallas

1959	Philadelphia	*La Bohème* Clarice Carson
1959	San Francisco	*I Pagliacci* Cond. Arturo Basile Mary Costa, Jon Vickers, Robert Weede, Frank Guarrera
1959	Los Angeles	*La Bohème* Licia Albanese, Geraint Evans, Giuseppe Gismondo, Lorenzo Alvary
1959	New York, Carnegie Hall	*Iphigénie en Tauride* Martina Arroyo, Gloria Davy
1960	London, Covent Garden	*La Traviata* Joan Sutherland, John Lanigan, Nello Santi
1960	London, Covent Garden	*Aida* Gloria Davy, Rita Gorr
1960	New York City Opera at Vermont	*Rigoletto* Cond. Julius Rudel Lisa di Julio, Giuseppe Gismondo, Joshua Hecht
1960	Canadian Opera Company (COC)	*Otello* First performance of Otello for COC
1960	London, Covent Garden	*La Traviata* Virginia Zeani
1960	Vancouver	*Madama Butterfly* Teresa Stratas, Richard Verreau
1960	Pittsburgh	*Il Trovatore*
1960	Philadelphia	*Lucia di Lammenmoor* Roberta Peters
1961	London, Covent Garden	*Aida* Regina Resnik, Arturo Sergi, Amy Shuard

1961	London, Covent Garden	*The Queen of Spades* Cond. Alexander Melik-Pashayev Marie Collier, Richard Lewis
1961	Toronto, CBC TV	*Falstaff* Ilona Kombrink, Franz Kraemer, Ernesto Barbini
1962	London, Covent Garden	*La Traviata* Cond. Alberto Erede Joan Sutherland, André Turp
1962	Florence, Italy	*Iphigénie en Tauride* Cond. Pierre Dervaux Rita Gorr, Robert Massard
1962	London, Covent Garden	*Aida* Galina Vishnevskaya, Charles Craig
1962	Russia, Moscow, Bolshoi Leningrad	*Rigoletto*
1962	London, Covent Garden	*La Traviata* Mary Costa
1962	Vienna Staatsoper	*La Traviata* Cond. Oliviero de Fabritiis Gabriella Tucci, Giuseppe Zampieri
1962	Philadelphia	*Il Trovatore* Cond. Franco Patané Franco Corelli, Sandra Warfield, Lucilla Vdovich
1962	London, Covent Garden	*Rigoletto* Renato Cioni, Ivana Tosini
1963	Paris Opera	*Tannhäuser* Cond. André Cluytens Régine Crespin, Rita Gorr, Mireille Martin, J.P. Hurteau, Gerard Serkoyan, Hans Beirer
1963	Philadelphia	*Un Ballo in Maschera* Cond. Anton Guadagno Giuseppe di Stefano, Claramae Turner,

		Norman Scott, Louis Sgarro, Antonietta Stella
1963	Toronto, CBC TV	*Otello* Cond. Ernesto Barbini Ilona Kombrink, Richard Cassilly, Victor Braun, John McCallum
1964	Rome, Caracalla, Italy	*Un Ballo in Maschera* Cond. Carlo Felice Cillario Prod. Margharita Wallmann Margherita Roberti, Lucia Danieli, Gianni Raimondi, Jolanda Meneguzzer, Silvio Maionica, Antonio Cassinelli
1964	Palermo, Italy	*Don Carlo* Cond. Antonino Volto Prod. Wallman Giulietta Simionato, Jacques Dupond, Jerome Hines, Eva Ligabue
1964	Houston, Texas	*Un Ballo in Maschera* Jon Vickers, Elinor Ross
1965	Paris Opera	*Hop Signor* (Premiere) Cond. Manuel Rosenthal Jacquiline Brumaire, Jean Giraudeau, Xavier Depras
1965	Toronto, CBC TV	*Tosca* Cond. Ernesto Barbini Renata Tebaldi
1965	Toronto, CBC TV	*Rigoletto* Cond. Ernesto Barbini Giuseppe Campora, Jan Rubes, Jolanda Meneguzzer
1966	Canadian Opera Company	*Macbeth* Cond. Ernesto Barbini Margaret Tynes, Luigi Infantino, Ermanno Mauro
1966	Parma, Italy	*Otello* Tito Del Bianco, Rosanna Carteri

1966	Philadelphia	*Don Carlo* Cond. Anton Guadagno Franco Corelli, Raina Kabavianska, Nicolai Ghiaurov
1966	Canadian Opera Company	*La Traviata* Maria Chiara, Luigi Infantino, Ernesto Barbini
1967	Toulouse, Paris	*La Favorita* Veronica Cortez, Tony Poncet Gerard Serkoyan
1967	Naples, Italy	*Saffo* Cond. Franco Capuana Dir. Marguerita Wallman Leyla Gencer, Tito del Bianco, Franca Matteucci
1967	Turin, Italy	*Un Ballo in Maschera* Carlo Bergonzi, Rita Orlandi Malaspina, Franco Capuano
1967	New Orleans	*Manon Lescaut* Montserrat Caballé, John Alexander
1967	Toronto, CBC TV	*Oedipus Rex* Cond. Robert Craft Marilyn Horne, Joseph Rouleau, Ernst Haeflinger
1967	Montreal Expo	*Otello* Cond. Zubin Mehta Teresa Stratas, Jon Vickers, Carlo Maestrini
1968	Toronto, Massey Hall	*Rigoletto* Cond. Seiji Ozawa Reri Grist, George Shirley, Joan Maxwell, Garnet Brooks, Jan Rubes, Thomas Paul
1968	Canadian Opera Company	*Tosca* Cond. Ernesto Barbini Prod. Leon Major Marina Krilovici, Ermanno Mauro

1968	Paris Opera	*Aida* Cond. George Sebastien Leontyne Price, Felicia Weathers
1968	New York, Carnegie Hall	*Alzira* Cond. Jonel Perlea Gianfranco Cecchele, Elinor Ross
1968	Philadelphia	*Otello* Cond. Anton Guadagno Renata Tebaldi, Jon Vickers
1969	Ottawa, National Arts Centre	*Rigoletto* Cond. Mario Bernardi Urszula Koszut, Pierre Duval
1969	Toulouse, France	*Otello* Anne Norelli, Pier Miranda Ferraro
1969	New York City Opera	*Rigoletto* Cond. Julius Rudel Patricia Brooks, Michele Molese
1969	New Orleans	*Rigoletto* Nicola Moscona
1969	Orlando, Florida	*Tosca* Gabriella Tucci, Nicholas di Virgilio
1970	New York City Opera	*Pelléas et Mélisande* Cond. Julius Rudel Prod. Frank Corsaro Patricia Brooks, André Jobin
1970	New York City Opera	*Roberto Devereux* Cond. Julius Rudel Placido Domingo, Beverly Sills
1970	San Francisco	*Tosca* Cond. Kurt Adler Dorothy Kirsten, Placido Domingo
1970	Canadian Opera Company	*La Traviata* Urszula Koszut
1970	New York City Opera	*Rigoletto* Louise Lebrun

1970	Montreal	*Rigoletto* Colette Boky, Richard Verreau
1971	Canadian	*Lucia di Lammermoor* Cristina Deutekom, Ermanno Mauro
1971	Canadian Opera Company	*Macbeth* Elinor Ross
1971	Montreal Opera Company	*Samson et Dalila* Cond. Jean Delaurier Regina Safarty, Pier Miranda Ferraro
1971	Montreal	*Carmen* Shirley Verrett, Claude Corbeil, Michele Molese
1972	Philadelphia	*I Puritani* Cond. Anton Guadagno Luciano Pavarotti, Beverly Sills, Paul Plishka
1972	Boston	*Les Troyens* Regine Crespin, Maralin Niska, Christa Ludwig, Jon Vickers, Shirley Verrett, Ronald Dowd
1972	New York, Carnegie Hall	*William Tell* Cond. Eve Queler Jerome Lo Monaco
1972	California, Hollywood Bowl	*Rigoletto* Cond. James Levine José Carreras, Carol Neblett
1972	Vancouver	*Lucrezia Borgia* Cond. Richard Bonynge Joan Sutherland, John Alexander, Huguette Tourangeau
1972	Metropolitan Opera	*Otello* Cond. James Levine Jon Vickers, Teresa Zylis-Gara
1972	Metropolitan Opera	*Pelléas et Mélisande* Cond. Sir Colin Davis Judith Blegen

1973	Metropolitan Opera	*Rigoletto* Mady Mesplé
1973	Covent Garden	*Lucia di Lammermoor* Cond. Richard Bonynge Joan Sutherland, Luciano Pavarotti
1973	Quebec	*I Pagliacci* Heather Thomson, Pedro Lavirgen
1973	Houston, Texas	*La Forza del Destino* Salvatore Nova, Suzanne Marsee, Clarice Carson
1973	Cincinnati	*Aida* Cond. Anton Guadagno James King, Martina Arroyo
1973	Canadian Opera Company	*Rigoletto* Maria Pellegrini, Leigh Munro
1974	Montreal, CBC TV	*Falstaff* Clarice Carson, Louise Lebrun, Andre Lortie, Pierre Duval
1974	San Francisco	*Luisa Miller* Cond. Jésus Lopez-Cobos Katia Ricciarelli, Luciano Pavarotti, Giorgio Tozzi
1974	Hartford, Conn.	*La Forza del Destino*
1975	Canadian Opera Company	*Il Tabarro* Costumes: Suzanne Mess Lucine Amara
1975	New Orleans	*Herodiade*
1975	Festival Las Palmas, Canary Islands	*Macbeth* Prod. Tito Copabianco
1975	Metropolitan Opera	*Un Ballo in Maschera* Cond. Henry Lewis Teresa Kubiak, Nicolai Gedda, Roberta Peters, Maureen Forrester
1975	London, Covent Garden	*La Traviata* Cond. Richard Bonynge Joan Sutherland, Alfredo Kraus

1976	Metropolitan Opera	*Aida* Carlo Bergonzi, James Morris, Elena Obraztsova
1976	Metropolitan Opera	*Aida* Cond. James Levine Montserrat Caballé, Placido Domingo, Jerome Hines, Mignon Dunn
1976	Metropolitan Opera	*Aida* Tatiana Troyanos, James McCracken
1976	Metropolitan Opera	*Esclarmonde* Cond. Richard Bonynge Joan Sutherland, Giacomo Aragall, Nico Castel
1976	Memphis	*Il Trovatore* Gilda Cruz-Romo, Rolf Björling
1976	Calgary	*I Pagliacci*
1976	Washington Opera	*Thaïs* Noelle Rogers
1976	New Orleans	*Aida* Cond. Richard Woitach Martina Arroyo
1976	Cincinnati	*Tosca* Dorothy Kirsten, John Alexander
1977	Cincinnati	*Most Happy Fella* Cond. Anton Coppola Benita Valente, John Fox
1977	New Orleans	*Ernani* Ezio Flagello
1977	Washington, D.C.	*Tosca* Stage Director: Fabrizio Melano, Gilda Cruz-Romo, Barry Morell, Allan Monk
1977	Seattle	*Tosca* Raina Kabavianska, Barry Morell

1978	Metropolitan Opera	*Adriana Lecouvreur* Cond. Jésus Lopez-Cobos Stage Director: Nathaniel Merrill Montserrat Caballé, José Carreras, Fiorenza Cossotto
1976	Metropolitan Opera	*Tosca* Cond. James Conlon Teresa Kubiak, José Carreras
1978	Metropolitan Opera	*La Favorita* Nicolai Gedda, James Morris, John Alexander, Bianca Berini
1978	Metropolitan Opera	*Aida* Carlo Bergonzi, Martina Arroyo
1978	Wolf Trap, Washington	*I Pagliacci* Marianna Niculescu, James McCracken
1978	Met. in the Park	*Il Trovatore* Veronica Cortez, Rolf Björling
1978	San Diego	*Rigoletto*
1976	South Carolina	*Rigoletto*
1979	Ottawa, National Arts Centre	*Cendrillon* Cond. Mario Bernardi Prod: Brian McDonald Frederica von Stade, Maureen Forrester, Gabrielle Lavigne, Ruth Welting
1979	Canadian Opera Company	*Simon Boccanegra* Patricia Wells, Gino Quilico, Carlo Bini, Don Garrard
1979	Milwaukee	*Macbeth*
1979	Pittsburgh	*La Traviata* Colette Boky
1979	Seattle	Tosca Raina Kabavianska, Barry Morell
1979	Tulsa, Oklahoma	*La Navaraise, I Pagliacci* Cond. Antonio de Almeida

1979	Metropolitan Opera	*La Gioconda* Cond. Giuseppe Patané Renata Scotto
1979	Cincinnati	*Rigoletto* Cond. Anton Guadagno Benita Valente
1979	Edmonton	*Macbeth*
1979	Long Beach, California	*La Traviata*
1980	Ottawa, National Arts Centre	*Thérèse* Cond. Mario Bernardi Mignon Dunn, Alain Vanzo
1980	Metropolitan Opera	*Un Ballo in Maschera* Cond. Giuseppe Patané Luciano Pavarotti, Katia Ricciarelli, Judith Blegen
1980	Fort Worth, Texas	*Il Trovatore* Placido Domingo
1980	Metropolitan Opera	*I Pagliacci* Giuseppe Giacomini
1981	Metropolitan Opera	*Un Ballo in Maschera* Carlo Bergonzi, Teresa Zylis-Gara
1981	Paris Opera	*Cendrillon* Faith Esham, Karen Hunt
1981	Cleveland	*Samson et Dalila* Bruno Baglioni, John Macurdy, Grace Bumbry
1981	Ottawa, National Arts Centre	*Rigoletto* Ruth Welting, Neil Shicoff
1981	Metropolitan Opera Carlo Bergonzi 25th Anniversary	Luciano Pavarotti
1981	Metropolitan — Live from Lincoln Center	*Rigoletto* Cond. James Levine Luciano Pavarotti, Eda Pierre
1982	Metropolitan Opera	*Il Trovatore* Leontyne Price, Veronica Cortez, Giuseppe Giacomini

1982	Met. in the Park	*Il Trovatore* Grace Bumbry
1982	Metropolitan Opera	*Macbeth* Cond. James Levine Olivia Stapp
1982	Canadian Opera Company	*Rigoletto*
1983	Montreal	*Macbeth* Marita Napier, André and Richard Turp
1983	Metropolitan Opera	*Adriana Lecouvreur* Renata Scotto, Neil Shicoff
1983	Metropolitan Opera	*Don Carlo* Cond. James Levine Mirella Freni, Grace Bumbry, Placido Domingo, Jerome Hines
1983	Metropolitan Centennial Gala	
1983	San Francisco	*Samson et Dalila* Marilyn Horne, Guy Chauvet
1984	Lucca, Italy	*Tosca* Lando Bartolini
1984	Montreal	*Rigoletto* Constanza Cuccaro, Joseph Rouleau
1984	Montreal	*La Traviata*
1985	Frankfurt, Germany	*Falstaff* Cond. Michael Gielen
1985	Montreal	*Ernani* Ermanno Mauro, Nicole Lorange
1986	Metropolitan Opera	*Falstaff* Cond. James Levine Judith Blegen, Carol Neblett
1986	Metropolitan Opera	*Aida* Cond. James Levine Luciano Pavarotti Anna Tomowa-Sintow, Florenza Cossotto

1987	Metropolitan Opera	*Manon* (Massenet) Alfredo Kraus, Gino Quilico
1988	Nice, France — Opera de Torante	*Falstaff*
1989	Edmonton	*Aida* Carol Neblett, Ermanno Mauro
1989	Hamilton, Ontario	*I Due Foscari* Cond. Daniel Lipton Eduardo Villa
1989	Metropolitan Opera	*Il Barbiere di Siviglia* Marilyn Horne, Thomas Hampson
1989	Tokyo, Japan	*Aida* Katia Ricciarelli, Grace Bumbry, Paul Plishka, Bruno Sebastian
1989	Hamilton Opera	*The Barber of Seville*
1989	Metropolitan Opera	*I Pagliacci*
1990	New Orleans Opera	*La Traviata* Marilyn Mims, John Poird de Hann
1990	Montreal Opera	*Adriana Lecouvreur* Cond. Michelangelo Veltri Diana Soviero, Ermanno Mauro
1990	Montreal, Place des Arts	*Nabucco* Cond. Otto Werner Mueller
1991	Montreal, Opéra du Québec	*Rigoletto*
1991	California	*Anniversary Tour* Luciano Pavarotti, Susan Dunn
1991	New York City Opera	*Most Happy Fella*
1991	Washington Opera	*Rigoletto*
1992	Paris Opera	*Le Barbier de Séville* Jennifer Larmore, Gino Quilico
1992	Metropolitan Opera	*Un Ballo in Maschera* Aprile Millo, Florence Quivar

1993	Metropolitan Opera	*I Pagliacci* Placido Domingo
1993	New Orleans	*Falstaff* Cond. Klauspeter Seibel Mignon Dunn, Amy Burton
1993	Palm Beach Opera, Fort Lauderdale Opera	*The Barber of Seville* Cond. Anton Guadagno Patricia Schumann, Maurizio Comenici, Giorgio Lormi, David Pittsinger
1994	Metropolitan Opera	*Adriana Lecouvreur* Cond. Robert Abbado Mirella Freni, Luis Lima, Stefania Tocyska
1994	Montreal, Place des Arts	Quilico, Millo, Petrowska Concert
1994	Ottawa, National Arts Centre Opera Lyra	*Rigoletto* Cond. Yves Abel Rebecca Caine
1994	Metropolitan Opera	*I Pagliacci*
1994	Met. in the Park	*Tosca*
1995	Tel Aviv Opera	*The Barber of Seville*
1996	Quilico, Petrowska benefit concert for the Academy of Vocal Arts, Philadelphia	
1996	Quilico, Petrowska benefit concert for the North York International Academy, Toronto	
1996	Quilico, Petrowska benefit concert for the Ottawa Capital Opera Society, Ottawa	

Discography

Bellini	'I Puritani'. Guadagno cond., Pavarotti, Plishka, Quilico (Riccardo). 1972 3 Historical Recording Enterprises HRE-311-3
	'I Puritani'. London Phil O, Rudel cond., Quilico (Riccardo). 1973 3 Audio Treasury ABC ATS-20016/3-Angel AVC-34013
	'I Puritani'. Guadagno cond., Quilico, Pavarotti, Sills. 1972. Philadelphia. Legato Classics. LCD-176-2
Christmas Music	Quilico, Gino Quilico, Loman. CBC Series. SMCD-5119
Darwin	'Song for a City'; Verdi: 'Rigoletto', 'Cortigiani'. Royal Phil O, Bonynge cond. 1975. Decca SXI-6719
Donizetti	'Il Duca d'Alba'. O and Chor of the Teatro G. Verdi di Trieste, Schippers cond., Quilico (Duca). 1959. 20 Melodram 002
	'Gemma di Vergy'. New York Opera O, Schola Cantorum, Queler cond. 1977. 3-Co Master M3-34575/3 CBS Master 79-303

	'Maria Stuarda'. London Phil O, John Alldis Choir, Ceccato cond. 1971. 3-Audio Treasury ABC ATS-20010/3-Angel AVC-34032/ (selections) Angel AV-34015
	'La Parisina d'Este'. New York Opera O, Schola Cantorum, Queler cond., Quilico (Azzo). 1974. 3-MRF 107-S/3 BIR BIRS-134-3
	'Roberto Devereux' (selections). London Phil O. Angel AV-34015
	'Roberto Devereux'. Julius Rudel cond., Sills, Domingo, Quilico. N.Y. City Opera. Melodram Connaisseurs 27.
Dubois	'Les Sept Paroles du Christ'. Duchesneau sop, Turp ten, Chor de Montréal, Renaud cond., Lagace org. 1960. Apex ALF-71700
Gluck	'Iphigénie en Tauride' (selections). René Duclos Chor, Conservatoire de Paris O, Prêtre cond. 1961. Angel S-35632/EMI ASDF-231 (CD)
Great Verdi Arias	Edmonton SO, Mayer cond. 1984. CBC SM-5043/RCI 609
Handel	'Hercules'. Vienna Radio O, Vienna Academy Chor, Priestman cond., Quilico (Hercules). 1967. 3-RCA Victor Red Seal LSC-6181
Loesser	'The Most Happy Fella'. E. Loesser cond., Quilico. 1999. Jay Records
Massenet	'Esclarmonde'. National Phil O, John Alldis Choir, Bonynge cond., Quilico (The Bishop). 1975. 3-Lon OSA-13118/Decca 425-651-2 (CD).
	'Thérèse'. New Philharmonia O, Linden Singers, Bonynge cond., Quilico (Andre Thorel). 1973. Lon AOSA-1165
Milhaud	'Pacem in terris'. Utah Symphony, University Choir, Abravanel cond. 1964. Vanguard 71134
Monteverdi	Smith — Morawetz — Vaughan Williams — Cadoret — et al. Newmark pf. 1967. CBC Expo 22

Opera Gala	Campra 'Quittez vos fers, goûtez un sort plus glorieux' from *Tancrède*. Provincial Instr Ens. 1973. DG 2538 244
Pacini	'Saffo'. Teatro San Carlo of Naples O and Chor, Capuana cond., Quilico (Alcandro). 1967. 2-Hunt HUNICD-541
Puccini	'Tosca'. Lorange sop, Aragall ten, Bisson bar, New Philharmonia O, Guadagno cond., Quilico (Scarpia). 1978. 2-Safiro SA ZOR-1011
Ricordi d'Italia	Italian songs. Claudio Vena O and chor, Vena cond. (1991). Analekta AN-29101 (CD)
Two of a Kind	10 Arias by Verdi, Mozart, Bizet. Quilico (baritone), Petrowska (piano). 1996. York Fine Arts 00195.
Chants Français et Russes	French and Russian songs. Quilico (baritone), Petrowska (piano). 1998. Welspringe Productions WELCD002-98.
Verdi	'Aida' (extracts). Royal Opera House, Birgit Nilsson Pritchard cond. 1963. Lon OS-25798
	'Luisa Miller' (selections). Kobos cond., Quilico (Miller). 1974. Unique Opera UORC-239
	'Rigoletto'. Rudel cond., Carreras, Quilico (Rigoletto). 1973. 2-Robin Hood RHRS-513-B
	'Il Trovatore' (excerpts). Lamoureux O, Raymond Saint-Paul Chor, Fournet cond., Quilico (The Count). 1966. Philips 837-469 in French
	Great Opera Arias. Edmonton Symphony O, Mayer cond. 1986. CBC Series SMCD-5043
	'Rigoletto'. Levine cond., Quilico, Carreras, Neblet. 1972. Hollywood Bowl, Los Angeles, CIN records (live). CCCD-1017/18
	'Rigoletto'. Rudel cond., Quilico, Carreras, Wise. 1973. New York. SRO Records. SRO-843-2

Videography

Leoncavallo	'I Pagliacci'. Vickers, Quilico, Savoie, Likova, Mueller cond. (1995) CBC TV (VHS VAI69203)
Puccini	'Concerto Italiano'. CBC Festival Orchestra. Tebaldi, Quilico. Barbini cond. (1963). CBC telecast (VHS VAI Distribution)
Verdi	'Un Ballo in Maschera'. Metropolitan Opera O and Chor, Pavarotti, Ricciarelli, Patané cond. 1980. Home Vision BALO-4/Paramount 2363/Pioneer Artists 84089
Verdi	'Don Carlo'. Metropolitan Opera O and Chor, Domingo, Freni, Levine cond. (1983). Home Vision DONO-3/Paramount 2363/Pioneer Artists 84075
The Voice Lesson	Quilico and Petrowska. (1994). (VHS York Fine Arts YFA00897).
Verdi	'Il Trovatore'. Vickers, de la Pergola. CBC TV

About the Author

Author, artist and concert pianist, Christina Petrowska enjoys an international reputation as a major interpreter of 20th-century music. Following one of several Carnegie Hall recitals in 1977, the *New York Times* described her as "a pianist of extraordinary talent...with a phenomenal ability to play the most difficult music cleanly." She has been hailed for her outstanding technique and understanding of the music — both emotionally and intellectually. She approaches the repertoire with a spirit of discovery and is able to communicate to an audience its complex mysteries.

Born in Canada, Christina Petrowska made her debut in New York's Town Hall at the age of 14, at which time the New York Times declared her a "promethean talent'. While attending the Juilliard School as a scholarship student, she discovered her intense identification with the 20th-century literature. As Toronto's *Globe and Mail* notes: "At 14, when most students are just beginning to realize there's more to music than Chopin waltzes and early Beethoven sonatas, Petrowska was playing Copland and Hindemith. Gradually she built her portfolio until it included some of the most intellectually and technically demanding piano music in creation."

From 1962 to 1980 New York was home where Petrowska presented and performed in a series of concerts in Carnegie Hall, Alice Tully Hall, Lincoln Center, Town Hall and the Museum of Modern Art, in addition to touring extensively across the U.S., Canada and in Europe. "A pupil of Rosina Lhévinne, Christina Petrowska revealed her heritage promptly in the crystalline finger technique, the clean crisp styling, the vibrant tone color and trills that border on the phenomenal" was the reaction by the *International Herald Tribune* to a Paris debut.

A graduate with Bachelor of Music and Master of Science degrees from Juilliard, she returned to reside in Canada where she has spearheaded several new organizations of series of concerts and performances. She has also performed at Rideau Hall in Ottawa for the Governor General, the Prime Minister and visiting foreign dignitaries. In 1985 Petrowska toured the Middle East, giving 11 recitals in four countries; in 1989 she concertized in London, England and returned to New York for a critically acclaimed recital in Merkin Concert Hall.

Petrowska has for many years championed the works of Canadian composers, many of which were created especially for her. She has recently premiered concertos for piano and orchestra by Violet Archer with the Vancouver Chamber Orchestra, George Fiala at Roy Thomson Hall, Alexina Louie with the National Arts Center Orchestra and the Esprit Orchestra, Steven Gellman with the Ottawa Symphony, George Koumendakis at the Athens Music Festival in Greece, Luis de Pablo and Claudio Ambrosini in Montreal with the Société de Musique Contemporaine du Québec and Larysa Kuzmenko with the Winnipeg Symphony and the Toronto Symphony. In addition, her work with major international composers, among them Krystof Penderecki, Karlheinz Stockhausen, Pierre Boulez, György Ligeti, Luis de Pablo and her late husband, Michel-Georges Brégent, has firmly established her in the global contemporary music community.

Petrowska has been a regular performer for the Canadian Broadcasting Corporation since her New York debut as a teenager. Her CBC record of Debussy Preludes and Messiaen Vingt Regards has won unanimous praise. The *Ottawa Citizen* said "Petrowska is one of the finest pianists Canada has ever produced. The recording is excellent and I recommend it without reservation." William Littler of the *Toronto Star* headlined his review: "Petrowska Just

Right — the Pianist's Performance of the "Messiaen" Represents a Considerable Achievement." *Le Droit* stated: "Her intelligent playing, brilliant technique and refined sensitivity make these interpretations undeniably valuable." Her recording "Virtuoso Piano Music of Our Time" on the JLH label, made its debut on the Space Shuttle Columbia with Canadian astronaut Steve Maclean, a York University alumnus, where Petrowska is Professor of Piano and Musicology. The *Toronto Star* described the album: "The playing, as usual with Petrowska, peddles brilliance with a capital B."

Recent recordings include a CD of Glenn Buhr's Piano Concerto with the Winnipeg Symphony, which was nominated for a 1995 Juno Award. A new recording "Two of a Kind" with baritone Louis Quilico was released recently as well as a solo CD "Mystic Streams."

Petrowska and Quilico met and married in 1993 and have given numerous recitals together in Montreal, Toronto, Philadelphia, Edmonton, and on Winnipeg CBC radio and TV and plan several future CD's. They make their home in Toronto with Petrowska's two daughters.

In addition to her musical activities, Petrowska is an accomplished visual artist and writer. Some of her drawings were published in Spain as part of a biography on the Spanish composer Luis de Pablo. She has also had a book of poetry published in New York and has written many articles for music publications. Her book *Opera Illustrated: An Artistic Odyssey*, published by Captus Press, received rave reviews, not only from opera stars such as Placido Domingo, who stated "This is a wonderful and illuminating book about opera"; Luciano Pavarotti who wrote "Bravo"; Sherrill Milnes: "For me, these sketches successfully portray opera in art. I found myself fascinated by the detail and originality. Petrowska has hit on an entirely different genre that is both unusual and rarely seen"; but from the press: "A magnificent book," *David Ha Shavu a*, Tel Aviv; "It is a book to return to, to be held in one's thoughts and digested carefully in the heart. Readers will indeed find themselves in that rarest of positions, moving beyond the boundaries of the ego to look inside, transported into the heart and soul of the artist," *Opera Canada*; "A rich and resourceful contribution to the world of opera and dramatic art," *La Presse*; "This combination of musician and artist has produced an unusual and rare work of art," The Canadian Opera Company.